CW01511464

The PLYMSTOCK
c o n n e c t i o n

THE HISTORY OF A DEVON PARISH

IVY M. LANGDON

WESTCOUNTRY
BOOKS

First published in Great Britain in 1995 by Westcountry Books

Copyright © 1995 Ivy M. Langdon

All rights reserved. No part of this publication may
be reproduced, stored in a retrieval system, or transmitted
in any form or by any means, without the prior permission
of the copyright holder.

British Library Cataloguing in Publication Data
Catalogue Data for this book is available from the British Library

ISBN 1 898386 14 5

The cover illustration is from a watercolour by William Payne (c.1800)
showing Hooe Manor, formerly Belle-Vue, home of the Harris family
(courtesy Devon Record Office)

WESTCOUNTRY BOOKS
Halsgrove House
Lower Moor Way
Tiverton
Devon EX16 6SS

Telephone: 01884 243242
Facsimile: 01884 243325

Printed and bound in Great Britain by The Devonshire Press Ltd., Torquay.

CONTENTS

ACKNOWLEDGEMENTS

I wish to record my gratitude to the late James Barber MA, FSA, AMA for reading and advising on the text of Chapter 1 and also for translating the 1586 *Survey of the Manor of Plymstock* which was in a difficult-to-read Latin. This valuable information would not have been available without his help. Also, the architectural details in Chapter 5 were all supplied by Mr Barber, who encouraged and supported my endeavours right up to his sad death in 1993. I am also deeply indebted to Mr Edgar Harris BSc, President of the Plymstock and District Civic Society, for his encouragement and practical help with the preparation of the manuscript.

My grateful thanks are due to Mr P.A. Kennedy, former Devon County Archivist, for obtaining permission from the Bedford Settled Estates, 'On behalf of the Trustees', to publish information from the Bedford Records. Also for his permission and that of Mrs V. Swete, to reproduce watercolour illustrations taken from the journals of the Rev. John Swete. In addition, I am grateful to the late Professor H.P.R. Finberg for permitting me to draw on his book *Tavistock Abbey*. My thanks are also due to Dr Keith Ray, Plymouth City Archaeological Officer, for supplying up to date contributory notes.

My thanks are also extended to Maurice Bond, OBE, FSA, Hon. Custodian of the Muniments, for arranging my visit to The Aerary, St George's Chapel, Windsor, and to Mrs Shelagh Bond, MA, FRHS, for her helpful advice. My thanks also to the staff of the following: The Public Record Office in Chancery Lane; The British Library; Lambeth Palace Library; Devon Record Offices at Exeter and Plymouth; and the Plymouth Central Library, Local Studies Library. All have been unfailingly helpful and courteous. I, of course, am entirely responsible for any errors this book may contain.

Lastly, but by no means least, I acknowledge the support given to me by my late husband Joe who helped in so many practical ways to make my research and writing possible.

Ivy M. Langdon
Elburton, 1995.

My sincere thanks are due to the following who, by sponsorship, have made this publication possible:

The Plymstock & District Civic Society
The Plymouth City Council,
The Plymouth Athenaeum,
The Billacombe Residents' Association,
Mr Edgar R. Harris, BSC, President of the
Plymstock & District Civic Society,
Mr Brian Y. Langdon,
Mrs Glenda M. Hills,
Mrs Betty W. Symons,
Miss Ann M. Hunt,
Mr Robert Rowland,
Mr Richard Snell.

FOREWORD

The casual visitor to Plymstock might be forgiven for thinking of it as essentially a twentieth century suburb of Plymouth with little history. The parish church is almost the only prominent building which belies this judgement. Mrs Langdon's *The Plymstock Connection* is, however, eloquent proof that this assessment is quite untrue.

A native of Plymouth, Mrs Langdon has lived in Plymstock for nearly forty years. She soon showed her interest in the area by serving on Plymstock Parish Council until it was dissolved in 1967, and she was later elected to represent a local ward on Plymouth City Council. In 1965 Mrs Langdon took a very active part in founding the Plymstock Civic Society which is still flourishing and has, by sponsorship, helped make possible the publication of this book.

At an early stage in her residence, because no history of the parish has ever been published, Mrs Langdon started accumulating relevant data in the local Record Office, later extending her researches by frequent visits to libraries in Exeter, London and Windsor (the Canons of St George's Chapel are patrons of the vicariate). The gathering of information in this way from early records and original documents involved a tremendous amount of work and much travelling, but it does mean that the resulting whole is really authentic and scholarly. I know myself the extreme care Mrs Langdon has taken to follow up every clue which might help to make the story of Plymstock's past more complete and accurate. She has long been striving to complete a complex historical jigsaw puzzle.

I feel sure that Mrs Langdon's book will long be considered the definitive work on this subject. It will be much valued because it fills a gap in the recorded history of Plymouth and presents much material which has never before been assembled.

Edgar R. Harris B.Sc
Plymstock, 1995

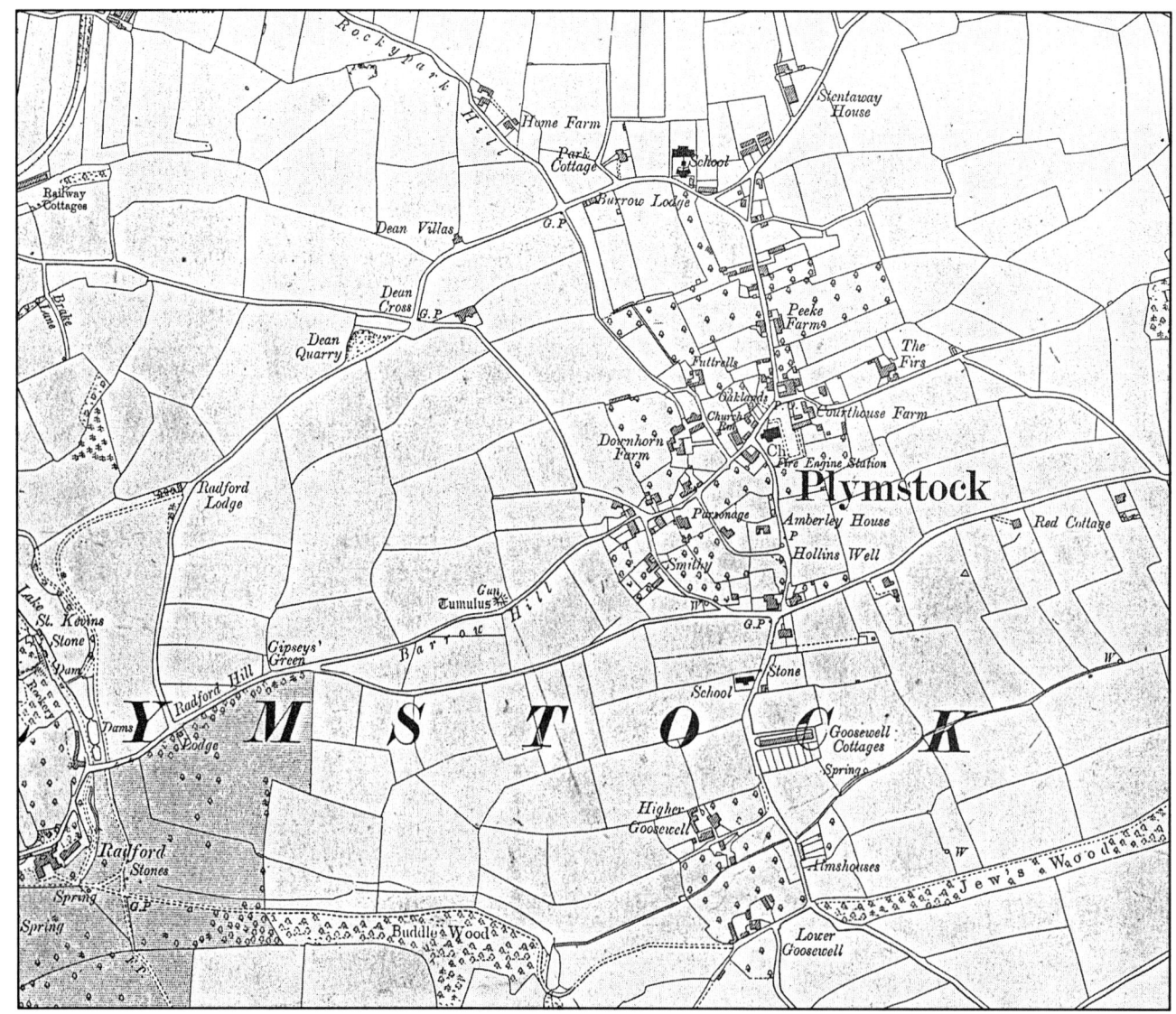

Plymstock: taken from the 1915 Ordnance Survey map.

Oreston: taken from the Ordnance Survey map of 1888 (see Chapter 6).

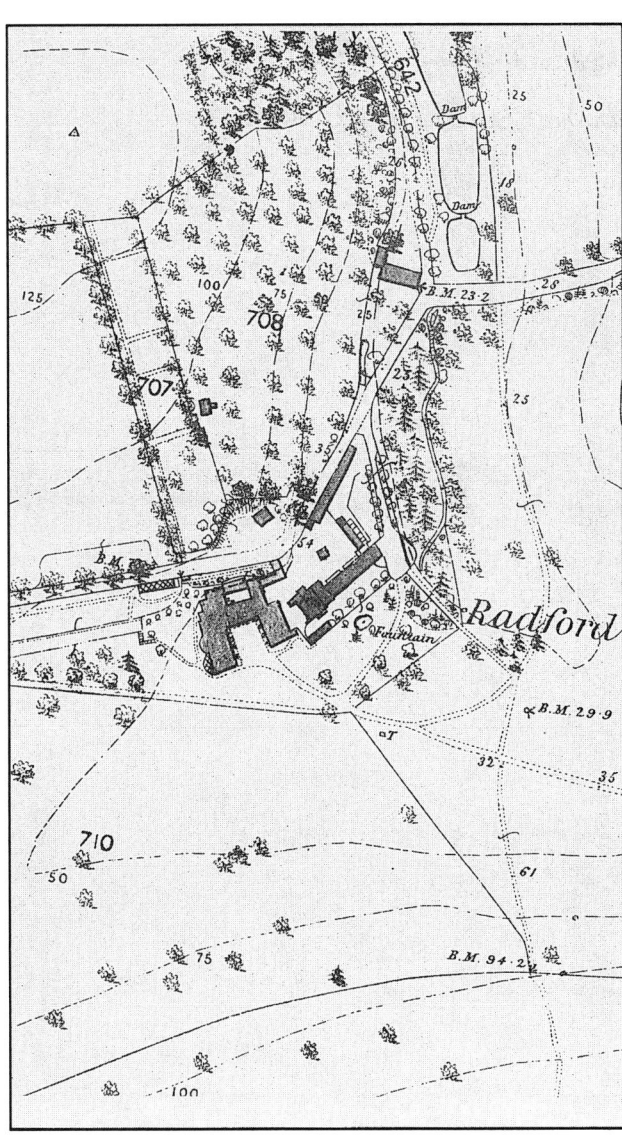

Radford: taken from the Ordnance Survey map of 1933 (see chapters 13 and 14).

Frontispiece:
Radford House – home of the Harris family.
From a watercolour (c. 1800) by William Payne (courtesy Devon Record Office).

Chapter One

PLYMSTOCK'S ANCIENT HERITAGE

The ancient parish of Plymstock, now merged with the city of Plymouth, is a canvas on which an evolutionary process of overwhelming magnitude has been recorded; its contours, deep valleys, plateaux and coastline, all being the result of some cataclysm or major upheaval in the early days of its formation. On this ancient backcloth the impress of many succeeding generations of immigrant people has been superimposed. Although several remarkable discoveries have been invaluable in enabling archaeologists to date particular periods of settlement, the resulting picture built up layer upon layer over many thousands of years is becoming more blurred and indistinct as time passes and it is only dimly that traces of their shadowy past can now be discerned.

Many millions of years ago, during Devonian times, southern Britain was submerged beneath a warm sea. During the middle period of this system of rock formation, in a shallow sea, calcareous marine life abounded, their shells forming limestone. In clear water areas coral reefs grew and built up the vast deposits of limestone which, in modern times, formed the foreshore of Plymouth from Devil's Point to Cattewater, extending to Mount Batten, Radford, Oreston, Pomphlett and Elburton. At least since Tudor times this stone has contributed to the local economy, the few remaining limekilns bearing witness to the burning of the rock into lime for manuring the land. Today, two large quarries, Plymstock and Moorcroft, are worked for aggregate and cement manufacture.[1]

The Palaeolithic (Old Stone Age), which covered an immensely long period, was characterized at the end by the four major phases of advance and retreat of the ice sheets of the Great Ice Age. At its greatest severity the glaciation advanced as far south as the Bristol Channel, reaching the northern shore of Devon and Somerset.[2] During these glaciations arctic conditions prevailed, interspersed with warmer inter-glacial periods when melted ice, carrying with it silt, peat and stones, flooded the valleys and coastal fringes where forests grew and flourished in the rich soil. At the close of the fourth and last glaciation the level of the seas was very low, the southern shore of Devon being out in the Channel, possibly in the vicinity of the Eddystone Reef.

Limestone is noted for its caverns and fissures, and in 1817 the bones of the rhinoceros were found in a cave at Oreston.[3] A series of caves broken into in 1822, when stone was being quarried for the construction of the breakwater, yielded bones of the mammoth, cave lion, cave bear and woolly rhinoceros. Human bones were also found, but unfortunately were thrown away as it was not thought that man could have been contemporary with such animals.[n.1]

In 1886 a fissure at Cattedown revealed the bones of many now extinct animals, which included the bison. Also found was a flint core of a type used by

Neanderthal Man. At a higher level in the fissure a bed of cave breccia, when blasted open, was found to contain the bones of at least 18 human beings. Fortunately the flint core and skull fragments were rescued from the ruins of the Plymouth Athenaeum when it was destroyed by enemy action during World War II.[4] These ancient relics of early man's existence are now in the Plymouth City Museum.

The Mesolithic (Middle Stone Age), which commenced in Britain about 8000 BC, has been described as a transition period between the age of the hunters and that of the agriculturists. This age has afforded the earliest positive evidence of human occupation in the Plymstock area, for, in 1885, Mr Francis Brent F.S.A. recorded the occurrence at Staddon of many specimens of flint, consisting of all the varieties of the smaller implements, together with a number of unwrought pebbles and flint pieces. These tiny implements, known as microliths, consisted of worked flints and arrowheads which were hafted, several at a time, on to bone or wood shafts, forming an arrow or spear.[5]

With the onset of the Mesolithic culture the cold, bleak conditions of the Palaeolithic Age gradually gave way to more seasonal change, with cold winters and warm summers; then becoming generally moist and warm. These conditions encouraged the growth of lush forests which covered the low-lying ground, leaving only the uplands free of dense growth. Due to their lack of tools suitable for forest clearance the Mesolithic people were obliged to keep to the higher ground and this may account for their presence at Staddon.[6]

With the departure of the larger animals from Britain the Mesolithic hunter was compelled to adapt his methods accordingly; his smaller implements being more suitable for dealing with the type of animal then prevailing, such as the red deer, wild pig, elk, etc. His diet was supplemented by the gathering of wild berries, nuts, edible plants and roots, and by fishing and collecting shellfish, of which there would have been a plentiful supply around the rocky coast. [7]

During the later stages of the Mesolithic period, about 5000 BC, the final retreat of the ice to its northern limits released vast quantities of water. When this inundation took place the sea rose to a much higher level than at present, resulting in raised beaches. The 'Sound' and the 'Cattewater' were formed and a forest in Bovisand Bay was drowned.

Plymstock's first farmers

The immigration of the Neolithic (New Stone Age) people to Britain followed a quite revolutionary change in living habits which had commenced about 8000 BC in parts of Asia, where wheat and barley grew wild and the wild predecessors of our domestic animals lived. It was in these regions that a system of food production slowly evolved, and man, instead of being entirely dependent on his own prowess and nature's bounty for his subsistence began to cultivate land, propagate seed and domesticate and breed animals. This new way of life led to a more settled existence and the forming of communities. Instead of sheltering in caves or in pits dug in the ground Neolithic Man now built a house for himself and his family; timber, wattle and daub, mud bricks and plastered branches being used for their construction.[8]

Over the years this new culture spread westward across Europe and then from southern France and Spain northward to Brittany and the Channel Islands. Eventually, about 4000 BC, small groups of people began to cross the Channel to settle in Britain, bringing with them a few belongings, seed corn, domestic animals and a knowledge of various crafts such as pottery-making and weaving. With their polished stone axes and by a process known as bark-ringing and burning, the newcomers cleared cultivation plots in the forest where they grazed their cattle and sowed their seed corn. These ancient people thus laid the foundation for Britain's agricultural economy.[9]

Although archaeological experts have not so far committed themselves to a positive belief that a Neolithic settlement existed at Plymstock, the discovery of several artefacts indicate their presence in this area. In 1887 the *Transactions of the Devonshire Association* contained a detailed description of the contents of a kitchen midden, situated on the section of beach between Mount Batten and Turnchapel. This large deposit of kitchen refuse was thought to be the accumulation over a very long period of ancient dwellers by the shore. Among the contents was a flint core, from which successive flakes had been struck, the flakes undoubtedly being intended for the manufacture of small tools and weapons. The midden also contained pieces of rough pottery which were thought to be portions of a funeral urn, fragments of red pottery, the bones of deer and pig, and a quantity of marine shells, indicating that shellfish formed a prominent feature in the diet of these people. Expert opinion at that time considered that this midden originated in the Neolithic Age, the view being also expressed that a late Mesolithic origin was not improbable.[10]

Human remains were also found in close proximity to the midden when an earth bank, just above high water mark, began to break away and revealed the frontal part of a skull. This discovery was reported to Mr Gage Tweedy, a Plymouth archaeologist, who arranged for an examination of the bank. Eventually a complete skeleton was revealed, the remains being in a crouched or sitting position and facing north-west; it was later stated that eight or nine skeletons buried in exactly the same way had previously been found nearby. Communal burials in artificial earthen banks with the bodies facing the setting sun were characteristic of interments during the Neolithic Age. This skeleton was found to be a female who was short in stature, being just under five feet; the head was large in proportion to the body, with a shallow, retreating forehead and prognathous and massive jaws.[11] This may, alternatively, have been one of the Beaker Folk who commenced to arrive in this country about 2000 BC, for these people have been described as a race of short, powerfully-built ugly men and women.[12] Their method of burial was sometimes similar to that of the Neolithic people, being also a contracted form of inhumation either communally or, more normally, as individual burials.

Further evidence came to light in 1919 when a Neolithic axe-head just under four inches in length was found during the construction of the Royal Air Force Station at Mount Batten. This implement is one of the exhibits in the Plymouth City Museum, the caption stating it to be made of an igneous rock, a greenish, volcanic tuff which occurs at Great Langdale in Cumbria. The existence of this specimen and its subsequent identification with Great Langdale, where there was a Neolithic axe factory, shows the extent of trade contacts in those early days.

The Neolithic period is further represented by casual finds of three flint arrowheads and ten scrapers at Elburton, and a greenstone axe at Horn Lane, Plymstock.[13] More recently, another Neolithic stone axe was discovered nearby when the Broadway car park was extended.[14]

Another possibly significant discovery in the farmyard at West Hooe in 1967, was the recognition of two large stones, about five feet by two, as 'standing stones' of some kind. This belief may be supported by two fields on the hillside behind and to the east of the farm buildings being named 'Higher Hingstone' and 'Long Hingstone'. The view was expressed by the Rev. L.E.H. Pike, former vicar of Hooe and a keen local historian, that these stones were Neolithic and that an 'improving' farmer may have moved them to the yard for convenience of ploughing.[15]

The Plymstock Tithe Map, 1842, identifies these fields as Nos 711 and 713 respectively.[15a] Also shown on this Survey are five circular areas in fields to the south–west of the farm buildings, and another to the west on the Turnchapel/Mount Batten peninsula. These may have been burial mounds of possibly Neolithic or Bronze Age date.[15a]

When, during the late 1960s and 1970s, extensive housing development took place on the fields of West Hooe, these stones disappeared, so without the opportunity for archaeological investigation it will never be known whether they played an important part in the life of Plymstock's first farmers.[n.2]

The Bronze Age

With the introduction of bronze into Britain about 2000 BC the Neolithic Age gradually merged with the

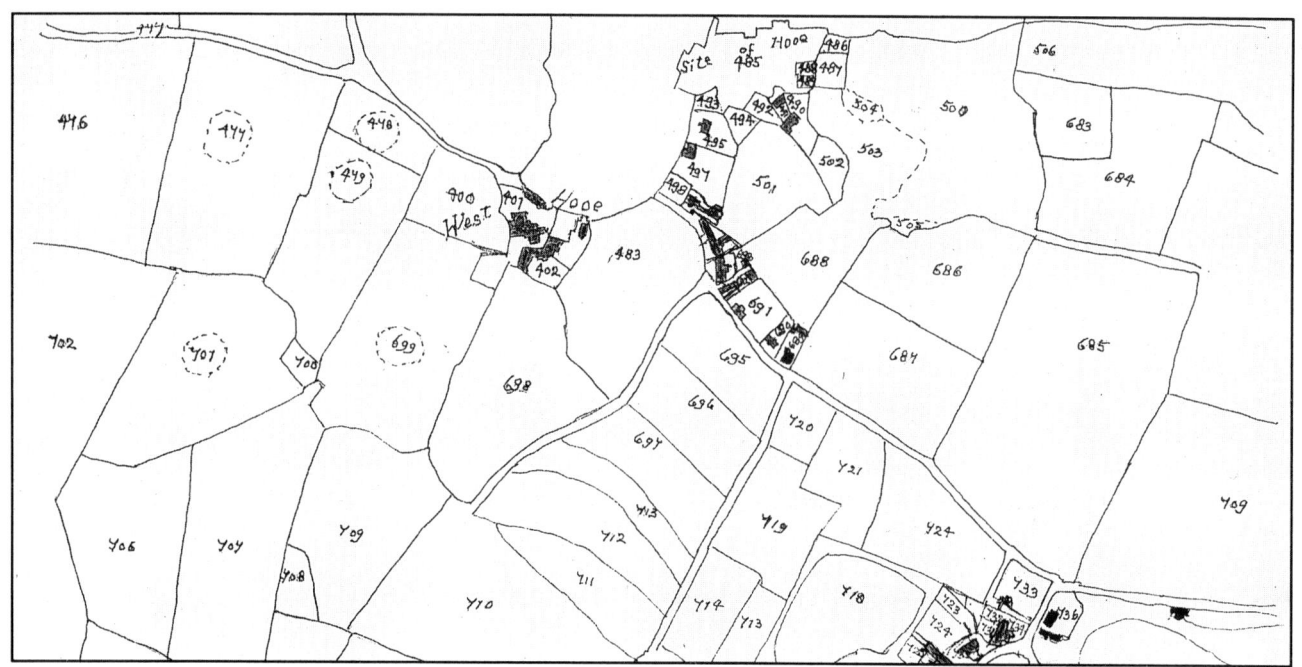

Part of the Plymstock Tithe Map, 1842. Field 711 is Higher Hingstone and Field 713 is Long Hingstone.

Bronze Age. There is good reason to believe that during this time Mount Batten was an important trading centre, probably for tin obtained by streaming on Dartmoor and the upper reaches of the River Plym, and brought to the coast along the ancient trackways. Tin was essential for the making of bronze and merchants would have visited the South West to procure this valuable commodity. The climate, dry and warm during most of this age, made settlement possible on the high ground of Dartmoor and the remains of Bronze Age hut dwellings can still be seen on many parts of the moor.

An interesting find was made at Oreston on 24 October 1868, when Ephraim Dodridge, a quarryman, whilst removing rock from the base of a limestone ridge in a field named 'Rocky Parks', came across a flat stone about two feet below the surface. On removing it he found, piled upon a ledge of the natural rock, 16 bronze celts of various sizes (many of these apparently unused, some of them much deformed), four bronze spearheads (three with studs) and a bronze chisel. This find, known as 'The Plymstock Hoard', was thought to have been the stock-in-trade of a merchant smith who visited Plymstock in the sixteenth or fifteenth century BC. The Duke of Bedford, the owner of the Plymstock estate, presented the greater part of this find to the British Museum, where it is on display.[16] The residue of the find is in the Royal Albert Museum at Exeter.

Bronze artefacts found in 1919 and in 1939 on the foreshore of Mount Batten are thought to have been part of a bronze-founder's hoard. Some of these were perfect, finished articles, others damaged castings, possibly rejects, and some lumps of unworked bronze, thought to have been the surplus left after pouring the molten metal into the stone moulds. These all belong to the Late Bronze Age.[17]

On the summit of Burrow Hill is a presumed Bronze Age burial mound; a Scheduled Ancient Monument, No. 882. On its apex is the Plymstock War Memorial, and nearby is a cannon, a relic of the Civil War. An air photograph of adjoining land (A.P. 623315) shows three circular crop marks, which are probably ploughed-out burial mounds. It has been suggested that this site may be a small Bronze Age cemetery.[18]

It was the practice during the Bronze Age to burn the dead on a pyre which would be surrounded by a circular trench, some of which had an inner ring of post-holes. An authoritative source believes there to be some connection between the Beltane fire ritual and the rite of cremation. It has been suggested that some of our Bronze Age barrows are the actual graves of sacrificial victims of the Beltane or Hallowe'en festivals.[19]

Recent archaeological investigation of a trench at Mount Batten has brought to light a small group of pottery sherds considered to be contemporary with other Late Bronze Age-style metalwork. Intensive occupation began in about the eighth century BC, continuing into the Iron Age.

The Iron Age

During the five centuries preceding the Roman occupation of Britain, a key settlement of Celtic Iron Age people developed in the vicinity of Mount Batten. During the fifth and fourth centuries BC groups of people from the Continent crossed the Channel to settle in various parts of southern Britain; these were followed by more groups in the third and second centuries and by another massive influx during the late-second and mid-first centuries BC [20]

A map of south-west Britain prepared by Claudius Ptolemy, a famous geographer in the second century AD, shows the whole of the peninsula; Devon, Cornwall and a part of Somerset, to be the kingdom of Dumnonia, which was ruled by its own native king and tribal chieftains. [21]

These people brought with them a knowledge of iron smelting, introducing the method to the Bronze Age people, who had formerly regarded iron ore as waste. Iron was found to be malleable and tools and weapons no longer had to be cast. These and domestic utensils became ultimately within the reach of everyone, although bronze was still used for luxury goods. [22]

Agriculture was the principal means of livelihood of these people, their wealth being counted in cattle. The Dumnonii did not have a coinage of their own, preferring instead to trade by their ancient custom of barter. It is known they had long and close trading connections with Armorica, exporting metals and metalwork, and importing Armorican pottery and raw glass, as well as trade in other commodities. [23] It appears also that neighbouring tribesmen, the Dobunni from Somerset and the Durotriges from Dorset, visited Mount Batten to trade, for in March 1832, during quarrying operations along the coast of this peninsula, five gold and eight silver coins were found which were identified as the currency of these tribes. [24]

During this period a fort was constructed at Staddiscombe and remains of this circular earth and stone bank can still be seen on high ground to the north of Court Gate Farmhouse, where it commands a wide view of the surrounding countryside. The field in which it stands is significantly named Castle Hay. Inter-tribal warfare was common in Britain and the Staddiscombe camp may have provided protection for the Mount Batten settlement by guarding it from surprise attack.

Probably because of their dealings with the merchants of other countries the Dumnonii had a reputation for friendliness and hospitality to strangers and this may account for their apparent acceptance of the Romans and their ability to co-exist with them; a fact confirmed by the discovery in 1863 of a Late Iron Age cemetery on the south–west side of Stamford Fort. This came about by chance when it was found that a gun on one of the emplacements could not be trained down into Jennycliffe Bay. Irish workmen engaged to cut away the slope of the hill came across a number of graves and some bronze articles. When they reported the matter to the engineer-in-charge, Captain Moggridge, he immediately informed Mr Spence Bate, a Plymouth archaeologist, who arranged to be present while an examination of the graves and their contents was carried out. As the men were under contract the task of demolishing the hill proceeded rapidly, various articles being thrown out of the graves as they were found. [25]

These graves were pits, 4 to 4$\frac{1}{2}$ feet deep, cut in the soft, slatey rock and lined with rough, worn blocks of limestone; the bodies being placed in them in a sitting position and covered with more of the blocks. Among the contents were three bronze mirrors, beautifully decorated with the Celtic running-scroll ornament-ation; bracelets, brooches, rings, fragments of an amber-coloured glass bowl and pottery were also found. Some of the articles were of Roman origin and it has been established that this cemetery continued in use right up to the end of the first century AD. The quality of the goods found indicates a high status for this settlement. [26]

Roman trading post

It has been established that Mount Batten was a Roman trading station during the period of their occupation of Britain from AD 43 to 410.

Vespasian, a legionary commander, was given the task of annexing southern Britain and after attacking a number of British forts his Legio II Augusta reached *Isca Dumnoniorum* (Exeter), setting up a legionary base which they occupied from AD 55 to 75. It is now known that they continued westward into Cornwall, where they constructed a fort at Nanstallon, just west of Bodmin, between AD 55 to 65, which is thought to have concluded their annexation of the whole of the south-west peninsula.[27] Mount Batten, with its known overseas and coastal trading connections was almost certainly included among their conquests.

Forty-seven Roman coins, which cover the period of the occupation, together with fragments of roofing tiles, bronze, and pottery artefacts, attest their continued presence at Mount Batten. Also, in 1888, a figurine of the Roman god Mercury was dug up in the lake-side garden of Mr Apworthy at Hooe, who gave it to Torquay Natural History Museum. Some doubt has been expressed as to the authenticity of this figure, which is now considered to be a nineteenth century forgery.[28] Other evidence was found in controlled archaeological examination by Professor Barry Cunliffe between 1983 and 1985. There have also been isolated finds of Roman coins at Plymstock, Oreston and Elburton.*

Sub-Roman and late-British period

During the sub-Roman and late-British period, 400-700 AD there was a hiatus at Plymstock. Following the departure of the Romans from Britain during the first

*Records of these are held at Plymouth City Museum.

half of the fifth century there was a general disclocation of trade and this would have affected the settlement at Mount Batten. Although some trade from the Mediterranean is known to have continued in the south-west, finds of this period are not represented in the Plymstock area, which suggests the British occupants may have abandoned their settlement at Mount Batten either before or soon after the Romans evacuated the port. Known landing places for the eastern Mediterranean trade are Bantham at the mouth of the Avon and Mothecombe on the Erme. [29] In addition to a diminution of trade, Britain, deprived of the protection afforded by the Roman military forces, was beset by barbarian races; among these the Picts, Scots and Saxons were predominant.

During these troubled years a number of refugees from the south and west of Britain crossed the Channel to Armorica, a country with which Dumnonia had long trading associations. The migrations resulted in this country becoming entirely British in character and for many centuries, until it became Brittany, it was known as Lesser or Little Britain.

The Saxons did not subjugate Dumnonia quickly or easily and many battles were fought before Egbert, King of the West Saxons, completed the long process by which the Britons of the south-west were gradually brought under English rule.[30]

NOTES AND REFERENCES
PLYMSTOCK'S ANCIENT HERITAGE

1. E.M. Durrance & D.J.C. Laming, *The Geology of Devon*, 9 &199.
2. British Regional Geology, *South-West England*, 3rd ed., 8.
3. *The Literature of the Oreston Caverns*, Trans. of the Plymouth Institution, V.5, 1872, 249-316.
4. *Human Remains in a Bone Cave at Cattedown*, Trans. of the Devonshire Association, V. XIX, 255-60, R.N. Worth.

5. James Barber, M.A. *Archaeological Discoveries in Plymouth & District.*
6. *Larousse Encyclopedia of Ancient and Medieval History.*
7. Margaret Lattimore, *The Mesolithic Age in Britain*, A Study of Plymouth, V II, 108 & 111.
8. Sonia Cole, *The Neolithic Revolution*, British Museum, (Natuural History), 61.
9. Ibid, 31.
10. R.N. Worth, *Kitchen Midden*, T.D.A., 1887, V XIX, 58. M. Lattimore, Study of Plymouth, V.II, 111.
11. *Mount Batten*, T.D.A., V.XXIII, 119.
12. Aileen Fox, *South West England*, 1973, Chap. IV, 63.
13. C. Gaskell Brown, *Plymstock: an Archaeological Study and Policy.*
14. Plymouth City Museum.
15. Rev. L.E.H. Pike, *Rubbing Stones at Hooe Barton*, Plymstock & District Civic Society bulletin.
15a. *Plymstock Tithe Map & Apportionment Book*, Devon Record Office.
16. *The Plymstock Hoard*, Bedford records, S.31, D.R.O.
17. J.Barber, *Arch. Disc.*
18. C. Gaskell Brown, *Plymstock Arch. Study.*
19. T.C. Lethbridge, *The Buried Gods*, 118.
20. Prof. Barry Cunliffe, *Mount Batten: A Prehistoric and Roman Fort*, Monograph No.26, 101.
21. R.N. Worth, *Roman Devon*, 6.
22. A. Fox, *S.W. England*, Chap. VII, 131-2.
23. Ibid, 133.
24. R. Hansford Worth, T.P.I., 1931, 223.
25. C. Spence Bate, T.D.A., V.6, 223. Victoria County History, *Stamford Hill*, 367.
26. Prof. B. Cunliffe, *Mount Batten*, Mon. No.26, 102.
27. A.H. Shorter, L.D. Ravenhill, K.J. Gregory, *Southwest England*, 88.
28. Prof. B. Cunliffe, *Figure of Mercury*, Mono. No.26, 134.
29. A. Fox, *S.W.England*, 195.
30. F.M. Stenton, *Anglo-Saxon England*, 235.

NOTES CONTRIBUTED BY DR KEITH RAY, CITY ARCHAEOLOGICAL OFFICER, PLYMOUTH CITY COUNCIL

n.1   Finds from a series of caves and fissures in the limestone of the area just to the north of Oreston were noted by Mr J Widbey and others during and after quarrying for the Plymouth Breakwater between 1816 and 1859. Large quantites of fossil animal bones were retrieved and were examined by such nationally renowned figures as Dean W. Buckland and William Pengelly. They date from the last interglacial and last glacial periods of the Ice Ages, and include rhinoceros, cave hyaena, lion and elephant from the former period, and bear, deer, wolf, fox, ass, horse and mammoth from the latter period. Human bones were found in the Oreston Third Bone Cave in 1822, but a fragment has only recently (1994) been identified among bones now curated by the British Geological Survey in Nottingham. Further human bones were discovered in Pomphlett Cave in 1839, but were discarded as of no interest, and bison, deer and bear bones were found in the same quarry in 1878.

n.2   Two finds of polished stone axeheads have been reported in the Plymstock Broadway area. They date from the neolithic period (4000 BC - 2000 BC), and represent settlement of the area by people who built stone and earthen long barrows as burial places, and who raised standing stones for ritual observances. At first they buried human remains in caves and fissures however, and a femur found in the Kitley Caves has recently been dated to around 4000BC. They also exchanged objects with their neighbours and a green-grey smooth stone axehead found in the 1900s at Mount Batten has been shown to have ultimately come from as far away as Great Langdale in the Lake District. That such trade continued into the Bronze Age is suggested by the famous hoard of bronze objects (17 flanged axes, 3 daggers, 1 spearhead and a chisel) dating to c.1200 BC found under rocks in a field just north of Oreston in 1868. In the later Bronze Age from 1000 BC, trade became more frequent and extended overseas, with industrial activity focused on Mount Batten. Iron Age settlements developed there, on the hill next to Hooe Lake Quarry above Turnchapel, and at Court Gates Farm, Staddiscombe where the remains of a fortified Iron Age farmstead survive today.

Chapter Two
SAXON SETTLEMENT AT PLYMSTOCK

Plymstock formed a part of the South Hams, land between the Dart and Plym rivers, with Dartmoor on its northern boundary. The Old English word *homme* or *hamme* was used by the Saxons to describe this part of South Devon which was colonized by them during the early ninth century.

Land features and some early names are to be found in royal charters, the earliest for the South Hams being a testimonial grant dated AD 833 by Egbert, King of the West Saxons, to Beornwyn, one of three sisters, of a part of her father's estate, the original document having been lost.[1] This was for *ten manentes in Derentune homm*, which is considered to be the well-known Dartington estate, with the River Dart forming its eastern boundary.

Of particular importance to Plymstock is the *Om Homme* Charter, dated 26 December AD 847, when Aethelwulf, Egbert's son and successor, with the advice

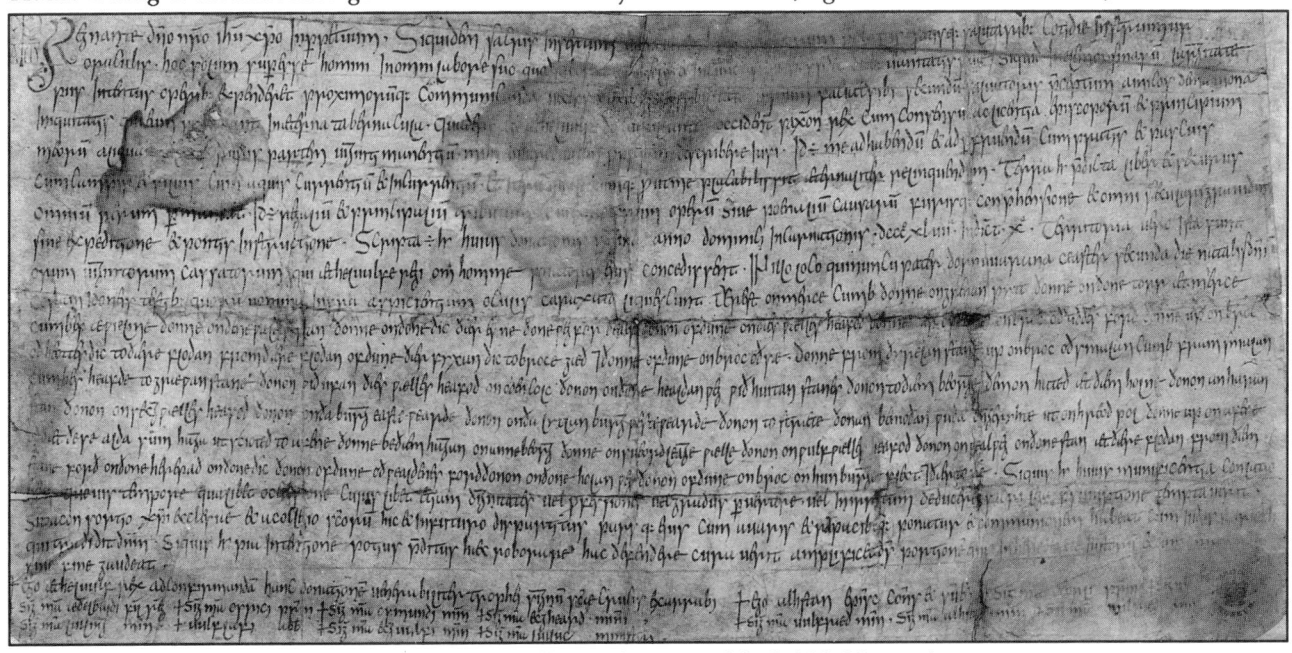

The Om Homme Charter (courtesy of the British Museum).

and permission of his bishops and nobles, granted to himself *twenty manentes om homme*. Apart from military service and the building of bridges, both expressly reserved, this land was freed thenceforth from all secular tribute to the king or ealdorman.[2] Anglo-Saxon kings did not possess a despotic authority and were bound to act by the advice of their nobles, many of whom were rulers of their own territories, though they themselves were vassals of the king.

Leading historians of the twentieth century consider this charter to be of great importance, for it makes clear the meaning of 'bookland' and implies that until the king owned the land in a personal capacity he was not able to give it away to whom he pleased or to free it from secular burdens.[3]

Manentes has been interpreted as *hides*, which may be misunderstood as meaning a land-measure. At that time *manentes* and *cassati*, which are interchangeable and both used in the charter, was the primitive unit of land-holding which varied in size. Forest and uncultivated or waste land as well as water, all of which must have covered a vast area, although included within the charter bounds did not form part of the twenty *manentes*.[4]

Central to the bounds, which are in two parts, is the River Avon, with its tributary the Glaze Brook. Written in Saxon, the first part has been translated as follows:

First on merce cumb – *boundary valley – then on the green pit then on the tor at boundary valley's source then on denewaldes stone then on the dyke where Esne dug up the way then on over the down as far as the wells head then from there down on the brook to the tide ford then up on the brook to the heottes dyke to where it floods from where it floods over the down to where the vixen dyke goes to the brook and then down on the brook to the sea.* [n.1]

The actual position of these landmarks has been the subject of much speculation and difference of opinion, being examined by the late Mrs Frances Rose-Troup, one-time president of the Devonshire Association, and also by the late Professor H.P.R. Finberg, who explored the area he considered to be covered by this charter.

Mrs Rose-Troup placed their commencement in the valley of the Glaze Brook on Brent Moor and traced the bounds westward to end in the sea at an estuary of the Plym. Then from Glaze Meet she plotted the second part to end in the sea at Dartmouth. [5]

Professor Finberg commenced at the mouth of the River Erme and continued across country to the River Avon. Commencing again at Thurlestone, a well-known holed rock formation, he traced the bounds to the River Dart.[6]

It is obvious some of the landmarks can be applied to various places in the South Hams, so it is not surprising there are divergent opinions. However, 'boundary valley' does appear to be the valley of the Glaze where the East and West Glaze flow together, for this is a known mark point for other charters such as *Hiwisce* and *Brent Moor*, later granted to Buckfast Abbey. The author's opinion in respect of this controversial subject is an alternative suggestion to the one put forward by Mrs Rose-Troup, who brings the western bounds via Dendles Wood and the Tory Brook to Plympton, is that the 'wells head' may be Plym Head, and 'on the brook to the tide ford' the course of the Plym River as far as the ancient crossing at Efford – the ebb or tide ford across the estuary: [n.2] 'Up on the brook' would then be Tory Brook, which originally joined with the Plym near to this crossing. 'To the heottes dyke to where it floods' may have been the causeway where trackways from the north and north-west converged. The socket stone and broken shaft of a cross embedded in the south bank of the brook marked this crossing which was flooded at high tide. The route southwards crossed the west end of the Ridgeway at the top of a steep hill (Station Road). 'From where it floods' could be understood to mean that the bounds after reaching this crossing followed the south shore of the brook round Harewood (boundary wood) to the head of the Plym estuary. There are many references to flooding before

Ancient marked stone at Hardwick Farm.

reclamation of this creek was finally completed in 1848, Tory Brook being channelled alongside the turnpike road between Plympton and Marsh Mills.[n.3]

As suggested by Mrs Rose-Troup, the bounds may then have continued over the hill past Hardwick, [n.4] along a road skirting Saltram to the 'vixen dyke' which she placed at Wixenford where a deep depression between two strips of woodland 'goes to the brook and then down on the brook to the sea'. This was once an inlet of the Plym called Schilleston Bay, now reclaimed land known as Chelson Meadow.

Ancient parishes sometimes adopted the old Saxon boundaries and an account of *The Beating of the Parish Bounds* which took place at Plymstock on 4 September 1937, shows that the parish bounds proceeded from the Plym estuary, called the Laira, through Chelson Meadow, being followed through Wixenford Bottom and Farm to the parish boundary stone in the road leading from Plympton to Plymstock. [7]

There are other factors which support the inclusion of Plympton in the charter, one being that in 855 Aethelwulf granted a tenth part of his lands throughout his kingdom to the church. [8] This famous donation was followed by the endowment of a monastery at Plympton, which in 904 was the subject of a charter when Edward the Elder granted certain manorial lands in Somerset to Asser, bishop of Sherborne, in exchange for 'that monastery which in the Saxon tongue is called Plymentun'. [9] This exchange appears to have been the precursor of a wider ecclesiastical policy, for in 909, following the death of Asser, Edward divided the ancient West Saxon see of Sherborne into three diocese, of which Sherborne, Wells and Crediton were the cathedrals. [10]

It is also considered probable the Hundreds of Wessex came into being during the tenth century by gradual division of the ancient *regiones* into districts of one hundred hides.[11] One of these primitive tribal *regios* extended from the Dart to the Plym.[12] The importance of the Plym as a boundary is confirmed when this river, from source to mouth, became the western boundary of the Hundred of Plympton. [13]

What may be considered a further indication of the extent of land covered in the *Om Homme* charter is a long–held tradition that Aethelwulf had a palace at Yealmpton, the name mistakenly recorded by Risdon as Aethelwold. This belief appears to be supported by the relics of an 'ancient chappel' of primitive designation in the grounds of Lyneham at Yealmpton, which was noted in 1699 as being 'wholly neglected'. In 1908, probable survivals of the actual fabric of the vanished chapel could still be seen in various parts of the grounds, such as a doorway of the stable and a well with some picturesque fragments of worked stone.[14] An additional note to John Prince's *The Worthies of Devon* gives the following information about Lyneham:

Of its Saxon origin, and its residence in the county before the Conquest, no recorded proof remains, but the one and the other rest on the firm authority of unquestioned tradition.

During the ninth century, the Saxon settlements were threatened by the incursions of the Danes who commenced a series of raids on the south coast, creating havoc and bloodshed wherever they went. The *Anglo-Saxon Chronicles* record the following for the year AD851:

Ealdorman Ceorl with the men of Devon fought with heathen men at Wicganbeorg made great slaughter and took the victory.

It is considered this battle took place at Wembury to the south of Plymstock, although not all historians agree. However, a map of Saxon England, dated 1819, attached to an early edition of *The Anglo-Saxon Chronicles*, indicates a place called Wicganbeorg on the site of the present Wembury. [15]

This famous victory was also recorded by Asser, bishop of Sherborne, in his life of Alfred the Great. A translation of this ancient manuscript contains the following excerpt:

In the year of our Lord's incarnation, 851 A.D., which was the third after the birth of King Alfred, Ceorl, Earl of Devon, fought with the men of Devon against the pagans at a place called Wicganbeorg [Wembury]; and the Christians gained the victory. [16]

It has fallen to twentieth century historians to cast doubt on the tradition that Wembury was the site of this battle, However, *wic* means: 'for security, hence a castle or fortress; also, a place of security for boats, hence a bay or creek.'[17] *Beorg* means a fortified camp; the formation of temporary encampments being a prominent feature of these raids.[n.5] To those who may argue the unsuitability of the rocky coast at Wembury for such a landing, the Danes used longboats with a shallow draft which could be navigated into the inner curve of Wembury Bay, the mouth of the River Yealm then providing a secure haven.

There has also been much diversity of opinion as to the origin and meaning of Plymstock's name. According to one eminent authority, such names are hybrids, one element being Brittonic and the other Saxon.[18] According to William Crossing, Plym is a Celtic name which is derived from *pilim* meaning 'to roll.' Another authority said the name was derived from the Gaelic *Plun*, which implies a harbour. The matter may be settled by John Hooker, an Exeter Antiquarian who, writing in 1599, tells us:

Plympton taketh his name of the Ryver of Plymme which fleeteth past by it and Rysseth on Dartmore syde about a four or five miles of. This Towne was sometymes a Haven Towne but by means of the Tynners the same by the sands in the course of yeres is cleene quirted and choked and noe haven there now at all. [19]

As further evidence that Plympton was once a 'Haven Town' of the Plym, a French ship was arrested there during the late thirteenth century. [20 n.6]

The meaning of the second element in Plymstock's name is not so easy to determine, one authority stating that *stock* implied a stockaded site of border warfare and another that 'stocks were originally military outposts in frontier positions.'[21] More recent scholarship claims that *stocks* were offshoots or dependencies which might be some distance from the mother-settlement.[22] *The Place Names of Devon* tells us *stocks* were outlying areas to which the herdsmen drove their cattle for summer grazing.

Any or all of these opinions may be supported by the remains of a curved bank in open land to the south-west of the parish church and Downhorn Farmhouse. This bank was surveyed in 1978 when a pipe-trench was found to consist of hard-packed clay, shillet, a layer of chalky limestone and some flecks of charcoal. [23] Whether this bank once formed the basis of a stockade against hostile attack or as a protection for cattle cannot now be established with any degree of certainty.

NOTES AND REFERENCES
SAXON SETTLEMENT AT PLYMSTOCK

1. Mrs F. Rose-Troup, Devonshire Association Transactions, Vol. LXI, 276.
2. W. De Gray Birch, *Cartularium Saxonicum*, No. 451.
3. F.M. Stenton, *Anglo-Saxon England*, 308. *English Historical Documents*, Vol. 1, 481.
4. F.W. Maitland, *Domesday Book and Beyond*, 359.
5. F. Rose-Troup, D.A.T., Vol LXI, 249-80.
6. Prof. H.P.R. Finberg, *West Country Historical Studies*, 13-20.
7. Plymstock Parish Council Minutes, 1937; West Devon Record Office.
8. *The Anglo-Saxon Chronicles.*
9. W. de Gray Birch, *C.S.*, No. 610.
10. F.M. Stenton, *A.S.E.*, 1971, 439.
11. F.M. Stenton, *A.S.E.*, 1971, 300.
12. Prof. W.G. Hoskins, N. 1, 52; 538.
13. *Place Names of Devon* Maps.
14. *Devonia*, April, 1908. Rev. John Prince, *The Worthies of Devon*, 1701, Sir John Crocker.
15. *The Saxon Chronicle*, trans. and ed. Rev. J. Ingram B.D., 1823.
16. J.A. Giles, *Six Old English Chronicles*, 1908.
17. Rev. J. Bosworth, *Anglo-Saxon Dictionary*, 1838.
18. Prof. K. Jackson, *Language and History in Early Britain*, 144-5. Map, 220.
19. John Stevens, *Plympton Documents*, MS, 13.
20. State Papers, *Calendar of Close Rolls*, 1279-1288, 514
21. Rev. O. Reichel, D.A.T., XXX, 298. J.J. Alexander, D.A.T., 1921, 170-1.
22. H.P.R. Finberg, *Tavistock Abbey*, 1951, 41.
23. Plymouth City Museum Archaeological Dept.

n.1. Esne; a man of the servile class.

n.2. John Leland (d.1552), whose *Itinerary* included a tour of Devon, recorded the following:

From Plymouth by good enclosed ground but hilly to a place where I crossed the Plym Ryver at the Ebbe was about three miles... After that I passed over Plym Ryver. I rode about half a mile along by Tory Brook, whose colour is always redde by the sande that it renneth on and carryeth from the Tynne Works with it: and so to Plymtoun Marie etc.

n.3.   Mention of drowned tenements appears in a Plympton Grange Rental of tenements formerly in the possession of Plympton Priory. Undated, but believed to be during the reign of Elizabeth. A tenement, *Lyncadale*, stood in the sands close to Tory Brook near the entrance to Colebrook. (Trans. Plym. Inst. XVIII, 131-4).

n.4.   An ancient stone by the roadside at the entrance to Hardwick Farm bears an inscription which has not been deciphered.

n.5.   Earthworks near Wembury are traditionally described as Danish. (M. Lattimore, *The Story of Plymouth*, 140).

n.6.   The King (Edward I) wrote from Windsor to the Constable at Plympton ordering the release of this ship which belonged to his Majesty the King of France without hindrance because the lord king grants his licence to the merchant of the King of France on condition dues were paid.

Chapter Three
CHILDE OF PLYMSTOKE

Although the legend of Childe of Plymstoke has come to be accepted as part of the folklore of Devon no one has ever doubted the truth of his existence or that he died of exposure on Dartmoor where a monument known as Childe's Tomb was erected in the vicinity of Fox Tor. Although for centuries his identity has been shrouded in mystery all the known evidence points to him as being Eadwig, a younger son of King Ethelred II and his first wife Aelfgifu, who is known to have possessed an estate at Plymstock, formerly belonging to the royal manor of Plympton. [1]

Because it was politically expedient that the death of the young prince should appear to be accidental and not contrived, and also to justify the subsequent transfer of his Plymstock lands to Tavistock Abbey, the truth was blurred and a fanciful picture built up which generations of moor dwellers carried by oral tradition until it was first recorded by historians during the seventeenth century. [2]

The basis of this legend is that Childe, while hunting with his companions on Dartmoor, became separated from them and lost his way. In spite of killing his horse in order to shelter within the carcass he was frozen to death, leaving a message written in blood that:

> *He who finds and brings me to my tomb*
> *The land of Plymstoke shall be his doom* [n.1]

This legendary story has been much embroidered over the years and even at the present time imagin-

The monks of Tavistock discover the body of Childe on Dartmoor. (From a painting by W.R. Huck, 1952).

ative versions are still published under the guise of truth, one misconception being that Childe was a personal name when in fact the Saxon *cild* was a title given to the son of an important personage. As a young member of the old English royal house this would have been an appropriate title for Eadwig.

When King Ethelred died on 21 April 1016 he was succeeded by the third son of his first marriage, Edmund, called Ironside, who was crowned king in London while at the same time Cnut, the Danish king, was chosen by the witan at Southampton. [n.2] Although successful in early battles against the Danish forces, Edmund's army was later routed at Ashingdon in south-east Essex.[3] Edmund was then persuaded to enter into a treaty with Cnut whereby they became joint rulers of England, Edmund retaining Wessex and conceding Mercia to Cnut. On 30 November, Edmund died in mysterious circumstances and was buried at Glastonbury near to his grandfather, King Edgar.

The chronicler, Florence, a monk of Worcester (d.1118), tells us that after the death of Edmund, Cnut questioned the witnesses of the treaty made between him and Edmund earlier that year, as to whether his brothers and sons should be allowed to reign in the kingdom of the West Saxons if Edmund were to have died in Cnut's lifetime, and that those questioned gave false testimony, imagining that Cnut would reward them and be more gracious towards them. Afterwards they swore on oath to elect Cnut as their king and utterly renounced the brothers and sons of Edmund and repudiated them as kings:[n.3]

Now one of the aforesaid athelings was Eadwig, the illustrious and much honoured brother of King Edmund, and by most evil counsel they there resolved that he should be exiled.[4]

According to the *Anglo-Saxon Chronicle* for 1017, Cnut banished Aedwig atheling, whom he afterwards ordered to be slain, and Eadwig king of the churls. In spite of the variation in the name it seems certain they were one and the same and that Eadwig was referred to in this derogatory manner because of his association with the peasants on his Plymstock estate. Cnut, determined to remove any threat to his sovereignty, asked Aethelweard, son of Aethelmaer the Great, to lay a trap for Eadwig in order to kill him, promising great honours. Although Aethelweard

pretended to agree he had no intention of complying, for he had close family connections with the old English royal house. Florence observes that Eadwig, the true successor: *was a minnow prince of friendly habit who deceived the guard and escaped to the west.*[n.4]

William, a monk of Malmesbury, who wrote *A History of the Kings of England*, gives a different version of the fate of Eadwig, King Edmund's brother and the rightful heir to the throne of England:

Edwin his brother, a youth of amiable disposition, was driven from England at the command of Cnut, and suffering severely for a considerable time, both by sea and land, his body, as is often the case, became affected by the anxiety of his mind and he died in England, where he lay concealed after a clandestine return, and lies buried at Tavistock.

William visited many monasteries in his search for information and this must have been the story told to him at Tavistock as to the manner of Eadwig's death.[5]

At that time the abbot of Tavistock was Lyfing, and although he has been described as a man of great eloquence, prudence and capacity, it has also been noted that he was undoubtedly worldly-minded, greedy and unscrupulous. He became a personal friend of Cnut, whom he accompanied on his visit to Denmark in 1019, and was also with him on his visit to Rome in 1026-7, when he brought back Cnut's letter to the English people. Following his return from Rome he was consecrated bishop of Crediton and also received Cnut's promise that the see of Cornwall (St Germans) would later be united with the see of Crediton.[6]

The Saxon Chronicle for 1020 records that after Cnut's return from Denmark there was at Easter a great council at Cirencester where ealdorman

Aethelweard and Eadwig king of the churls were outlawed. This edict probably led to Eadwig's hiding place being discovered and, ultimately, to his death.

Cnut died in 1035 and was succeeded by Harold, his son by Aelfgifu of Northampton, with whom Lyfing also gained favour, for in 1038 he was granted the see of Worcester which he held in plurality with Crediton. Finally, on the death in 1043 of his uncle, Brihtwold, bishop of Cornwall, this bishopric was merged in perpetuity with that of Crediton.

When Harold died in 1040, Harthacnut, son of Cnut and Emma, returned to England from Denmark to claim the throne. Because of the murder of his half-brother Alfred, younger son of King Ethelred and his second wife Emma of Normandy, when he came to England in 1036 to visit his mother at Winchester, it is said that he burned with great anger against Earl Godwine and Bishop Lyfing, whom he held responsible for this cruel deed. For his complicity Lyfing was deprived for a time of his see of Worcester, only regaining it the following year after he paid the king a large sum of money. [7]

In considering Lyfing's involvement in the murder of Alfred, who was also a half-brother of Eadwig, the suspicion grows that he may have arranged for the young prince to be led astray and then deserted by his companions, so that his death would appear to be accidental; the story of the message written in blood being invented in order to gain possession of Eadwig's Plymstock lands.

The fact that Plymstock figures decisively in the legend points to the young prince Eadwig as being the Childe whose death from exposure on Dartmoor created a legend that has refused to die. Whilst William of Malmesbury quite naturally accepted the story he was told at Tavistock Abbey, that Eadwig's death was brought about by mental anxiety, an examination of the evidence gives grounds for belief that his death was not the result of stress but was engineered by the clever Lyfing, whose reward was the intimate friendship of Cnut, with all the personal advancement that followed, and the appropriation of Eadwig's Plymstock lands to Tavistock Abbey.

Proof of Eadwig's place in the annals of Tavistock Abbey occurs in 1287, when Robert Champeaux, abbot of Tavistock, assigned to the abbey's almoner the tithes of Woodley in Lamerton for the purpose of honouring the abbey's four chief benefactors; Eadwig's name appearing as *the lord Edwyn*. On the anniversary of their death the great bell of the abbey was tolled, the monks were served with wine at dinner, and bread was baked and given to the poor. A surviving almoner's account for the year ending Michaelmas 1396, names Eadwig as *Edwynus de Plymstoke*. [8]

Further evidence appears in Bishop Stapeldon's Register under the date 14 January 1321-2, when in response to a petition from Robert Champeaux, he approved and confirmed the erection of a perpetual chantry in the parish church of Whitchurch. The four priests were to pray for the souls of the four great benefactors of Tavistock Abbey. The list is headed by Ordulf, founder of the abbey, followed by his wife Aluina of good memory, [n.5] Edwyni and Luvyngi.

Childe's Tomb

According to William Crossing, Childe's Tomb continued perfect until the year 1812, when it was practically destroyed by the workmen of a Mr Windeatt who had been granted an allotment or newtake and was building a farmhouse nearby. Some of the stones were used for doorsteps and others for a bridge over a

Childe's Tomb, Dartmoor.

stream. Restoration work was carried out in 1890, when nine of the original twelve granite stones which formed the stepped pedestal were replaced on the site and a new cross and socket-stone placed on top. Sad to say, no real effort was made to restore this monument to anything like its original appearance.[9]

The site of this tomb was examined by Crossing in 1887, when he recorded the existence of a kistvaen, of which one end and the cover-stone had been removed. Situated on a little mound about 15 feet in diameter, the three remaining stones of the kistvaen appeared to be of a later date than the examples generally found. He considered that although the plan of it was similar it was evidently of less antiquity. His findings suggest that Childe may have been originally interred at this spot and that some time before William of Malmesbury's visit to Tavistock, which must have been before 1125,[n.6] his body was removed and re-interred in the abbey church.

Although the shafts of most of the crosses on Dartmoor are set into the ground, an ancient map of the area which has been tentatively dated to 1240, or possibly earlier, shows two crosses, Syward's Cross and Hobajon's Cross, both set on to a square stepped base. Childe's Tomb does not appear on this map, which would support its dating to the late thirteenth or early fourteenth century.[10] The earliest known illustration of this monument, drawn and etched by P. H. Rogers in 1826, shows the cross with an octagonal plinth also set on to a square stepped base.[11] The suggested dating falls within the abbacy of Robert Champeaux and would, therefore, be in accordance with the other measures adopted by him to give the young prince Eadwig his rightful place among the abbey's principal benefactors.

Also during this period the conventual church of St Mary and St Rumon at Tavistock was rebuilt and on 1 August 1318 Bishop Stapeldon dedicated this church and two altars in the nave.[12] In it had been buried Ordulf, the founder of the abbey, and Eadwig, brother of King Edmund Ironside. Interesting remains of this church in the prevalent style of the thirteenth century can still be seen in the parish churchyard. These were illustrated in 1866 by Mr E. Appleton F.I.B.A. who, in view of the flat stones in front of this arch, considered it to be an altar stone.[13]

Remains of the Abbey Church, Tavistock.

However, excavations carried out in 1914 and in 1920 showed that the masonry was a fragment of the north cloister arcading which backed on to the abbey church. A site plan of the abbey buildings at Tavistock, prepared by Mr C. Ralegh Radford following the 1920 excavations, illustrated the position of the abbey church in relation to the parish church.[14] The abbey church was extremely narrow in proportion to its length, being only 21 paces wide compared to its length of 138 paces.[15]

There is an obvious lapse of time between Eadwig's outlawry at Easter in 1020 and his subsequent death on Dartmoor during a 'bitter snow', which must have been during the following winter; so may we suppose that his hiding place at Plymstock being discovered he was persuaded to take up residence at Tavistock Abbey. Florence hints at a reconciliation with Cnut – if so, this may have been a ploy to allay suspicion – but goes on to say that Eadwig the atheling, deceived by the treachery of those whom he had considered hitherto his closest friends, was killed, though guiltless. [16]

NOTES AND REFERENCES
CHILDE OF PLYMSTOKE

1. H.P.R. Finberg, *Lucerna*, 187-8.
2. Thomas Fuller, 1608-61, *The History of the Worthies of England*, 1662.
3. *The Anglo-Saxon Chronicle.*
4. Florence of Worcester, *English Hist. Docs*, c.500-1042.
5. William of Malmesbury, *Gesta Regum*, trans. by Sharpe.
6. *Dict. of National Biography*, Lyfing, sometimes Lyving.
7. F.M. Stenton, *Anglo-Saxon England*, 421-3.
8. Finberg, *Lucerna*, 187-8.
9. William Crossing, *The Ancient Stone Crosses of Dartmoor*, 50-63
10. C. Spence Bate, *The Original Map of the Royal Forest of Dartmoor*, Trans. Devonshire Association, V. 5, 1872, 510–48.
11. N.T. Carrington, *Dartmoor*, pub. 1826.
12. *Bishop Stapeldon's Register.*
13. *Trans. Devon. Assoc.* V. 1, 1862-6, 124-5.
14. Lady Radford, F.R. Hist. Soc., *Tavistock Abbey*, Trans. Exeter Diocesan, Architectural & Archaeological Society, V. IV, II
15. Finberg, *Tavistock Abbey*, The Abbey Buildings, App. c.
16. Florence, *Eng. Hist. Docs*, c.500-1042, 312
17. Gabriel Ronay, *The Lost King of England*, 27-8.

n.1.   Doom in this sense means lot or portion.

n.2.   Council of wise men.

n.3.   Cnut also banished the two infant sons of Edmund Ironside to Denmark under the care of Earl Walgar. When, in 1027, Walgar was warned of Cnut's intention to have the boys killed, he took them first to Sweden, where they found temporary refuge, and then in 1029 to Kievan Russia, where he placed them in the care of their aunt, Ingegerde, wife of Yaroslav the Great. [17]

n.4.   The original paragraph in Latin for this information has been taken from Lappenberg, *Cnut*, 200, n.1. Flor. Wigorn. a.1017: *Verum sequenti rege pacificatus est Eadwius: Eadwius vero clito, deceptus illorum insidiis quos eotenus amissimos habuit, jussu et petitione regis Canuti, eodem anno innocentur occiditur.*

n.5.   Ordulf's wife is generally known as Aelfwynn, a form of the Old English Elewyn, Aluina being a Latinised version.

n.6.   William of Malmesbury's most important work, *Gesta Regum Anglorum* was concluded by 1125.

Chapter Four
THE MANOR OF PLYMSTOCK

The Saxon manor of Plymstock remained in the possession of the abbot and convent of Tavistock after the Norman Conquest; Lyfing, who acquired this manor after the death of the young prince Eadwig, was succeeded in AD 1032 by Aldred, who was followed in 1043 by Sitric, the last English abbot, who died in 1082. Sitric was succeeded by Gaufrid, the first Norman abbot, who died in 1088.[1]

The Domesday Survey, 1084-6, records the following:

The abbot has a manor called Plemestocha, which abbot Sitric held on the day on which King Edward was alive and dead, and it rendered geld for half a hide. This can be ploughed by four ploughs. Of it the abbot has half a virgate and one plough in demesne, and the villeins have one virgate and a half and three ploughs. There the abbot has four villeins, and nine bordars, and five serfs, and four head of cattle, and seventy sheep, and thirty-four goats, and half an acre of meadow, and thirty acres of pasture. This manor is worth forty shillings; and when the abbot received it it was worth twenty shillings.[2]

The villeins were the freemen, who held tenements composed of a dwelling and a few acres of land. The bordars, a lower class, rendered menial service for a cottage and a plot of land held at the will of the lord; when not required to work on the demesne farm he could be employed elsewhere within the manor. The serfs had no property and no rights. In early times they lived in the outbuildings on the lord's demesne farm, but by the end of the twelfth century many changes had come about; although the slave, now known as *nativus,* had been given a measure of freedom and independence such as enough wood to build himself a cottage and a smallholding to enable him to feed himself and his family, he was still not free. He was bound to his lord and must obtain permission if he or his family wished to leave the manor for a period of time. It was the duty of the reeve to see that this rule was observed. That this bondage extended to descendants of the *nativus* is shown in 1532, when the Plymstock reeve was fined for neglecting to distrain a *nativus* whose son and daughter had gone to live outside the manor.[3] It seems that if a *nativus* or any member of his family stepped out of line he risked losing his smallholding and his cottage.

From very early days wheat was grown at Plymstock, as well as pill-corn and barley. The fertile limestone soil combined with its sheltered position between the high Staddon ridge to the south and the Plympton ridge to the north, was particularly suitable for corn–growing, the yield being greater and the market value higher than average.[4]

The Plymstock manor with 913 acres formed part of the ancient parish of 3550 acres, being bounded by Elburton on the east, Lower Goosewell and Radford

Pomphlett Creek – from a watercolour by John Swete, 1794.
(By permission of the Devon Record Office and Mrs V. Swete. D564 V.7 p.35).

on the south, the Cattewater on the west and the Saltram estate on the north. The manor was composed of two quite separate settlements; Plymstock being purely agricultural, with scattered farmhouses, cottages and fields, and Oreston, a fishing village on the shore of the Cattewater. The abbot's demesne or barton farm was at Pomphlett bordering the northern boundary of the manor, with its farm buildings, orchards and fields clustered round the farmhouse. Here also was the lord's common land called *Broxton* on which the villeins had a customary right to pasture their cattle. The farmhouse was situated at the head of a creek of Cattewater, the tide reaching a point near to the farm buildings where it was joined by the Billacombe Brook. When, during the fourteenth century, the abbot's grist mills were constructed over

29

Pomphlett Farmhouse.

the creek, the Plymstock tenants were bound to bring their corn to be ground at the manor mill instead of using the hand quern. Mill receipts run from 1392 to 1521. A lease dated 24 January 1532 conveyed Pomflyt Mills in the parish of Plymstock to Nicholas Rede and his two sons at a rental of £5.6s.8d. per annum.[5] Up to

Site of the Old Mill at Pomphlett, taken in 1965.

this time the manor tenants were required to repair the sluice of the mill and to clean out the leat which carried the Billacombe Brook to the mill-pond. Until the main A379 road was widened during the 1960s this leat could be seen alongside the old turnpike road. It is not clear just when the abbot ceased to cultivate his barton farm, but by the time the abbey was dissolved in 1539 this large farm had been divided into two tenements (see below).

In addition to their duties at the mill the Plymstock tenants were required to perform a number of errands; collecting a variety of commodities such as fish, wine and cider and carting them by barge to Morwellham, perhaps for use by the abbot at his country seat at Morwell,[6] or to be taken by road to the abbey at Tavistock. When the abbot needed a further supply of corn for his granaries one of the Tavistock burgesses would be sent with a message to the reeve at Plymstock, being recompensed for his trouble with a treyquarter loaf of bread. It would then be the duty of the reeve to arrange for delivery, packhorses being used for this purpose.[7]

Tavistock Abbey, in common with other large monasteries in Devon, was called upon in the spring of 1539 to surrender its house, lands and possessions to the Crown, the abbot's suzerainty over the Plymstock manor, which had lasted for well over 500 years, coming to an end. Letters Patent dated 4 July 1539 confirm that the king, Henry VIII, by authority of parliament, awarded to John Russell, knight, Baron Russell, and the Lady Anne his wife, all the lands formerly belonging to the dissolved Abbey of Tavistock. With this Act of State a new chapter begins for the Plymstock manor.

The new Lords of The Manor

John Russell was the son of James Russell of Dorset and his first wife Alice, daughter of John Wyse of Sydenham-Damerel in Devonshire. His meteoric rise to royal favour commenced in January 1506, when the ship carrying the Archduke Philip of Austria and his wife Joanna from the Netherlands to Spain encountered stormy weather and was driven ashore at Melcombe Regis in Weymouth Bay. The royal visitors were received by Sir Thomas Trenchard of Wolfeton, where John Russell, who had acquired a knowledge of foreign languages while travelling abroad on the family business, was introduced to him. Russell, in company with other Dorset men, escorted Philip to Windsor Castle, where he acted as his interpreter.[8]

Henry VII, who for some time had been anxious to make friends with Philip, welcomed him with open arms, for Philip was now in a strong position on the Continent. In his own right he was Duke of Burgundy and Lord of the Netherlands and since the death of Isabella of Castile he was King of Castile in right of his wife Joanna. Henry made the most of this unexpected twist of fate, entertained Philip royally and before he departed entered into a treaty of mutual defence against any aggressor. For the valuable service he had rendered to the Crown John Russell was taken into the royal household and made a gentleman of the privy chamber.

After the death of Henry in 1509 John Russell found favour with the new king, Henry VIII, often travelling to the Continent on confidential state missions. After the siege of Morlaix, where an arrow wound caused him to lose the sight of his right eye, he was knighted. In 1526 he married Anne, daughter of Sir Guy Sapcote, and the following year he visited Pope Clement on a diplomatic mission. After the dissolution of the monasteries Russell was appointed President of the Council for West Parts, which had been set up to quell any unrest, and was created Baron Russell. Henry also appointed him one of the sixteen counsellors of his infant son and at the coronation of Edward VI in February 1547, Russell was appointed the Great Steward of England. Three years later he was created Earl of Bedford.

Russell's only son, Francis, succeeded as second earl after his father died in 1555. When Elizabeth came to the throne in 1558 she appointed him a privy councillor. Like his father, Francis was a trusted envoy and is reputed to have been a kindly man who was much liked by his compatriots. He was godfather to Francis Drake, the famous seaman. Although he had several children by his first wife, Margaret, his two elder sons predeceased him and his third son, Francis, was killed by the Scots on 27 July 1585, leaving a son, Edward, who succeeded to the earldom the following day when his grandfather died on 28 July. [9]

The following year a survey was carried out of all the possessions of Edward Earl of Bedford, which included the manor of Plymstock. The State required that:

Every tenant of the manor, dying possessed of any of the customary lands of the manor, having a wife at the time of his death, such wife by the custom is to enjoy all the lands whereof her husband died seised, during her life, if she shall so long live sole and chaste. [10]

The introduction to this Survey notes:

that all the land within the manor, except the Lord's house, is customary land and the tenants hold their land without any copies of the Court Roll, but only by entry in the Court Book or Roll. The tenants for the most part pay no rent money but rent corn although some of them pay both money and corn. The measure for their rent corn is 'olde Winchester', their place to pay it is at the Abbey House of Tavistock now one of the Earl of Bedford's mansion houses, where the 'olde bushell' is still extant.

This payment of rent corn is further evidence of an early settlement, for Sir Frank Stenton, an authority on Anglo-Saxon England, tells us:

in the past, bishops and abbots, like kings, had been accustomed to take rents in kind from their properties.

For every tenant who died a heriot had to be paid to the lord of the manor of as many best beasts as the number of tenements or cottages held by him at the time of his death.

The Survey then lists the tenants of the manor, the size of their tenements, the amount of their rent wheat and their rent money. Fifty newly-built cottages follow and for these the payment was rent money ranging from 6d. to 12d. All the amounts shown were payable three times a year.

Released from the bonds of service imposed by Tavistock Abbey, life must have been much easier for the Plymstock tenants. The new cottages are just another example of improved living conditions, for previously the bordars would have lived in huts constructed of wattle and daub covered with thatch or turves. The better-off tenant farmers were now able to build dwellings with living rooms and chambers approached by a circular pole staircase. Some examples of these vernacular dwellings at Plymstock are now listed as Buildings of Architectural or Historic Interest.

The list of properties is headed by two tenements with 90 acres of land, obviously the old Pomphlett Barton Farm, the tenant in possession of these was Phillipa Sheare, widow, aged 60, the tenant in reversion being Alicia, aged 54, wife of William Ellys. The payment was 16 bushells of rent wheat and £3.6s.8d. rent money. All the other holdings were much smaller tenements with a dwelling and fields intermixed with those of their neighbours.

The second entry is a tenement of 20 acres of land held by John Lange senior, aged 80, with John Lange, aged 40, being the tenant in reversion. The rent wheat was twenty bushells. Lang's Tenement was at Oreston, where this family as well as the Ellis family, were well-known right up to the present century.

Two interesting entries follow: Margaret, wife of Richard Lawry, aged 40, holds one domus and half acre of land for which the rent is 2s.; and Joan Rodde, widow, aged 60, holds one parva domus, the rent being incorporated with that of Henry Rodde, aged 30, who held one tenement of two acres and paid six bushells of rent wheat.

The appellation *domus* was often used in medieval days for a religious house, *messuage* describing a farm or tenement house and outbuildings. It is possible this was the chaplain's residence and the half acre of land the former orchard fronting the house on the corner of Horn Lane (see Chapter 7). The *parva domus* would have been the 'Littlehouse' mentioned in a Deed of 1650 as lying near a place called 'The Tree', which was situated in the road at the junction of Dunstone Road with Church Road (see Manor Plan 1755). There was once a tiny cottage and a piece of ground opposite Candishes Tenement, now the Plymstock Inn, which has long since been incorporated in the churchyard.

The land on which the *domus* stood, as with the church and the tithe barn, was land of the manor and there is evidence that by 1600 it had been replaced by an imposing Elizabethan dwelling named Downhorne, the lessee being Thomas Barkley, Gentleman. A pond by the roadside at the junction of Horn Lane with Church Road was anciently known as the 'Prior's Pond', and thought to have been used for the ducks and geese given in tithe. An item in the Surveyor of Highways accounts for 1694 reads: 'to mend horn lane and abots pool.' [11] The manor plan of 1755, the Tithe Map of 1842 and the Ordnance Survey Map of 1915 all show a definite kink in the road at this place. This pond was filled in and the site is now occupied by three shops.

Also of interest in the 1586 Survey is the tenancy of a cottage to Simon Gallesworthy, a forbear of the well-known author, John Galsworthy. This may have been a cottage called Triggs at Burrow Hill, near its junction with Furzehatt Road, which was occupied in 1755 by Robert Galsworthy. Triggs was demolished sometime between 1755 and 1800, a pair of semi-detached houses being built on the site. Alternatively, this entry may apply to a cottage at Oreston, for later records show the Galsworthys holding property there.

The list of cottages is followed by details of a Lease of Pomphlett Mills, granted by Francis Earl of Bedford on 1 August 1574 to Thomas Rede (deceased), Nicholas Rede, aged 45, and John Rede his son (also deceased) of two grinding mills within the parish of Plymstock, the fine being £13.6s.8d. and the annual rent £5.6s.8d. (see above).

The Survey closes with special mention of the Courthouse, formerly occupied by Humphrey Brymsdon and Clemente his wife, and granted by Indenture dated 20 March 1582 to Humphrey Hake and Elizabeth his wife of the whole Capital *messuage* named the Corte House and two enclosures adjacent containing five acres of land, one called the Poundhouse and one the Columbarium (dovecote). The land was Culver Park (an orchard and herb garden) and Well Park. The fine was £3.6s.8d., the annual rent 45s. and no heriot was required (see Manor Plan 1755).

This was the lord of the manor's house where his courts were held, the chairman being the lord or, more likely, his steward. An *Olde Survey Booke* of 1690 mentions 'The Great Hall' and 'The Dining Room'. No doubt both were used on Court days. The business was concerned principally with the tenants' lands and the succession to these lands. The reeves, one for Plymstock and one for Oreston, reported any death that had occurred after the last court was held and presented the cases, usually only minor offences such as trespass on another's holding, allowing their tenements or their hedges to be badly repaired and, in one case, pasturing too many cattle on the lord's common at Broxton to the grievous harm of others. For all these and similar offences, a fine, usually 3d, would be imposed. All tenement holders were required to attend the courts and absentees were fined.[12]

Humphrey Hake, as lessee of the Corte House on favourable terms, would have been the official responsible for the proper ordering of the court, the reception of the manor representative and the reeves, and no doubt for providing suitable refreshment. He was also bound to perform the office of reeve if elected or appointed. Humphrey Hake, aged 40, was also tenant in possession of one of the newly-built cottages, his daughter Agnes, aged five, being the tenant in reversion. The rent for this cottage was 12d. A descendant of this family, Thomas Hake, kept a school at Plymstock and, as a result, suffered badly under the Commonwealth government (see Chapter 11). Despite their troubles the Hake family survived and, like the Lang and Ellis families of Oreston, continued up to and during the present century.

When Edward, third Earl of Devon, died in 1627 the earldom passed to his cousin Francis, son of Sir William Russell, fourth son of the second earl. In 1651 Francis died of smallpox, being succeeded by his eldest son William, who became the fifth earl and was created first Duke of Bedford in 1694. William's wife, Anne, was a daughter of Robert Carr, Earl of Somerset and erstwhile favourite of James I. Tragedy struck this family, for their eldest son, John, died in infancy, Francis, the second son, died in 1678 and William, the third son, was tried on a charge of high treason in 1683, being sentenced to death by the Recorder of London, Sir George Treby of Plympton St Maurice. William Russell, known as 'The Patriot', was executed in Lincoln's Inn Fields on 21 July. On the accession of William and Mary in 1689 Russell's name was vindicated by the reversal of his attainder. William's son, Wriothesley, succeeded his grandfather as second Duke of Bedford.[13]

From time to time further surveys were made of the Duke of Bedford's Plymstock estate, notably in 1755, when a large plan was produced, each tenement property and field bearing a letter and a number: the ancient tenements in Old English lettering and the remainder in plain capitals. The cottages are only numbered. The Plan is coloured and each field has a border in a deeper shade; the tenement fields being intermixed, this makes for easier identification. An accompanying book identifies each property under the name by which it has always been known and gives the name of the tenant at that time. [14]

The only other major survey is the Plymstock Tithe Map 1842, which covers the whole of the civil parish. Each building and each parcel of land is numbered, the Tithe Apportionment Book grouping these together under the names of their owners. Land measurements and the names of the occupiers are also given. Only three copies of this map and book were made; one for the Tithe Commissioners (now at the P.R.O. at Kew), one for the Devon County Council (now at the D.R.O. at Exeter) and one for the Plymstock Parish Council (now at the W.D.R.O. at Plymouth). [n.1] (See also Chapter 10.).

At the time of the disposal of the Duke of Bedford's Plymstock Estate by Public Auction in 1911, most of the original tenement holdings were broken down into convenient lots and purchase of these by individuals and by building speculators opened the way for the eventual expansion of Plymstock. An extract from the 1915 Ordnance Survey Map, CXXIV S.W., shows that very little change had taken place since the 1842 Survey.

The sporadic building which took place following the First World War resulted in untidy ribbon-type development, which lacked an overall plan. Then, in 1925, the Plympton St Mary Rural District Council commenced the preparation of a Planning Scheme for Plymstock. This took several years to pass through the various stages of draft plan, advertisement and approval, until, in 1939, the scheme received the approval of the Minister for Health. At its third reading in September 1939 the Plymstock Planning Scheme received the approval of both Houses of Parliament. [15]

This scheme incorporated some valuable covenants, one being an agreement made on 8 February 1930 between the Rural District Council of Plympton and the Right Honourable Edmund Robert Earl of Morley that: (a) about 40 acres of land at Billacombe should be reserved for public open space and (b) that Dunstone Plantation, containing about 8.36 acres, should be reserved for public open space. The land at Billacombe was conveyed to the Council for a nominal sum and Dunstone Plantation was given to the Council in 1935. (See also Chapter 20).

Unfortunately, due to the Second World War, the provisions of the Planning Scheme were not put into effect. Some of these have since been revoked, although the covenants mentioned above still remain binding. The post-war years led to the preparation of a joint Plympton/Plymstock Development Plan, which was approved in 1953. A 1960 Ordnance Survey Map, SX5152 & 5153, shows that by that time considerable residential development had taken place around Plymstock and during the next two decades considerable infilling took place within the confines of the village.

On 1 April 1967 the councils for the Plympton St Mary rural district and the Plymstock parish were dissolved, the greater part of this parish being amalgamated with the city of Plymouth, the remainder going to the parishes of Wembury and Brixton. [16]

Comparison with an extract from a 1989 Ordnance Survey Map, SX55 S.W., indicates the rapid pace of development which has encompassed the once isolated villages of Elburton, Hooe and Staddiscombe.

In 1965, under the auspices of the Civic Trust, a Civic Society was formed for Plymstock and District, which keeps a watchful eye on planning applications. The Society has also carried out various environmental improvements, one example being land in the centre of the village at Elburton which was laid out as a garden, provided with a seat and planted with trees. The village cross now stands on this site. An ongoing project, commenced in 1974, is an arboretum in Radford Park, this work being carried out by enthusiastic volunteers.

An Historical and Architectural Survey of all the older properties in the centre of Plymstock was carried out in 1970 for the Civic Society. The making of this Survey was prompted by the simultaneous threat to the future survival of such ancient buildings as Downhorn and Burrow Farmhouses, when it became clear that prompt action was necessary if the ancient village of Plymstock was not to lose the bulk of its remaining character. As a result of this survey a number of properties were listed by the Department of the Environment either as Grade II or were placed on the Local List.

Of the surviving Plymstock properties, apart from the church, four are perhaps worthy of special mention as having a particular place in the history of the manor. They are: Courthouse Farm, Downhorn Farm, the former Workhouse and Burrow Lodge.

Courthouse, already mentioned above, is obviously the most important because of its medieval links with the manor. The first documentary evidence of a building on this site is a Deed, dated 1302, which recites that:

A certain Wall was at the common charges of the Abbot and Convent of Tavistock and the Prior and Convent of Plympton; raised in the Manor of Plympstock between the Court of the said Abbot and the Grange of the said Prior. It was thereby covenanted between the said parties that this Wall should be common to them, And that the Prior and Convent of Plympton and their successors might build, repair and sustain their House upon the said Wall for ever; And that the said Abbot and Convent might on their side whenever they pleased, build, repair & sustain a House for ever and affix their timber to the said Common Wall. [17]

Downhorn Farm – from an oil painting c. 1920.

It would appear from the position of the Prior's tithe barn that the east wall may have been affixed to this Common Wall. Also, the *Olde Survey Booke*, 1690, under 'Corte House' mentions the Herb Garden. The records of Tavistock Abbey show that this garden at Plymstock yielded a small revenue from the sale of herbage.

Downhorn Farm – originally Down Horne – is easily the most attractive ancient building in the manor. It was almost certainly built for Thomas Barkley, Gentleman, of Okenbury, Kingsbridge. J.C. Bellamy noted in 1853 that 'stained glass with coats of arms was, formerly, in a window.' [18] This was probably the Barkley Arms: sable; a fesse ermine between three cinquefoils argent. Thomas Barkley's son and heir, Thomas, was baptised at Plymstock Church in 1603. Subsequently three daughters and another son,

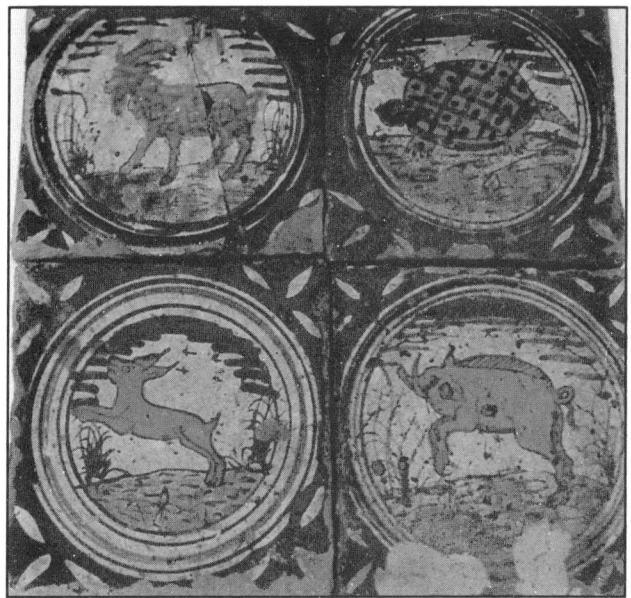

Late sixteenth century tiles from the Netherlands, discovered at Downhorn.

Ancient entrance at Downhorn.

37

Henry, were baptised at Plymstock. Thomas Barkley's signature appears in the Plymstock Rate Book in conjunction with the signatures of John Harris, who succeeded to Radford in 1625, and Richard Franklin, cleric, 1617-37. [19] Nothing more is known of this family and, in 1655, Thomas Riche, Gentleman, was granted a 99 years lease of Down Horne, formerly in the possession of Thomas Barkley: the estate being held on the lives of Thomas Riche the father, Thomas Riche, his son, and Ellen Bogan, daughter of William Bogan of Little Hempston near Totnes. [20]

Thomas Riche's son, Thomas, married Ellen Bogan the same year, their only child Ellen, b.1662, marrying William Corham, a nephew of the Blakes of Combe Farm, Elburton, in 1680. Thomas Riche, the father, d.1664 and in 1685 Ellen Riche, then also widowed, assigned the lease of Down Horne to her son-in-law, William Corham, who died in 1704. [21] More land had been added and in 1709 William and Ellen's son, William, held 43 acres. [22] A rental of the Manor of Plymstock dated 1742 shows William Corham, 55 years, and Rebecca Corham, 54 years, as holding Down Horne. A William Corham, probably a son, died in 1750 and William Corham Esq. died in 1753. In 1755 the Manor Survey shows that Rebecca Corham holds on two lives, 'House, 2 Barns, Stable, Yard & 3 gardens, also The Orchard, total holding 43 acres 33 perches'. Rebecca Corham, then aged 67 years, appears to have been the last surviving member of this family. No record of her burial has been found in the parish registers.

In 1768 Thomas Emmett was granted a 99 years lease of Down Horne, still containing 43 acres 33 perches, by John, fourth Duke of Bedford, on the lives of the lessee, 32 years, Elizabeth his wife, 33 years and Thomas his son, three years. By 1781 Thomas Emmett must have died, for a lease of Down Horne was granted to Tubal Lewis on the lives of Thomas Emmett, 16 years, Catherine Lewis, 35 years, and Jonny Lewis, 9 years. [23]

The Census Returns for 1891 show that Richard Kingdom, 62 years, was a farmer at Down Horne, and in 1923 a Plymouth Directory shows that Richard Kingdom, almost certainly a son, was farming at Down Horne. As with other Bedford properties Down Horne would have been sold in 1911.

The Parish Workhouse, built 1823-5, replaced the old Poorhouse by the church. The Plymstock minister, James Lampen Harris, obviously took a great interest in the well–being and comfort of the inmates, for a letter to the Duke of Bedford's London Agent thanks the duke for his prompt compliance to a request for financial assistance to put a ceiling in the attics as a protection against heat in summer and cold in winter. He also described the diet of the House, which was adequate and varied. The garden nearby supplied the House with vegetables. At that time, 15 November 1827, there were 26 grown persons and 18 children. His report concludes: 'When we get Oakum from the Dockyard they receive a fourth part of their earnings and are happy and contented.'[24]

This state of affairs was not to continue for many more years, for the unpopular Poor Law Act of 1834 withdrew much of the poor law administration from the parochial authorities, one outcome being the grouping of parishes under a central body; Plymstock coming under the Plympton St Mary Union, which was composed of twenty parishes (see also Chapter 8).

Plymstock Workhouse was closed, probably about 1837, when the inmates were transferred to the Plympton Workhouse, which was administered by a Board of Guardians. The Census Returns for 1841 show that this Workhouse had a total of 178 inmates, their ages ranging from 3 months to 75 years.

The Overseers of the Poor at Plymstock continued as administrators of Poor Law Relief (see Chapter 8) and were also held responsible for the misdemeanours of their parishioners. One example affecting a neighbouring parish is an Order that the Overseers of Brixton do apply for a Warrant to apprehend Elizabeth Summers for absconding from the Workhouse with the Union clothes so that she may be sent to Bridewell (prison) for the offence. [25]

Life was much harder under the new system with its strict rules and regulations. Formerly, at Plymstock, there were no written rules of discipline except that 'Inmates were expected to conform to House and not absent themselves without the leave of the Master or Mistress.'

In 1851 the Census Returns show that 'Old Parish Workhouse' was occupied by Samuel Gould, his wife and two daughters. It is not even mentioned in the 1841 Census, so was probably unoccupied at that time.

Burrow Lodge is well-known locally as the house built by Dr George Bellamy using timber purchased when the famous battleship *Bellerophon* was broken up. Dr Bellamy, who entered the navy in 1793, served during the Napoleonic Wars and was Surgeon on this ship during the Battle of the Nile in 1798. *Bellerophon* also took part in two other great sea battles during the wars with France; the Glorious First of June, 1794, under Lord Howe and the Battle of Trafalgar, 1805, under Lord Nelson.

George Bellamy was a colourful character who became mayor of Plymouth in September 1811. During his mayoralty the military authorities claimed the whole of Plymouth Hoe to the exclusion of the

Burrow Lodge, Plymstock.

townspeople. Bellamy and members of the corporation marched up on the Hoe and threw down the barriers which the government department had erected. Bound stones were set up in order to establish the right of the corporation. They did, however, concede the right of military troops to exercise on the Hoe – a right which continues to the present day. Although he became involved in local affairs Dr Bellamy continued his naval career and during the year following his mayoralty he was on board the royal yacht *Mary* when he was made physician to the Duke of Clarence, later William IV. He was placed on the retired list in 1817. [26]

Bellerophon continued throughout the long wars with France to defend Britain from the threat of invasion until, on 15 July 1815, while cruising in Basque Roads off Rochefort, Captain Maitland accepted the surrender to the British government of Napoleon Bonaparte, who was taken on board at 6 a.m. Ten days later on a fine morning at the end of July *Bellerophon* entered Plymouth harbour.

The sight of the 74-gun man o'war attracted a large crowd of waterborne sightseers, all anxious to catch a glimpse of the defeated Emperor. At last, Bonaparte, wearing his old world-famous green coat, came up the gangway and mounted the poop deck.[27] While Admiralty orders were awaited a young Plymouth artist, Charles Lock Eastlake, hovered round the vessel in a boat, taking rapid sketches. Seeing Eastlake at work, Napoleon held his pose and later sent ashore a uniform and decorations for the artist's use.

Subsequently, Eastlake produced a small full-length portrait of Napoleon which was so much admired that another larger portrait incorporating other figures was commenced. This painting was sold by the artist for 1000 guineas.

Orders were at last received that Napoleon would not be permitted to land in England, but was to live henceforth on the island of St Helena. With hopes of hospitality and protection dashed, Napoleon did not appear on deck again. On 8 August *Bellerophon* sailed

The Bellerophon *(a prison hulk, renamed* Captivity*) lies at Hamoaze, Devonport.*

40

out into the Channel, where Napoleon was transferred to H.M.S. Northumberland under the command of Captain Cockburn, whose orders were to carry him to his place of exile.

In October 1863, in his 90th year, George Bellamy died, two years after the death of his wife Mary. They were both buried at Charles Church, Plymouth. So ended a life spent in courageous service to his country. Also, without his timely intervention the citizens of Plymouth would have been denied their right of recreation and enjoyment on the Hoe.

NOTES AND REFERENCES
THE MANOR OF PLYMSTOCK

1. Dr G. Oliver, *Monasticon Dioceses Exoniensis*, MDCCCXLVI.
2. *Exeter Domesday.*
3. H.P.R. Finberg, *Tavistock Abbey*, 258.
4. Finberg, *Tavistock Abbey*, 241
5. *Bedford Records*, D. Bundle, (74) No.5.
6. H.P.R. Finberg, *West Country Historical Studies*, Morwell, 159.
7. Finberg, *Tavistock Abbey*, 82.
8. John, Duke of Bedford, *A Silver–Plated Spoon.*
9. *Dictionary of National Biography.*
10. *State Papers – Domestic*, (Case G. Eliz. No.2) 1581–90; Public Record Office.
11. The records of the *Plymstock Parish Council*, W.D.R.O.
12. *Elizabethan Court Roll*, November 1574, Bedford Records, D.R.O.
13. *Dict. Nat. Biog.*
14. *Plymstock Manor Survey 1755*, Bedford Records, T1258 M/E24. D.R.O.
15. *Public Record Office.*
16. *The Plymouth Order 1866.*
17. *Bedford Records*, D. Bundle, (74) No.2.
18. J.C. Bellamy, *MS. History of Plymstock 1853.*
19. *Plymstock Rate Book*, W.D.R.O.
20. *Bedford Records*, The Olde Survey Booke 1690, 3. L1258 18/41.
21. *Bedford Records*, Downhorne Tenement, Deed, 24 June 1685.
22. *Bedford Records*, Survey Book, 1709.
23. *Bedford Records*, Lease, Sept. 29 1768.
24. *Bedford Records*, L1258 E. Letters, No. 122. Misc. Plymstock Workhouse 1807-37.
25. *Plympton St Mary Union* Guardians Minute Book.
26. J. Elliot Square, *The Book of Plymouth*, 94-6.
27. Emil Ludwig, *Napoleon*, 540-3.

PLYMSTOCK'S HISTORIC BUILDINGS

28. *Survey of Plymstock Buildings 1970*, Architectural information supplied by James Barber, Plymouth City Museum.
29. *Census Returns* 1861.

n.1. The former Plymstock Parish Council's copy of the written Apportionment is being held in private hands and only an abridged printed copy can be seen at the West Devon Record Office or at the Local Studies Department, Plymouth Central Library.

Chapter Five

PLYMSTOCK'S HISTORIC BUILDINGS

The following chapter includes a brief history and summary of the architectural details of each property,[28] together with its grading, where appropriate, as a Building of Architectural or Historic Interest.

The two maps here are extracts from the Plymstock Manor Plan 1755 and the Plymstock Parish Tithe Map 1842. Both are reduced in size from the original Surveys. These illustrate the changes that had taken place between the two dates; shading indicating additions or replacements. The M.P. letters and the T.M. numbers are for identification purposes only and do not relate to those shown on the original maps. The extract from the Ordnance Survey map (see page vi) shows the undeveloped land surrounding the village before the First World War.

M.P. A. *The Parish Church of St Mary & All Saints* Grade B
T.M. 1. (See Medieval Chapel and Parish Church)
M.P. B. *The Workhouse & Garden* adjoining the Church Yard The Church Wardens of Plymstock
M.P. C. *The Priory alias Tything Barn*
T.M. 2. Still there in 1875 but demolished soon afterwards.
M.P. D. *The Court House* for the Manor of Plymstock Grade II
T.M. 3. By 1842 Court House had become a farm with a total holding of 55 acres. When sold by public auction in 1911 Courthouse Farm comprised 86 acres.

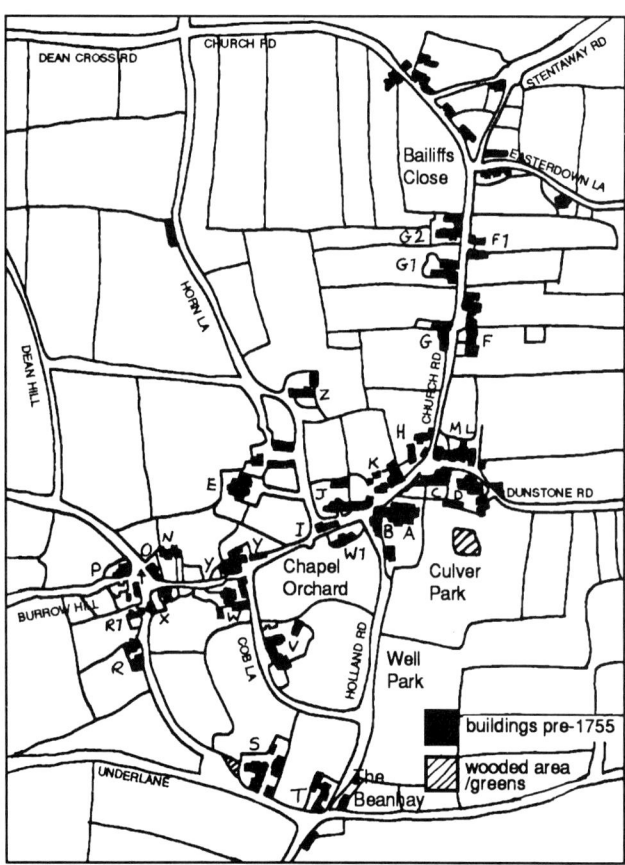

Map based on the Plymstock Manor Plan of 1755.

Court House, although much modernised at different periods, incorporates noteworthy features, such as the series of massive oak beams which support the ceiling of the ground floor north room: each beam has been adzed to shape and has chamfered edges with plain triangular end-stops and rests at either end on plain, massive granite corbels. The present fireplace has a modern mantelpiece and grate, but leads into the

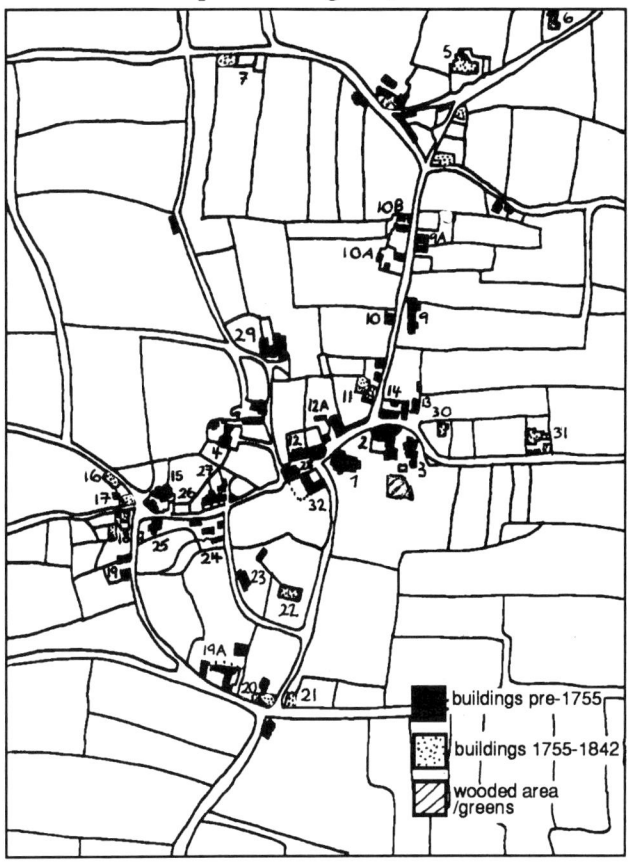

Map based on the Plymstock Tithe Map of 1842.

large, early chimney stack which is a prominent feature of the rear external elevation. An early granite or oak lintel may still be present behind or above the modern mantel-shelf. The roof trusses, which are thought to be mid or late seventeenth century in date, are in excellent condition. The oak beams are adzed unusually regularly to shape and all the members are secured to each other by wooden pegs; the principal rafters are also notched into each other at the apex.

M.P. E. *Downhorn Farm.* The front of this large house is distinguished by two (**T.M.4.**) rectangular projections, one of which is the porch, and the other containing the main staircase, which is wide and partly curved, is entered directly from the main living room – formerly the hall. This room has a deep moulded plaster frieze representing ornamental figures separated by blank shields. At the rear of the house are two tall rectangular stacks from prominent chimney breasts. In 1755 Rebecca Corham, in addition to the tenement holding of 43 acres, also held *Little Orchard* fronting the house on the corner of Horn Lane. This was the half acre of land attached to the domus mentioned in the Survey of 1586. Grade II

M.P. I. *Island House.* Occupied in 1755 by William Bartlett, when it was (**T.M.28.**) known as Woodwards Cottage. In 1842 Island House was occupied by Susan Taylor. Date of demolition not known.

M.P. F. *Peeks Tenement.* An ancient farmhouse with the dwelling at the south (**T.M.9.**) end and a barn or shippon at the north. The north end has been rebuilt and converted into a dwelling house. The original house is of seventeenth century date or even earlier. Like other Plymstock farmhouses, e.g. Downhorn and Burrow, it occupies a site continuously inhabited since early medieval or even Anglo-Saxon times. The staircase is of pole or newel type, winding up to the

Magnolia Cottage.

the lease of the old tenement and in 1843 the Rev. Frederick Pym occupied the early nineteenth century house. During the 1890s and well into the present century Oaklands was occupied by the Bishop family, remembered because one of their children, born 1897, who later became Major General Sir Alec Bishop, wrote an account for the parish magazine of life in the village during his boyhood. He described Plymstock as a rather remote and beautiful village.

Wages, were very modest in those days, and although we were not well off we were able to employ a cook, a housemaid, a groom, and a part-time gardener.

He mentions that the occupiers of farms and houses in the village were given the opportunity of buying at

first floor level within a square tower, which may be a later addition of seventeenth century date to an older structure. Grade II.

M.P. G.(T.M.10) *Magnolia Cottage.* This cottage is first mentioned in a Manor Survey of 1709 when it was *Bartlets Cottage* held by John Bartlet on the lives of himself and son. It then contained '1 Ground Roome and 1 Chamber.' It was enlarged early in the eighteenth century, before the extinction of the vernacular tradition. This quaint and picturesque cottage took its name from the magnolia which grew against the front wall. Although an Order was made on 5 March 1971 listing Magnolia Cottage as a Building of Special Architectural or Historic Interest, on 15 October 1971 Plymouth City Council approved Listed Building Consent for its demolition.

M.P. H. (T.M.11) *Oaklands.* This was a Georgian residence of considerable charm, which was built on the site of a dwelling house which once belonged to Forsters Leys Tenement. In 1755 Edward Avent held

Oaklands, Plymstock. This house was demolished and Selkirk House, a home for the elderly, has been built on the site.

very reasonable prices the properties they had been renting from the Duke and this enabled his parents and many other people in the village to become the owners of their homes. Transport at that time was limited to bicycles and a pony cart. The house was lit by oil lamps and candles. Summer recreations included tennis on their own lawn and expeditions in the pony cart to one of the beaches a few miles off for a bathe and a picnic. Sir Alec's father was a lay reader and often took the services at the Church of the Good Shepherd at Oreston. The Plympton Rural District Council later acquired this property with the intention of making it a home for the aged. This did not come about and when Plymstock was amalgamated with Plymouth in 1967 the ownership passed to the city council. Being vacant, the property soon deteriorated and during the 1970s Oaklands was demolished. Selkirk House, a home for the elderly, has been built on this site.

M.P. J. (T.M.12) *Three cottages* on the corner of Horn Lane and Church Road. Demolished about 1929 when the Church Hall was built on this site.

M.P. K. (T.M.12a) *Plymstock Inn.* This site originally formed part of Candishes Tenement and comprised a house, barns, stable, yard, two gardens and an orchard, the total tenement being 19 acres 38 perches, the fields lying in various parts of the manor. The Candish family were prominent at Plymstock during the sixteenth century, holding no less than four tenements in 1586, all of which paid rent wheat. In 1755 this tenement was in hand and afterwards leased to John White. By 1843 the tenement had been broken up, the house then being in the possession of Thomas Mann. In 1887 the *Western Figaro*, a weekly newspaper published by the Parade Printing Works, Plymouth, carried a drawing of Plymstock church tower and the north entrance, and showing also the front of this property bearing the sign *Church Inn.* Judging by the external elevations, and by the ground floor rooms, the present building would appear to be no older than the nineteenth century with more modern additions. It was sold as the *Plymstock Inn* in 1911. Local List.

M.P. L. (T.M.13) *74 Dunstone Road,* opposite the Court House. This property once formed part of the dwelling house belonging to Peeks Tenement, the lease being held in 1755 by John Pyke. This house is the west wing only of a large vernacular dwelling, the eastern part of which was removed between 1755 and 1842. The exterior suggests a building date in the seventeenth century, with characteristic massive stone chimney stacks to the west and north elevations. Grade II.

M.P. M. (T.M.14) *76 Dunstone Road.* At the time of the Tithe Map Survey in 1842 this property and 74 Dunstone Road were united in a single tenement. The rear portion was a bakery in later years. On the site of numbers 78 and 80 Dunstone Road was a cottage called *Woodcocks* and in 1843 Jane Taylor occupied a house on this site, as well as a cottage opposite which adjoined the Tithe Barn. The present properties are probably no older than mid nineteenth century.

M.P. N. (T.M.15) *Burrow Farm,* formerly Burt's Tenement, retaining this name until 1843. In 1586 John Burt paid $16\frac{1}{2}$ bushells of rent wheat. In 1755 this tenement was held by Francis Badcock, the total being 19 acres (scattered fields). Part of this tenement at Goosewell was sold to John Harris of Radford in 1807 and a field at Billacombe was sold to Lord Boringdon. Burrow Farm consists of two detached portions of an ancient farmhouse, linked into a modern dwelling by a relatively recent building occupying part of the site of the missing section of the original house. The present west wing consists of the hall and parlour of a late medieval long house, erected before 1600 A.D., together with a staircase tower enclosing a spiral staircase added to the original building, perhaps in the mid seventeenth century. This house, with its steeply pitched roofs and massive chimney stacks, is a fine example of the local vernacular architecture. Grade II.

M.P. O. *Saunders Cottage.* Still there in 1842, but later demolished.

M.P. X. (T.M.25) *Russell House.* A house and shrubbery, date of demolition not known.

M.P. P. (T.M.17) *Jessops Cottage.* This was the site of a dwelling belonging to Bridgmans Tenement. Leased in 1695 to John Jessop, together with a plot called the Bean Hay. After the death of John Jessop his widow married Silas Bickford and in 1717 the lease was granted to him. In 1769 the lease passed to Mr John Burrow. This cottage was demolished, a house named Creacombe being built in its place. The Census Returns for 1891 show that James B. Jacob, a funeral practitioner, occupied Creacombe Cottage. This also has been demolished.

T.M.16. *Elm Cottage.* This property was built alongside and in the grounds of Jessops Cottage, about 1760–70. Local List. This site appears to be the one referred to in a MS by J. Brooking Rowe in 1875:

> *On the site of an ancient property in the slope of Burrow Hill, Spanish coins and weapons have been found.*

At that time Mr William Lugg, the Assessor of Taxes at Plymstock, was the owner of some very valuable ancient coins found there and he possessed a sort of Museum of Antiquities procured from the locality. Amongst these was the cravat worn by Sir Walter Ralegh during his imprisonment at Radford in 1618. Items of interest in the garden included a sundial dated 1776.

M.P. R1. *Mortcomb Tenement.* In 1651 Richard Hake held this tenement, then Eleanor Candish. In 1690 the tenement was in hand. In 1755 it was held by Mary Edwards' Executors, the total holding being 16 acres. By 1842 the old tenement had been dispersed, the house being held by Thomas Doddridge. (Demolished).

M.P. R. (T.M.19) *Smithy.* Formerly belonging to the above tenement. This small building has been a blacksmith's shop since soon after the 1755 Survey, judging by a pencilled–in note on the entry. The house to which it originally belonged has been demolished and the smithy itself, reduced in size, was, in 1970, very much a going concern, adapting itself to a changing world after some two hundred years of active life. Because of its unique character this building was listed Grade II. Later becoming disused it fell into a very dilapidated condition, but has now been attractively restored as a dwelling–house.

M.P. S. (T.M.19A) *Gales alias Jackman's Tenement.* This holding comprised a house, barns, outhouses, yards, gardens and orchard and fields intermixed with those of other tenements. The old group of buildings has been demolished and a modern dwelling-house built on the site.

M.P. Q. (T.M.18) *Triggs Cottage.* Robert Galsworthy was the tenant in 1755. This cottage was demolished before 1790 and a pair of semi-detached houses, *Northenhay and Southern House* were built on this site about 1790, both altered about 100 years later. Each property retains its original later eighteenth century wooden street door-case and, internally, many late eighteenth century features are present.

M.P. T. (T.M.20) *Furzehatt House. Furzhats,* a much larger property than the present house stood on this site. According to the *Olde Survey Booke 1690,* the original building was held in two parts, one being the *Mynisters House.* The total acreage for the higher part of this tenement was 21 acres and the other part, which comprised the lower part of the house, part of the yard with the garden and orchard, was 16 acres. By 1842 the old tenement no longer existed, the house being in the possession of Thomas Neesham. Furzehatt is a pleasant late Georgian house built shortly before or after 1800. Grade II.

M.P. U. (T.M.21) *Benhay House.* This is a property of Regency character, built 1810–20. In 1755 a dwelling on this site was known as Woods Cottage. (See Chapter 15, Goosewell). In 1842 the new house included the Bean Hay, formerly leased with Jessops Cottage, (see above) and later occupied by Peter Franklin Bellamy, surgeon, second son of Dr George Bellamy of Burrow Lodge. [29] Grade II.

T.M.22. *Amberley House.* This property was built on land attached to Gaude's Tenement, some time after 1755. Although it does not appear on the 1755 Manor Plan it is shown on a 1784 Survey Map. In 1842 the house was occupied by James Courtenay.

M.P. 5. (T.M.23) *Oak Cottage.* This was formerly Gaudes Tenement House, the total tenement being 48 acres. By the time of the 1842 Survey this holding had lost its lands. The tenant of the house at that time was Elizabeth Cobbe. The name Gaude, variously spelt Gawd or Gawde, is much in evidence in the Plymstock Parish Registers from 1591, when George Gawde's daughter Elizabeth was baptised during that year, and throughout the first half of the seventeenth century. Also, on 30 September 1606, when John Harris of Lanrest in Cornwall purchased the remainder of the Lease of the Plymstock Tithes from Sir Anthony Rous and his son Arthur, George Gawde was one of the attorneys appointed by them to deliver over the chapel to him. Oak Cottage is an ancient farmhouse of several phases, now modernised and divided into three dwelling units. Grade II.

M.P. W. (T.M.24) *Candishes Tenement at Tree.* In 1755 the Revd William Cookson held this house and tenement, the total tenement being 19 acres. This holding must have been broken up, for in 1845 the house and barns had been demolished and a vicarage built on this site. (See Chapter 8). The vicarage has been removed to another building nearby and the old house is now the Treetops Day Nursery.

M.P. Y. (T.M.27) *Marchants, formerly Cloaks Tenement.* This appears to have been a large tenement which was divided in the latter half of the seventeenth century. Lately in the possession of John Warner, the portion leased to Silas Bickford comprised one dwelling house, one malt-house and several closes of land, containing in the whole ten acres. At the time of the 1842 Survey this tenement, then 19 acres, was held jointly by Silas Hodge and Jacob Hodge. The present house probably replaced the earlier vernacular dwelling shortly before the mid eighteenth century, about 1720-40, this dating being based on internal features. Grade II.

M.P. Y1. *Louville.* An attractive property similar in style and date to its neighbour, Marchants. The south front retains only a part of its original slate-hanging, but has a particularly effective Venetian window in the gable over the street door. The street door itself is original, with a nice open-work Victorian cast iron knocker. A date in the second quarter of the eighteenth century is indicated by the character of the ground floor front rooms, with half-panelling to chair-rail level and original panelled doors. Grade II.

M.P. Z. (T.M.29) *Bedford Cottages.* Now three dwelling units. These cottages once formed the dwelling house and an adjoining barn belonging to an old tenement known as *Futtrells.* In 1586 Jacob Futterell held two tenements and 20 acres of land, for which he paid 31 bushells of wheat rent. By 1670 this tenement had been divided into four parts, one, held by Charles Terdre, being a house, barn, garden, orchard and Horn Field, total four acres. A barn adjoining Charles Terdre's house was held by Richard Fillis, who also held one fourth part of the original tenement, his holding totalling 14 acres. A cottage was built on the site of this barn by George Bellamy which he called *Bedford Cottage* and on 20 January 1839 in consideration of £30, John Duke of Bedford granted unto George Bellamy his heirs and assigns for ever in fee farm, a dwelling-house or Cottage and Garden called Bedford Cottage within the Parish and Manor of Plymstock. *Eventide* is the eastern unit of this group. The only visible ancient features are the feet of its roof trusses in the first floor front: the ceiling of the room is curiously arched, suggesting that it *may* be following the line of arch-braced cross–ties, not accessible for inspection. The north wing of Eventide has probably been converted to domestic use from an early farm building. Grade II. *Glendene*: This is the central property and consists of the west end of the original farmhouse, probably of sixteenth century date. It has a massive chimney stack at the west end: an impressive semi-circular staircase tower projecting beyond the north wall and still contains a pole or newel staircase. Grade II.

M.P. F1. (T.M.9aA) *Elmleigh.* This was the site of Gimblett's Tenement house, leased in 1690 to William Hendy and his wife Margaret, to commence after the death of William Hendy's mother-in-law, Margaret Shaptoe. Rent was 5s. per year. In 1729 Gimblett's Cottage was leased to Thomas Edwards, Gentleman, and in 1755 the lease was held by Samuel Avent. In 1842 Elmleigh was occupied by David Jones. Elmleigh is among the most attractive of the Georgian houses of Plymstock. It is of two periods, a western block fronting on Church Road and erected in the second half of the eighteenth century, and an eastern addition of probable early nineteenth century date. The slate-hanging on the west and south elevations and the hipped roof of the western block are notable exterior features. Elmleigh became the home of the well-known Dr S. Noy Scott, who was followed by Dr C.J. Rooke. Grade II.

M.P. G2. (T.M.10b) *Carcleve:* in 1660 this property belonged to Horsmans Tenement, referred to in a lease granted to Edward Geddy in 1708, when its name became Geddys Home Tenement, the total holding being 16 acres. Carcleve is basically an ancient house, long and narrow, of several building periods. The only clue to a probable sixteenth or seventeenth century origin for the central sections of the building is provided by the feet of a number of massive adzed roof-trusses. The massive chimney stacks are embedded in the centre of the building, but all the open fireplaces are blocked over. Grade II.

T.M. 7. *Burrow Lodge.* This is a charming cottage in the Gothic style, built in 1835 by Dr George Bellamy (see Chapter 4, Manor of Plymstock), which still has its original door and window-frames, glazing bars and boldly carved barge-boards. Its appearance has been enhanced by recent restoration. Grade II.

T.M. 8. *Dean School.* This was the first National School for Plymstock. (See Chapter 12, Civil Parish). Now demolished, the site forms part of the Plymstock Broadway Shopping Centre.

Burrow Lodge, west gable inscribed GB 1835.

T.M. 5. *Plymstock Workhouse.* This building has been converted to five dwelling-houses which form a charming limestone-fronted entity, the west end being pleasantly slate-hung. (See Chapters 4 and 8, Manor of Plymstock and The Parish Church). Grade II.

T.M. 6. *Stentaway House.* This imposing house was built in 1834, when it was known as *Ashleigh.* More recently, this property has been converted into three dwelling-units, while the coach house has been developed as a dwelling named Stentaway Cottage. Grade II.

T.M.31. *The Firs.* This spacious and attractive house was built after 1784 on a part of the old Peeks Tenement. The Hawker family, wine merchants of Plymouth, occupied the house for a number of years. It is now Abbeyfield Retirement Home. Local List.

(Notes and References follow Chapter 4).

Chapter Six
ORESTON AND THE CATTEWATER

Oreston, often referred to as 'Osun', was a large fishing village with a small harbour and Town Quay, both now gone, for in the 1960s the harbour was reclaimed, taking the waterfront some hundred yards away from the old sea wall. The name is more correctly Orston, being a progression from Horstone and possibly the earlier Hoarstone, marking a boundary. This is credible, for the waterfront formed part of the western boundary of the Plymstock manor and the parish.

The Cattewater belongs to the Duchy of Cornwall, being part of the 'Water of Tamar' and in these waters to the eastward of a line drawn from the former Bear's Head Rock at Coxside to Mount Batten landing, the

Reclaiming the harbour at Oreston, 1965.

manor of Plympton owned the royalty of the oysterage and the passage between Oreston and Cattedown. Bear's Head Rock, a natural and unusual rock formation, was adjacent to the old Queen Anne's Battery until the commencement of the nineteenth century, when it was destroyed.

The ancient ferry for foot passengers which ran from Oreston across Horstone Passage to Passage House Inn at Cattedown was, until 1807, the only direct route to Plymouth from Plymstock and the surrounding villages and farms. There must have been a great deal of coming and going through Oreston, especially on Plymouth market days when farm produce would have been carried across.

In 1774 Eleanor Lambell of Oreston, who held a lease of one fourth part of this passage or ferry, sold it to two mariners, Thomas Cooper and William Wallon.[1] Then, in 1807, Lord Boringdon of Saltram, who had been busy acquiring the divided parts of the manor of Plympton, purchased one fourth part of the passage or ferry upon the River Plym between Oreston and Cattedown, and the fourth part of the two passage-boats, together with the use of the several landing places. With this transaction Lord Boringdon became the sole owner of this ferry.[2]

Then, in 1807, Lord Boringdon provided a flat-bottomed ferry-boat, open at both ends and capable of carrying animals and wheeled traffic. This ferry, named 'Flying Bridge', ran between Pomphlett and

'Oarstone'. A watercolour by John Swete, 1794. (By permission of the Devon Record Office and Mrs V. Swete. D564 V.7 p.39).

Prince Rock, being impelled by means of a strong iron chain which passed over trucks in the boat. Although its slow passage belied its name this ferry served for twenty years until the Laira Bridge was opened in 1827. [3]

In 1819 the Earl of Morley, formerly Lord Boringdon, granted a lease of the passage-boats to Mr John Keam for seven years at an annual rental of £106. The last of a series of leases, dated 1869, was to Mr Thomas Jordan for two years, the rental then being £20. [4] The inception of the new, more direct steam-boat service from Oreston to the Barbican in 1869 presaged the end of the old passage-boats.

In 1812 Lord Boringdon acquired an eighth part of the royalty of the oysterage in Cattewater from John Harris of Radford. The Oreston residents had a customary right to pick up oysters from the beach, but during the early years of the eighteenth century this right had been threatened by Captain Walter Avent, who was the lessee of a large waterfront cottage and quay and two cottages at the rear in what became known as 'Captain's Court'. This dispute led to the visit to Oreston in 1735 of Thomas Veale, a Master Extraordinary in Chancery, when several older residents made depositions that they remembered for many years past inhabitants gathering oysters on Oreston beach in the presence of the farmers of the oysterage who were at the same time dredging oysters in the river. They all remembered the privilege of gathering oysters 'as far as low water mark and selling them without any interruption till within fourteen years past.'

There must also have been some interference with the right of the boatmen and boatwomen to carry

*The old road from Plymouth to Cattedown
and thence by ferry to Oreston.*

Laira Bridge, opened 1827.

passengers across Horstone Passage, for on the same day depositions were made that for the space of 55 years past inhabitants have carried in their own boats passengers and goods between Oreston and Cattedown, and a fare of one penny was paid for the passage of each person. [5]

In 1741 Captain Avent forbade the farmers of the oysterage to gather oysters without his leave. A strong letter from the farmers pointed out that 'they held a grant of the Royalty of the whole Oysterage and Fishery by and under the Lords of the Manor of Plympton whose undoubted right it is'.

The oyster trade continued to flourish until the early part of the present century, when the third Earl of Morley granted a lease to Mr G.M. Courage of Leigham of the fishing in the River Plym and the oysterage in the Cattewater. Possibly during the First World War this trade diminished and then ceased altogether. Although Captain Avent's house on the waterfront still remains, the last of the two cottages was demolished in the 1970s and Captain's Court is no more.

At one time Oreston relied mainly on the fishing trade for employment and over a long period Oreston ships were engaged in the Newfoundland trade, numerous small vessels sailing across the Atlantic and returning with cargoes of salt fish. Another long-established employment, especially for young lads commencing work, was cracking stones from the quarries at Pomphlett, Billacombe and Radford, the stones then being carried in little ships called 'stone-knackers' along the coast to farmers who would burn the limestones in their own kilns. This trade was threatened in 1772 when the Corporation of Saltash petitioned parliament to grant twopence a ton for all goods carried by water on the River Tamar and Cattewater in the harbour of Plymouth. The inhabitants of the parish of Plymstock sent the following counter-petition to the House of Commons:

The Chief support of the Labouring people being the Limestone Quarries and carrying the limestones in barges up the said River Tamar to the several limekilns to be burnt into lime which is chiefly used for manuring the lands, and as the prime cost of the said limestones is but sevenpence a ton the additional duty of twopence a ton will greatly affect all the farmers so that they cannot afford to give an advance price for such lime, and their lands will be greatly impoverished, and the consumption being lessened several of these people who are now employed in the said quarries and barges will be deprived of livelihood.[6]

A further petition in 1783 from two gentlemen for 'cleansing and preserving Catwater' and granting them an impost of tonnage on shipping was before the House of Commons when the mayor and council of Plymouth stepped in and sent a resolution to parliament protesting against this petition.

Additional employment was provided when the construction of the Plymouth Breakwater, first

Building the Plymouth Breakwater.

proposed in a report by the engineer John Rennie in 1806, was approved by an Order in Council in 1811, the work commencing in 1812. Land between Oreston and Pomphlett was leased by the Duke of Bedford to the Admiralty and a large quarry opened for limestone blocks to be quarried for this major undertaking. A total of 4.5 million tons of stone was provided from the Oreston and Bedford quarries. John Rennie died in 1821, his work being carried on by his son, Sir John Rennie. The breakwater was finally completed in 1841 at a total cost of £1.5 million. [7]

An accumulation of unserviceable stone led to the formation of picturesque mounds at Pomphlett known as Ballast Hills. The Admiralty gave this stone to Sir John Jackson to be used for concrete for the beds and basins which were to be built at the naval barracks at Keyham. [8]

In 1858 John Bayly opened a timber yard along the waterfront at the south end of the village, where telegraph poles were pickled for the G.P.O. Times were hard and, as one writer put it; 'Lucky you were if you got a job in the pickle-yard carrying deals from six to six'.

The Hooelake ferry which ran from 'The Rock', a landing place at the entrance to Hooe Lake and Hooe Lake Point, once provided a useful link with the village of Turnchapel. Dick Frost was one of the last boatmen and when he gave up Sam Wright took over. Probably for lack of a boatman this service lapsed and the Rock, now gone, was incorporated in Bayly's Yard. Daddy Lander, who lived in Silver Lane, ran a ferry-boat from steps by the sea-wall to the Barbican to pick up beer barrels for the King's Arms.

William Lambell was obviously a prominent figure at Oreston in the eighteenth century, for in 1755 he held leases of three cottages and a part of Hendrick's and Hatch's tenement. One of these was Drake's Cottage with two outbuildings, yard and garden. [9] This site on the waterfront midway between Town Quay and the Rock was later developed as a shipbuilding yard. This was probably the yard of Messrs Soby and Company of Oreston who built the *Hamoaze* in 1800, a naval sailing lighter of 159 tons. She was used mainly for carrying stores around the coast, from Haulbowline to Portsmouth. An old building with a rounded wall on the corner of this site may have served as a Custom House, for inset between its first floor windows was a cast iron plaque bearing an early form of the Royal Coat of Arms, considered to be of late sixteenth or early seventeenth century date. When the sale of the Duke of Bedford's Oreston properties took place in 1911, this lot comprised two houses with gardens and outbuildings, and a commodious shipbuilding yard and dock with workshop, the tenant then being Mr Harper. This yard later became known as Lucas's Yard. At present it provides winter storage for yachts.

Another of William Lambell's properties was Lang's Cottage on the Parade. For many years this was a baker's shop, the horse used for the deliveries being brought through the passage of the house to its stable in the courtyard at the rear of the property.

During the nineteenth century Oreston developed a successful export trade, its ships carrying blacklead and starch from the Sutton Pool factories and cargoes of arsenic from the Tamar, probably shipped at Morwellham Quay. At the end of the summer ships would be prepared for the 'nut trade', the ships sailing down to Gijon or Riva de Sella on the north coast of Spain for cargoes of nuts. When loaded they would proceed either to London, Liverpool or Bristol. Some ships were engaged in the London trade, or occasion-ally made a voyage round Land's End and up to the Bristol Channel for a cargo of coal.

According to the Plymstock Manor Plan dated 1755, the King's Arms public house was situated at the south end of the Parade at the entrance to Rock Lane. An Ordnance Survey map dated 1888 (see page vii) shows the King's Arms in its present position on the Parade. In addition there was a Forester's Arms and the Old Inn, which in 1870 was run by Mrs Ann Hurrell.

In 1822 Mr James Rendel, an up and coming engineer, was engaged by the Earl of Morley to investigate the practicability of constructing a suspension bridge over the Laira. Plans were prepared and in 1823 an Act of Parliament approved its erection. The first site selected was found to be unsuitable and the new site chosen was unfavourable for the principle of suspension. In 1824 another Act of Parliament was obtained by which the 1823 Act was repealed and plans for a bridge of a different type were approved. The masonry of this was to be of limestone and granite and the bridge itself of iron. The first stone was laid by the Earl of Morley on 10 March 1825, and the bridge opened on 14 July 1827, when H.R.H. the Duchess of Clarence (afterwards Queen Adelaide) with her entourage passed over it. Properly named Laira Bridge, it became known as 'Iron Bridge'. In 1897 the Plymouth Corporation purchased Iron Bridge and freed it from tolls in 1924.

In 1955 Mr J. Paton Watson, the Plymouth City Engineer, said the superstructure was in very poor shape and it would be easier to build a completely new bridge, probably on another alignment. Plymouth would have to pay a quarter of the cost of the new bridge, estimated at £750 000. The Ministry of Transport would make a 75 per cent grant towards the cost of the scheme as it was on an a Class 1 road. Mr Paton Watson who designed the bridge said it would have five 108 feet spans, and piers would be sunk 120 feet below the riverbed. The new bridge was commenced early in 1960 and was opened on 1 June 1962 by Lord Chesham, Parliamentary Secretary to the Minister of Transport. The metal from the Iron Bridge was melted down and turned into high pressure boilers which were exported to all parts of the world.[11]

The railway bridge over the Laira (just north of the Iron Bridge) was constructed in about 1887 and was opened on 5 September 1892 when the first Plymstock train crossed to a halt at Pomphlett. When the Turnchapel branch line was opened in 1897 a halt was provided at Oreston.[12]

The Church of the Good Shepherd at Oreston was built between 1847 and 1858 on a site in Rock Lane (now Marine Road), and in 1913 the former Wesleyan Sunday School in Rock Lane was conveyed by the Trustees of the Duke of Bedford to the Rev. C.H. Wreford, Vicar of Plymstock, for a Parish Hall.[13]

The first Wesleyan Church at Oreston was built about 1816 on land purchased from the Duke of Bedford. Now known as old Chievely Hall this building is on the south side of the Plymstock Road near the Parade and adjacent to Minards House.

In 1864 the Duke of Bedford conveyed land at Oreston for a burial ground. This was further up the hill on the north side of Plymstock Road, and was also available for use by the inhabitants of the Coxside and Cattedown villages of Plymouth. Then in 1888 a new Wesleyan Church was opened on land adjoining the burial ground. Neighbouring Pomphlett had its own small Wesleyan Chapel at the top of Millway Terrace bordering the Honcray Road. This was later found to

be inconvenient and in March 1904 the foundation stone of the present church in Pomphlett Road was laid.

The village of Cattedown which once had its own Wesleyan Church and Sunday School has disappeared, the former dwellings and market gardens have given way entirely to industry. The old road to Plymouth is closed to pedestrians and is due for demolition. The quaint old Passage House Inn, burnt down in 1907, is now replaced by a modern public house which bears the same name.

Robinson Crusoe at Oreston

Alexander Selkirk, alias Selcraig, the Scottish seaman from Largo in the County of Fife, whose lonely exile on Juan Fernandez, an island in the South Pacific, 400 miles off the coast of Chile, inspired Daniel Defoe to write his world-famous story *Robinson Crusoe*, spent a short time at Oreston before departing on his final voyage.

Selkirk joined the Royal Navy on 12 March 1719, being entered as Master's Mate on board the *Enterprize* which was being commissioned at Deptford. Her commission ended on 18 October 1720 when she arrived in the Hamoaze at Plymouth. Two days later men from the *Enterprize* turned over to the *Weymouth* which 'lay between Drake's Island and the main at ye mooring'. and on 16 November the crew of the *Enterprize* were paid on board, Selkirk receiving £42.2.9d.[14]

Weymouth was still at this mooring a month later when at noon on 20 November a hard gale and squally weather caused her moorings to part and she ran aground. During the afternoon she floated again and that evening two launches came to her assistance. The following day she was taken into the Hamoaze where her guns and provisions were taken out, and on 3 December she was taken into Plymouth Dock in order to ascertain whether any damage had been sustained when she ran aground.[15]

During the time the *Weymouth* was at Plymouth Alexander Selkirk spent some time ashore frequenting and probably lodging at a public house which was kept by a spinster named Frances Candish. According to a later statement made by her 'Selkirk courted her for a wife to which she was very averse but being persuaded by her neighbours and friends she at last consented'. Their mariage took place on 12 December 1720 at St Andrew's Church, Plymouth, by licence, the ceremony being performed by the Rev. Robert Forster, formerly vicar of Plymstock.[16] After the ceremony Selkirk made his last will, leaving all his possessions to his wife.

On 21 December *Weymouth* set sail for Spithead where she was provisioned in readiness for a voyage to the Gold Coast. On 5 February 1721, in company with the *Swallow,* she sailed under orders to convoy the Royal African Company's Governors for Gambia and other places and to support them in restoring the credit of that company.

The *Weymouth's* voyage was ill-fated, for while the ship was at the Island of Princes, yellow fever spread rapidly among her crew, resulting in many deaths. During this epidemic 125 of the ship's complement of 280 men died. While they were at Elmina the *Weymouth's* log records that on 13 December 1721 'Mr Alexr Selkirk died'.

Described as a 'gay widow' Frances Selkirk journeyed to Largo to claim her inheritance. Although her right to the property could not be denied, Selkirk's family did not produce the effects Alexander had with him when he was marooned on the island. His sea chest and his coconut shell cup are deposited in the National Museum of Antiquities of Scotland at Edinburgh.

Frances remarried at Plymstock in 1723, her second husband being Francis Hall, a tallow chandler of Plymouth.[17] She died in 1729, aged 72 years. A public house named the Old Inn adjacent to the earlier King's Arms near the Town Quay, seems likely as the place where Selkirk stayed during the period *Weymouth* was at Plymouth. Although these buildings have been demolished, a plaque on the front wall of Minards House, opposite the site of the Old Inn, is a reminder of Robinson Crusoe's visit.

NOTES AND REFERENCES
ORESTON AND THE CATTEWATER

1. *Morley MSS,* Lease, 1774, W.D.R.O.

2. *Ibid* Conveyance, W.D.R.O.

3. John J. Beckerlegge, T.P.I., V.xviii, 188.

4. *Morley MSS,* Lease, 1869, W.D.R.O.

5. *Bedford Records,* Deposition, L1258/LP/18 *Bedford Records,* Letters, L1258/LP/18, bundle 29, W.D.R.O.

6. Bedford Records, Petition, 7 February 1752, W.D.R.O.

7. C.W. Bracken, *A History of Plymouth and Her Neighbours,* 190.

8. F.S. Bligh, *Hail and Farewell to Devonport.*

9. *Bedford Records,* Plymstock Manor Survey 1755.

10. J. Britton & E.W. Brayley, *The Lary Bridge* 20-22.

11. *Western Morning News,* Reports, 1959-62.

12. David St John Thomas, *Plymstock Trains.*

13. Parish Church Records, Conveyance, W.D.R.O.

14. Log of H.M.S. *Weymouth.*

15. *Ibid.*

16. *St Andrew's Parish Register.*

17. *Plymstock Parish Register.*

Chapter Seven

PLYMSTOCK'S MEDIEVAL CHAPEL

All the available evidence points to an early foundation for the medieval chapel of Plymstock as a natural progression from the time of Theodore, Archbishop of Canterbury, AD 669-690. This active archbishop, actively aided by Ine, King of Wessex, 689-726, brought about the unification of the clergy and their grouping together in minsters, which had under their control extremely large parishes, the priests going out periodically to visit outlying settlements in order to minister to the spiritual needs of the people who would gather at a cross for prayer and instruction. Sometimes a small chapel would be built; rough-rubbled, with narrow slit-windows and a rude-angled west tower. The interior might have wall paintings in order to illustrate stories from the Bible. [1]

Although founded at a later date, probably following Aethelwulf's famous donation to the church in 855, when he granted the tenth part of his land over all his kingdom for the glory of God and his own salvation, [2] the monastic church of Plympton became the religious centre of a large parish which covered a wide area of the South Hams, encompassing Plymstock and Wembury to the south, Brixton to the east and Shaugh Prior to the north.

The end for the old Saxon monastery at Plympton came in 1121, when the Norman bishop of Exeter, William de Warelwast, nephew and chaplain of William the Conqueror, considered the brethren were guilty of transgressing the church's law by having

Saxon Cross in Stentaway Road.

wives. He removed the five members, a dean and four canons, to Bosham Collegiate Church in Sussex,

Ancient font at Plymstock church.

settling in their place a band of Augustinian canons. Liberally endowed by its wealthy founder the new priory became the richest in Devon. When he died in 1137, William de Warelwast was buried at Plympton. [3]

A mid twelfth century concord, 1160-4, between Walter, abbot of Tavistock, and Richard, prior of Plympton, proves the existence of an early chapel at Plymstock, which had become a bone of contention between them, for the abbot owned the land on which the chapel stood, while the prior claimed his ancient right to the chapel, together with the tithes and the appointment of the chaplain.

There can be no doubt Prior Richard had the law on his side, for one of King Edgar's Ecclesiastical Laws reads:

First, namely, that God's churches are to be entitled to every right ... and all payment of tithe is to be made to the old minster to which the parish belongs, and it is

to be rendered both from the thegn's demesne land and from the land of his tenants according as it is brought under the plough. [4]

This amicable agreement confirmed:

that all strife, contention, and dispute may be taken away for ever concerning the chapel of Plymstock and that the said chapel shall belong for ever, with freedom and quietness to the church of Plympton,

But the abbot was not going to let the prior have things all his own way, for a number of conditions were incorporated, one being:

When any of the monks shall come to Plymstock, the chaplain of the prior shall give them free admission into the chapel, and a candle at supper and breakfast, and for service in the chapel. [5]

In 1304, when Robert Champeaux was abbot of Tavistock, a recognition of the rights of the abbey took place at Bickleigh Church in the presence of his notary and others when

John prior of Plympton acknowledges that he and his successors are bound to wait upon the abbots on the terms stated, to offer them counsel and help as far as possible, and also to supply the abbots with six white loaves, two flagons of wine, and five wax candles, when they visit their manor of Plymstock. The prior also confesses himself bound to present to the abbot, annually at Michaelmas, a fit chaplain for the church of Plymstock. These rights, which are immemorial, having been overlooked, Prior John has given to the abbot as a pledge of their future observance, twenty barrels of wine, of which the abbot has returned five. [6]

Additional evidence that an ancient chapel preceded the present building is the Saxon cross which has been erected on a wall in Stentaway Road. Regarded as being of great archaeological significance, it is scheduled as an ancient monument by the Department of the Environment. Also, outside the north porch of the church is a plain granite font. It is possible the cross and the font both belonged to Plymstock's first chapel.

This cross was the subject of speculation in 1883, when a correspondent wrote to the *Western Antiquary*: 'There is at the residence of Captain Daubeny an old cross and a gargoyle head in granite.' At that time Captain Daubeny lived at Stentaway House, and it is possible that because of the recent demolition of the Tithe Barn and the extension of the graveyard, the cross and the gargoyle head were removed by him and used to embellish the garden of his home. Later, the cross was relegated to an adjoining field where it is said to have served as a rubbing-post for cattle. It lay in this field for many years until, in 1939, it was rediscovered by Mr V. Almy, who reported his find to Mr E. Masson Phillips F.S.A. who, acting on behalf of the Old Plymouth Society, approached the owner of the field and suggested its erection at a more suitable site. Permission was readily given and in 1946 the cross was lifted and erected nearby on the wall of the telephone exchange. It was described by Mr Masson Phillips as an early tenth century Saxon wheel-head cross, with an incised inscription on the lower part of the shaft, previously below ground. This was later interpreted by Miss E. Barty as 'E L E' in Anglo-Saxon capitals, followed by the runic symbol for W or WYN, thought to represent the female name Elewyn. [7 n.1]

The present building consists of two quite separate periods of construction, the south aisle, nave, chancel and embattled west tower have been dated to the Decorated period of English Gothic, 1250-1350. The north aisle belongs to the Perpendicular period, fifteenth century. The Confirmation of Rights issued to the Priory of Plympton by Bishop Grandisson in 1352 contains a list of parochial chapels appropriated to it. This refers to the Plymstock chapel as dedicated to All Saints. [8]

During the episcopacy of Bishop Edmund Lacy, 1420-55, many parish churches were either rebuilt or restored and it must have been then that the Plymstock chapel was widened and the handsome carved oak rood-screen placed in the enlarged building. A large buttress built into the new north wall has two openings giving light to the interior, which

The large buttress which contains the rood stairs. The north wall of Plymstock church.

contained the rood-stairs. The blocked-up rood-loft door can still be seen just above the screen. When re-plastering of the wall was carried out recently the lower doorway was revealed, but has now been plastered over. The rood itself – the crucifix, usually with the attendant figures of the Virgin Mary and John the Baptist – together with the rood-loft were all torn down by the king's commissioners at the time of the Reformation.

When, in 1429, trouble flared up once again, this time concerning the presentation of a chaplain, independent arbiters were asked to decide the matter. Their judgement was:

> that the Prior and Convent of Plympton and their successors should for ever thereafter at their own proper charges find a 'fit chaplain' for celebrating divine service in the said chapel of Plymstock.

The award set out his duties explicitly, it being specified:

> that such chaplain should make continual residence within the bounds and limits of the said parish chapel for saying divine service therein and administering the sacrament. [9]

A Survey of Plymstock taken in 1586 records a *domus* – religious house – which appears to have been on the site of Downhorn Farmhouse. There is a well-known tradition at Plymstock that a tunnel once linked the house with the church. Although no documentary evidence has been found, two former residents have said that a trap-door in the floor of a room latterly used as a kitchen leads down to the entrance to a tunnel, high enough for a man to stand upright, which has been completely blocked up with loose stones. The present house is Elizabethan in

design and is first recorded as being occupied in 1600.[10]

The Norman font is the oldest feature in the church. It is circular, of dark red sandstone, and is decorated with the honeysuckle design which occurs

The Norman font.

on many fonts in Devon, the motif being upside-down, which is different to the usual Devon practice.[11] It once had an octagonal font cover in carved oak, thought to be of German origin and of seventeenth century date. The frontal chest in the Lady (formerly Harris) Chapel – a memorial to the Rev. C. H. Wreford and his wife, both of whom worked so hard to renovate this little chapel – incorporates some oak panels which once formed part of this font cover. The church had an oak wagon-roof, which was replaced in the 1870s by a sharp-angled roof of pitch-pine.[12]

The Plymstock chapel not only served the villages of Plymstock and Oreston, but also the outlying districts of Elburton, Staddiscombe and Hooe, for baptisms and marriages. An anomaly was that the tenants of the manor of Plymstock could be buried at Plymstock, either in the church or the small graveyard, while all other parishioners had to carry their dead to Plympton for burial.

Matters came to a head in 1448 when a request was made to the prior and convent of Plympton to grant an exceptional licence for the burial of Thomas Walter of Wembury in the parochial chapel of Plymstock or its churchyard, 'he having died while on a visit there and lain in the chapel unburied with noisome effect'. Parishioners at Plymstock had refused to take Walter to Plympton for burial for so long that they could not now, without inhumanity, offence and danger be compelled to do so.

This incident highlighted an obvious grievance, for in February the following year action was taken by John Harris of Radford, leader of the parishioners, against the priory about the right of burial at Plymstock. Pending a delayed arbitration between the prior and convent of Plympton and John Harris Esquire and his fellow parishioners, Bishop Lacy

Memorial to John Harris of Radford, Plymstock church.

requested the prior and convent that an exceptional licence be granted for burial at Plymstock of any parishioner not being a tenant of the abbot and convent of Tavistock. It was not until July 1450 that notification was received that, at the bishop's request:

the sub–prior and convent of Plympton have granted an exceptional licence for the burial of parishioners at Plymstock in this time of severe pestilence, during which time the parishioners utterly refuse to carry their dead to Plympton for burial.

This licence was granted without prejudice, pending judgement in the suit brought by the priory against the parishioners in the Court of Arches. [13]

It has not been possible to discover the outcome of this dispute, as the records of the Court of Arches were destroyed in the Great Fire of London. However, on 10 April 1477, the parish of Brixton was granted the right of burial, so possibly Plymstock also received a similar grant. The parish of Wembury was certainly the worst off of the three parishes as no cemetery was allowed there; all bodies had to be taken in all weathers to Plympton for burial until, during the reign of Henry VIII, the petition of the inhabitants was granted and a churchyard provided. [14]

Following Henry VIII's repudiation of Rome and the Pope's authority, parliament confirmed the Act of Supremacy 1534, declaring the king supreme head of the church. One of the signs of impending change occurred on 5 August 1534, when John Howe, prior of Plympton, with twenty of his brethren, subscribed to the king's supremacy. Realising the priory's end was near John Howe very astutely proceeded to capitalise on its assets, obtaining long leases of its property and charging it with pensions. Even the tithes of the several parish chapels belonging to the priory did not escape, for all were leased away into private ownership. At Michaelmas 1538 the Plymstock farm of tithes was leased to Walter Shere and Christopher Hornebrook for 25 years at a rental of £62, less the stipend of the chaplain £8, and for bread, wine and wax, 8s., leaving

an annual income to the prior of £53.12s. [15] Finally, on 1 March 1539, John Howe and his canons abjectly surrendered their house, lands and all their possessions to the Crown. Within two or three years the priory church – the old minster – and all the monastic buildings were destroyed, only the parish church of St Mary being preserved for the people. For his subservience the prior received a pension of £120 per annum, living out his retirement at Exeter College in Oxford. [16]

A Court of Augmentations was set up to administer the properties of dissolved religious houses and a valuation taken at that time shows that Plymstock *Firma Capelle* was worth £72. [17]

On 7 October 1547 Edward VI granted to the Dean and Chapter of Windsor the rectory and church of Plympton, with the chapels of Plymstock, Wembury, Brixton &c., late parcels of the possessions of Plympton Priory. [18]

Some early Plymstock ministers

Peter de Plymstoke	Bishop Bronescombe's Register 1257–1280
Magister Richard de Plymstoke [n.2.]	Bishop Bytton's Register 1291–1307
Simon de Plymstoke 1350 Cleric	Bishop Grandisson's Register 1327–1369
Henry Godeman 1421 Curate of Plymstock Chapel Also instituted to Revelstoke	Bishop Lacy's Register, Vol. IV

Thomas Hille 1449–1450   Bishop Lacy's Register, Vol. IV
Curate of Plymstock
Chapel

John Perys   Bishop Lacy's Register, Vol. III, 62
Curate of Plymstock
Chapel

NOTES AND REFERENCES
PLYMSTOCK'S MEDIEVAL CHAPEL

1.   Keith Feiling, *A History of England*, 50.
2.   F.M. Stenton, *Anglo-Saxon England*, 1971 edn, 308.
3.   Rev. R.J.E. Boggis M.A., *A History of the Diocese of Exeter*, 1922, 308.
4.   *English Historical Documents*, 2nd edn, ed. Professor D. Whitelock, 431.
5.   Rev. D.P. Alford, *The Abbots of Tavistock*, 1891, 83–7.
6.   Rev. D.P. Alford, *The Abbots of Tavistock*, 1891, 87.
7.   Transactions of the Devonshire Association, 1954, LXXXVI, 184-5.
8.   John Stabb, *Some old Devon Churches*, 1908. Plymstock.
9.   *Bedford Records*, D Bundle, 74, No.3. Devon Record Office. Letters Patent, 6 November 1429.
10. *The Survey of the Manor of Plymstocke*, P.R.O., S.P. 13/G, 007318, 1586.
11. Nikolaus Pevsner, *The Buildings of England*, Plymstock Church.
12. J. Stabb, *Devon Churches*.
13. Bishop Edmund Lacy's Register, V. III, 269.
14. Rev. K. Tagg, *Wembury Church*.
15. Dr George Oliver, *Monasticon Dioceses Exoniensis*, MDCCCXLVI, Plympton Priory.
16. Dom John Stephan, *Plymstock in Catholic Days*, 9.
17. Letters and Papers, Foreign and Domestic, Henry VIII, 1539.
18. Oliver, *Monasticon*.

n.1.   The tentative interpretation of this inscription by Elisabeth Barty of Newnham College, Cambridge (1965) is that Elewyn is a form of the Old English name Aelfwynn, the Latinised form being Aluina. This cross may possibly be a memorial to Aluina, wife of Ordulf, who supervised and completed the building of Tavistock Abbey, which was founded by his father, Ordgar Duke of Devonshire (d.971). Aluina is mentioned in a document dated 14 January 1321-2 when Bishop Stapeldon approved and confirmed a perpetual chantry to be erected in the church of St Andrew at Whitchurch. The four priests were to pray for Ordulf and his consort Aluina, of good memory, Edwyni (of Plymstock) and Luvyngi (Lyfing), the founder and benefactors of Tavistock Abbey. (Bishop Stapeldon's Register, 402-5).

n.2.   Plymstock has no reason to honour this man who bore its name, for his career in the church shows that he was a self-seeking and unscrupulous man who would stop at nothing to gain his own ends. He was well-educated, for this title Magister Ricardus de Plymstoke indicates that he was a cleric with a master's degree.
We first hear of him in 1274 after the important ecumenical Council of Lyons, when he obtained the Devon rectories of Exminster and Uffculme, which he held without being consecrated or obtaining a dispensation from the Pope. He was a pluralist, for he also held canonries in Lincoln and Wells cathedrals and is later recorded as a canon of Exeter Cathedral. He was clever and ambitious, causing much trouble to Walter de Stapeldon who was elected to the bishopric of Exeter in 1307. Richard was later excommunicated.

Chapter Eight

THE PLYMSTOCK PARISH CHURCH OF ST MARY AND ALL SAINTS

Although parish churches and their appendant chapels were spared the complete destruction that befell the monastic buildings, they were not to escape the attention of religious reformers when, after the death of Henry VIII in January 1547, his nine year old son Edward succeeded to the Crown.

Following Henry's dissolution of the monasteries and his appropriation of their possessions there had so far been little or no deviation from the old form of church service, but under Edward, who was much influenced by the Protector Somerset and Archbishop Cranmer, both ardent Protestants, the move towards a drastic reform of the liturgy accelerated. Also, foreign Protestants, notably of the Swiss school with extremist views, influenced events in England. These gathered strength, when in 1548 German Protestants flocked to England to escape the catholic domination imposed by Emperor Charles V.[1]

Although very little evidence exists to tell us what happened at Plymstock during this revolutionary period of England's history, we are able to consider how the progress of national events for a period of twenty years, until the Accession of Elizabeth in 1558, relates to entries in the first Plymstock Rate Book which dates from 1554. For instance, proclamations in 1548 ordered the removal of the rood and any attendant images from all churches and a further proclamation ordered the removal of rood lofts, although the removal of the rood-screens was

Plymstock church and Pauper House, from a drawing by Worsley, 1826.

forbidden. The commissioners appointed to carry out this task wantonly smashed stained glass windows,

The medieval rood screen, Plymstock church.

damaged carvings and otherwise defaced the churches. Then, in January 1549, parliament passed the first Act of Uniformity compelling the clergy to adopt the new English prayer-book when the Act came into force on Whit Sunday. Those bishops who objected were sent to prison and deprived of their sees.

All these changes were resisted in the West Country, the men of Cornwall sending a petition to the king setting out their various grievances. In brief, they wished to have the mass in Latin as previously, the Sacrament hung over the high altar and images set up again in the church. Archbishop Cranmer's detailed but autocratic reply to each of the many points made gave the petitioners no hope of the old religion being restored and the dissatisfaction which had been simmering over the changes and injustices brought about by the dissolution of the monasteries finally erupted. Groups of Cornishmen banded together and marched first to Trematon Castle and then on to Plymouth. Mob violence ensued and Protestant families in fear of their lives were forced to seek a hiding place. The insurgents, gaining support on their way, pressed on towards Exeter and Honiton. Fierce and bloody fighting took place when Lord Russell, lord of the Plymstock manor, supported by his son Francis and an army of foreign mercenaries, were compelled to use force to quell the insurrection. Ten of the ringleaders were taken to London, among them William Harris of Radford, an estate bordering Lord Russell's manor. Harris, with four others, was confined in the Fleet prison and possibly because he had surrendered he escaped severe punishment, although it is probable he was fined. He was released by order of the privy council on 1 November 1549. [2]

One result of this Rebellion was the order that all bells but one should be removed from the tower of every church in Devon and Cornwall, the bells having been used to rally the rebels. This order was apparently amended and the clappers only were removed. In 1553 there were:

> at the *Parochia de Plymstoke iiij bells yn the tower theire and one chalice committed to the custody of Henry Elys, Walter Birte, John Foster, Richard Yeate and other the parishioners there by indentur.* [3]

It seems the proclamations of 1548 ordering the destruction of images from the churches was not fully complied with, for in 1550 parliament approved an 'Act for the Abolishing and Putting Away of Divers Books and Images'. This Act ordained that if anyone had in their custody any books or images which had been taken out of any church or chapel and did not deface or destroy them or deliver them to the mayor, bailiff or churchwardens to be delivered up to the archbishop, bishop, chancellor or commissary of the said diocese to be destroyed, they shall for every such book retained and not delivered after the last day of June be lawfully convicted and fined twenty shillings for the first offence. If convicted of more than two offences they risked imprisonment.

The final ignominy came in January 1552 when a second Act of Uniformity brought in a revised prayer-book which went even further than the prayer-book of 1549 in satisfying the Swiss interpretations. Altars were to be replaced by wooden tables devoid of covering and ornaments. These drastic changes were to be short-lived, for Edward died in 1553, being succeeded by his sister Mary, a devout catholic. The change in influence was immediately apparent, for Mary's October Parliament repealed the whole of the ecclesiastical legislation of Edward's reign. With the country's brief return to Roman Catholicism came the opportunity for parishioners to repair some of the damage to parish churches and to replace altars and repair bells. This situation is reflected in the entries of Plymstock's first Rate Book when, in 1554-5, the expenses of the Parish include the following: [4]

> *Itm pd for stone for the Aulter and the Cros*
> *Itm pd for cuttynge some of the stone*
> *Itm pd for stone and lyme for settynge of the stone*

The replacement of the altar and the cross was obviously the first consideration of the parish and several years elapsed before further major work was carried out.

Despite her early personal popularity and the good beginning to her reign, Mary's determination to bring the country under the jurisdiction of Rome, her persecution of the protestants, and her unpopular marriage to Philip of Spain, brought her the hatred of the nation and she died in 1558, a lonely and embittered woman.

Mary was succeeded by her sister Elizabeth, who adopted a more tolerant attitude towards religion. Her first parliament brought in the Acts of Supremacy and Uniformity 1559, their provisions being nowhere near so one-sided and inflexible as those of Edward or of Mary. Although the first prayer-book of Edward was brought back, it was slightly modified to include a variation in the communion service which would be acceptable to the Catholics, and an offensive reference to the Bishop of Rome was deleted. The Act of Supremacy also changed the queen's title to that of 'Supreme Governor' instead of 'Supreme Head' of the church. In fact the country entered upon a more peaceful period for the churches and they were able once more to get on with looking after the spiritual needs of the parishioners and keeping their buildings in good repair.

As evidence of a more settled period for the parish, Plymstock's Rate Book gives us further details of repairs and additions to the church:

1571 *Itm pd for boards for the mending of the rood loft*

Itm pd for a quantity of large nails

Also during this year the church roof was repaired:

Itm pd to ? Barnacott for a hundred large nails and a pound of lead
Itm pd for settynge home of helling [roofing] stones and lyme and sande
1574 *Itm pd to janor [joiner?] for the mendynge of the housel [chancel] doors*

Itm pd for the helling of the church
Itm pd to the helier [slater or tiler] for the hellyng of the church

In 1576 an item is shown for 'the mendynge of our bell' and for 'the putting in of the same'. A further item refers to a visitation of the Dean and a payment to the 'Dene of iiijd' (4d). Additional items are paid 'for the making of the church stuffe', which indicates some new covering for the altar.

The first Plymstock Registers for baptisms, marriages and burials date from July 1591, the entries being in Latin until 1670, when English was used. Also, the year commenced on March 25, until, in 1752, the new-style calendar was adopted.[5]

In October 1591 the dreaded plague spread through the parish, resulting in the death of many inhabitants. Forty-six perished in four months. Some families were sadly depleted; for instance, Henry Forster, his son and two daughters died. This family lived in Church Road in a tenement called Forster's leys. This old tenement was replaced by the Georgian house Oaklands, which was demolished in the 1970s. Selkirk House, a home for the elderly, now stands on this site. The Byrt family, some of whom lived at Burrow farm, still to be seen in Church Road, but then known as Byrt's Tenement, lost nine members during this epidemic.

Sunday in the Middle Ages was the regular day for transacting business matters, being the only day people came together. This custom prevailed until about 1840 at Plymstock, the clerk reading at the church door a notice of any sales about to take place in the coming week, the farmers standing around to hear the particulars. Another custom was that of the clerk reading at the desk after the service, the poor rates as assessed on each payer for an ensuing period. [6]

The parish register notes that an 'Act for Burying in Woollen' came into force on 1 August 1678, from which time none were to be 'put in, wrapt, or wound up or buried in any shirt, sheet or shroud made or mingled with flax, hemp, silk, hair, gold or silver other than what was made of sheeps wool only, or in a coffin lined with any of these materials'; and this Act required that an affidavit should be made before a J.P. or Master in Chancery. Parliament protected cloth manufacture by forbidding the import of foreign cloth and the export of raw wool.

Under the old Elizabethan and early Stuart laws parishes were expected to have a poor-house for the aged and sick, and a workhouse where the able-bodied could be employed and the children taught to work. A building called the Pauper-house was situated directly in front of the west entrance to the church at Plymstock, being built over and to the sides of the lych-gate. Formerly the stocks stood outside this building, but after its demolition they were placed in the yard adjoining the tower door. The date of their removal from there is not known.

A new workhouse was built in 1823, when land at the top of Stentaway Road was leased by the Duke of Bedford to five trustees for a new poorhouse for Plymstock.[7] As a result of changes in Poor Law administration Plymstock workhouse was closed. The exact date for its closure is not certain, but believed to be about 1837 to 1839. (See Chapter 4, Manor of Plymstock).

After the lease lapsed the building was converted to five dwelling houses, a first floor room in the largest being reserved for the Poor Law relief. This room could be reached only by a separate covered outside staircase and contained what was known as the 'Pay Table', where those in need were given one shilling and a loaf of bread. This dispensation took place on one morning each week.

It is hard to imagine in these days of social security payments and retirement pensions, the extremes of poverty suffered by many, especially when women were widowed and perhaps left with a family to feed and clothe. The Rev. Vincent Warren, lessee of Pomphlett Barton Farm, did his best to ameliorate such cases when he made his will in 1790, for he left £2000 stock in the hands of trustees so that the income might be used to clothe ten poor boys and ten poor girls a year. He also made provision for four boys and four girls to be taught to read and the girls also to sew and knit.[8]

In 1828 the church was re-pewed with deal work and the rood-screen, which only narrowly escaped destruction due to the intercession of one person, was set back from the second to the first pillars, its original position. Unfortunately, all the painted panels disappeared. When, in 1887, this screen was restored, the work being carried out by Harry Hems & Sons, Ecclesiastical Art Works of Exeter, it was considered that originally painted panels had existed in the lower panels, which had been removed. These came to light in a Bristol antique dealer's premises in December 1913. The firm wrote to Plymstock Church offering them at a special price – £25 for 25 panels, one month being given for acceptance. These were subsequently examined by Canon Masters and the Rev. R. Cole, archaeologists, who thought that they ought to go back to the church. Canon Masters wrote to Plymstock that he had no doubt as to their authenticity and considered it was most important to recover them. He offered to send a contribution towards the cost. Despite this the offer was not taken up and the last letter from Little and Barber of Bristol, dated 5 February 1914, states the panels had been sold to a

Devonshire gentleman and they thought their ultimate destination would be near to their original home.[9] One letter mentioned the panels as representing Adam and Eve in the Garden of Eden, Isaac and Jacob and the prophets of the Old Testament, also David on one panel and verses of scripture at the top.

When Dr. J.C. Bellamy wrote his manuscript *History of Plymstock* in 1850 the colours of the screen; vermilion, green and gold, were all still brilliant. The screens were generally coloured with a thin spirit colour, which scarcely hid the grain of the wood and never disguised its texture.[10]

The following notes from Milles Parochial Collections, is of a brass that seems to have disappeared:

'On a brass plate in the chancel is the figure of a woman with her hands joyened in a prayer posture of ye taste of James ye first's reign. Underneath on a brass plate:-

> *Behold here Mary Blake doth rest*
> *Whose corpse reverts to dust*
> *Her soul she did commend to Christe*
> *Her stay and onely trust.*
> *Fifety eight years, and moneths seven*
> *She liv'd with some days odd,*
> *Which time she still consumed then*
> *In service of her God.*
> *Her warfare ended she in…*
> *Her strength and perfect peace,*
> *With whom for aye she hath possesst*
> *Such joys as never cease.*

She deceased the third day of December 1610.'[11] Mary was the wife of John Blake, Gentleman of Coombe Farm, Elburton.

A large ornate monument occpies the south-east corner of the former Harris chapel. Looking inward are two male figures in Tudor dress and a woman in a hooded, flowing gown. Two sizeable areas of blank slate must have carried separate inscriptions which have long since been removed as no record of the wording remains. If the dating of 1623 is correct,[12] this must be a memorial to John Harris of Lanrest, nephew and heir to Sir Christopher Harris of Radford and also probably to his eldest son, Christopher, both of whom died at Radford in 1623. Sir Christopher Harris died in January 1624/5 so possibly the inscription carried his name also.

In 1928 plans were put in hand for the restoration of the Lady (formerly Harris) Chapel and on 16 October a faculty was granted. A Lady Chapel committee was formed, the vicar's wife, Mrs Wreford, acting as secretary. While work was in progress a serious state of dampness was noted in the floor of the transept, making it imperative to have the floor re-laid. This work was obviously going to add greatly to the cost of restoration, which was being met entirely by voluntary subscriptions.

The Rural Dean, after inspecting the church, authorised Mrs Wreford to appeal to the ecclesiasical commissioners for a grant on the grounds that the Dean and Canons of Windsor, being Patrons of the Living, and therefore responsible for the repairs to the chancel might be ready to support them. The response was a request to be furnished with full particulars of the restoration scheme and whether any part of the work affected the chancel, and also to be furnished with a plan showing the position of the Lady Chapel in relation to the chancel. It appears a later conditional offer of £5 was made by the commissioners, but whether this was ever implemented is not known.[13]

Plymstock church from a photograph c.1900.
The cottages on the left of the picture were
demolished to make way for a church hall.

Messrs Pearn Bros did the structural work and made the altar table. The altar frontal of blue and silver Gloucester draping was made by M. Perkins & Sons Ltd of London, who also supplied matching material for the curtains. These materials were ordered through the good offices of the Rev. Mother of the House of Prayer, Burnham, Bucks, the committee thus gaining the benefit of the considerable reduction allowed to her. Messrs Pophams of Plymouth supplied the felt (floor covering?) and 24 chairs. The final cost of restoration amounted to £100.18s.7d.

Herbert Read of Exeter made the altar cross and two candlesticks of oak, which were carved and silvered in accordance with a design by T. H. Lyon Esq., at a cost of £21.7s0d. This item appears to have been paid by Mrs Wreford, as it does not appear in the final account presented to the committee. It is certain that Mrs Wreford and her friend, Mrs E. Olive Miller

of the Vicarage, Brixton, both worked very hard organising the furnishings for this chapel. [14]

The Parish churchyard

J.C. Bellamy, writing in 1850, tells us that all the ground near the tithe barn sloping from the north aisle was garden, while it was only recently that the south part of the churchyard was adopted for burial. In 1868 an exchange between the trustees of Francis, seventh Duke of Bedford, and the Ecclesiastical Commissioners, whereby the Duke's trustees gave 471 square feet of garden ground in exchange for a yard and part of the tithe barn, containing in all 522 square feet, led to the further enlargement of the graveyard and the demolition of the tithe barn. The extended graveyard was consecrated on 16 June 1898. Bellamy also tells us the tithe barn had a finely timbered roof. [15]

The Memorial Chapel

Plans for a War Memorial and thank-offering for peace were put in hand during the incumbency of the Reverend Robert G. Ball (1944-1953), which was to take the form of a Memorial Chapel at the east end of the north aisle. This would require the re-siting of the organ and the Exeter Diocesan Advisory Comittee, who visited the fine ancient church of St Mary and All Saints, welcomed the suggestion of putting it at the west end, Messrs Hele suggested the platform or floor of the gallery from which the bells are rung could be extended to hold the organ. Also, as the stained glass west window in the tower would be hidden, the committee advised its removal to the east end of the north aisle, where it would look very well over the new altar. Restoration work commenced in 1955, the organ being moved to a new west gallery, its present position. [16]

The new chapel with its Roll of Honour containing the names of those parishioners who gave their lives in the two World Wars was dedicated on 6 November 1957, to the Glory of God and in honour of St Michael and St George, by the Lord Bishop of the Diocese, Dr Robert Mortimer.

During the visit the diocesan committee advised that the chancel should be simplified and made more beautiful. They considered the east window to be good but the altar was short, without a frontal and flanked by curtains of brocade to hide the free-stone of the Victorian tablets of the law. As a result a faculty was granted for the high altar to be extended by a new mensa of English oak and to furnish it with new ornaments.

The six gilded candlesticks and central crucifix were given in memory of Winifred May Crocker and (Nurse) Bessie Mary Ashton; the two smaller candlesticks in memory of Edith Pearse. They were specially designed and made by Herbert Read of Exeter.

The Wreford Memorial

The carved oak panels of the former high font cover can be seen in the frontal press which stands in the Lady Chapel. This is in memory of the Rev. Charles H. Wreford and his wife, both of whom worked so hard to bring about the restoration of this chapel.

The choir stalls

The choir stalls are a memorial to Thomas Coulthard who was vicar from 1855 to 1884 and was the offering of his family in 1892. The twelve stations of the Cross were put up in memory of Mrs Ronald Mumford. [18]

The Exeter Consistory Court

In 1980 the Plymstock Parochial Church Council sought authority to carry out a re-ordering of the church. They asked for a faculty authorizing them to move the rood-screen to the west-end of the church, and to substantially clear the church of its furniture. In its place they wished to set up a central altar which would be surrounded (except on the eastern side) by moveable chairs. The font would be moved to the east end of the south aisle (Lady Chapel).

On Wednesday 8 October and Thursday 9 October 1980, a Consistory Court hearing was held in the church to hear the views of the petitioners and the objectors. it became clear that a large body of opinion was against the proposed re-ordering. This hearing was conducted by the Worshipful D.C. Calcutt QC, Chancellor of the Exeter Diocese. The judgment of the Court, which was made known on 4 November 1980, stated; 'that the ojectors, who are many, do not want the church to be re-ordered. Quite simply, they like their church as it is, and they want it to remain so.' The judgment of this Court was that the petition be dismissed. [19]

The church bells

The Plymstock team of bell ringers, captained by Mr Ivor Treby, have achieved distinction over the years gaining the following awards:

Six bell team: South Devon Competition; South and North Devon Final; Inter-Deanery Shield; The Old Plympton Deanery Shield; East Portlemouth Bowl; Arthur Seymour Cup; Pat Johnston Cup; and many invitation competitions.

Eight bell team; Winners of The Devon Association of Ringers competition

PARISH CHURCH OF ST MARY AND ALL SAINTS, PLYMSTOCK.
Ring of Six Bells – Tuned and Rehung by John Taylor & Co. Loughborough 1937

Two new trebles were added to the bells of this tower to complete a ring of eight in March 1979. The original number 1 and 2 were hung in a new frame placed above the remaining six bells. Frame and fittings were supplied by, and work done by Arthur Fidler & Son, Bow, Devon. The bells were dedicated and first rung on 4 April 1979.

No.	Note	Diam.	Inscription	Weight cwts qrs lbs			Date
Treble	G	2' 1"	A.M.D.G. D.D. K.Garbett. MCMLXXVIII	4	0	22	1979
2nd	F#	2' 2"	IN MEM. 1.P. Garbett. MCMLXXVIII	4	3	5	1979
3rd	E	2' 4¹/₄"	LAUDATE DOMINUM. Erected by Subscription AD1872 Mears and Stainbank, London	4	3	13	1872
4th	D	2' 7¹/₂"	John Harries Esq. I.P.1739	6	2	25	1739
5th	C	2' 8¹/₄"	Charles Backer Wardens Richard Badcock I.P. 1739	6	0	21	1739
6th	B	2' 10¹/₄"	Silas Bickford CB. RB. Wardens I.P. 1739	7	0	23	1739
7th	A	3' 1¹/₄"	Mears and Stainbank, Founders, London I Coulthard, Vicar	8	3	27	1871
Tenor	G	3' 6¹/₄"	I to church the liveing call and to the grave I summon all. I.P. 1739	13	1	10	1739

LIST OF PLYMSTOCK MINISTERS 1595 – 1986

Thomas Eversley	1595
Edmund White	1597
Richard Franklin	1617-1637 dec.
Nathaniel Adams	1637-1642
William Pyke (temp. pastor)	1642-1643
John Bishop incumbent	1643-1654
Henry Hatsell curate	1648-1654
Pastor Evans	1654-1655
Pastor Domming	1655-1660
Josiah King	1660-1670
Pastor Carew	1670-?
John Warner	1682-1709
Jonathan Oltramore	1709-1713
Robert Forster	1713-1720
William Taunton	1720-1721
John Shire	1721-1725
Edward Dunning	1725-1729
William Cookson	1729-1771
Richard Doidge	1771-1772
Vincent Warren	1772-1790
William Forster	1790-1812
Thomas Culme curate	1795-1796
Nicholas Mill curate	1796-1798
J.R. Fletcher	1813-1814
George Hunt	1814-1815
John Woollcombe	1815-1818
William Williams	1818-1826
James L. Harris	1826-1832
Orlando Manley	1832-1841
Frederick Pym	1841-1843
Edward F. Coke	1843-1852
William James	1852-1855
Thomas Coulthard	1855-1884
A. Quentin Sproule	1884-1894
C.B. Collyns	1895-1913
C.H. Wreford	1913-1944
Robert G. Ball	1944-1953
Donald Weston	1953-1955
Noel Round	1955-1969
Geoffrey Sunderland	1969-1986
Paul Hawkins	1986-

NOTES AND REFERENCES

1. Arthur D. Innes, *England under the Tudors*, 1905, 192.
2. Frances Rose-Troup, *The Western Rebellion*, 167-83. Appendix L. List of Insurgents, 340-46.
3. Beatrix F. Cresswell, *Notes on Devon Churches*, MS, Deanery of Plympton: West Country Studies Library, Exeter.
4. Plymstock Rate Book, West Devon Record Office.
5. Plymstock Parish registers, W.D.R.O.
6. J.C. Bellamy, *History of Plymstock*, MS, 1850, Plymouth Local History Library.
7. *Bedford Records*, Devon Record Office, Lease 1823, Plymstock Workhouse
8. Plymstock Charities – Ecclesiastical; D.R.O.
9. Plymstock Church Records, 968/PI, 112-22; D.R.O.
10. F. Bligh Bond, *Devonshire Screens and Rood-lofts*. Devonshire Association Vol.XXXV, 434-96.
11. Cresswell, *Devon Churches*, MS, 187; W.S.L., Exeter.
12. John Stabb, *Some Old Devon Churches*.
13. Personal information.
14. Personal information.
15. *Bedford Records*, Bundle 3, D.R.O.
16. Report of the Exeter Diocesan Advisory Committee.
17. Parish Church Guide Book, 'Recent Restoration Work' 13.
18 Parish Church Guide Book, and personal information.
19. Personal knowledge and the Judgement of the Consistory Court.

Chapter Nine

SOME WELL KNOWN PLYMSTOCK MINISTERS

Robert Forster

Robert Forster, a clerk in holy orders, was minister at Plymstock from 1713 to 1720, when he was appointed lecturer at St Andrew's Church at Plymouth. He is best known as the father of the outstanding classical and biblical scholar, Nathaniel Forster.

Robert Forster and Elizabeth Tindal, daughter of the vicar of Cornwood, were married on 4 March 1716, and on 3 February 1717 their son was baptised.[1] Nathaniel received his early education at the Grammar School at Plymouth. After a course of instruction under the Revd John Bedford he studied at Eton. In 1733 he was admitted scholar of Corpus Christi College, Oxford, where he became a Fellow of Corpus in 1739. After many scholastic attainments he graduated as Doctor of Divinity in 1750 and was appointed one of the chaplains to George II in 1756. Forster was thoroughly conversant with the Greek, Latin and Hebrew languages and published several works. He died in October 1757; it was said through excessive study.[2]

Not so well known is the fact that on 12 December 1720 Robert Forster officiated at the marriage of Alexander Selkirk, by licence, to Frances Candish of Oreston.[3] Selkirk was the Scottish sailor whose adventures on the solitary island of Juan Fernandez, off the coast of Chile, inspired Daniel Defoe to write his famous adventure story, *Robinson Crusoe*.

ALEXANDER SELKIRK
1878 — 1721
MAROONED ON JUAN FERNANDEZ ISLAND
IN 1704; HIS STORY BECAME THE BASIS OF
DANIEL DEFOE'S BOOK "ROBINSON CRUSOE".
STAYED IN ORESTON FARM FROM OCTOBER 1720,
MARRYING FRANCES CANDISH
ON 12TH DECEMBER.
HE DEPARTED ABOARD
H.M.S. WEYMOUTH
ON 20TH DECEMBER
1720

Text of the plaque affixed to the wall of Minards House commemorating Selkirk's marriage at Plymouth in 1720.

James Lampen Harris and Henry Bellenden Bulteel

James Lampen Harris was born in 1793, the fifth son of John and Catherine Harris of Radford.[1] He was ordained in the Church of England and appointed perpetual curate of Plymstock Parish Church in 1826. His cousin, Henry Bellenden Bulteel, born in 1800, the fourth son of Thomas Hillersdon and Anne Bulteel of Belle-Vue, became curate of St. Ebbe's in Oxford in 1826. Both were influenced by the new thinking regarding clericalism and, as will be seen, their careers run in tandem, each pursuing their fundamentalist beliefs in their own particular fashion.

After gaining a greater knowledge of the scriptures James Harris gave up his living at Plymstock in 1832 and joined the community of Plymouth Brethren, who followed a simpler form of worship. Among these learned men was the brilliant scholar, Samuel Prideaux Tregelles, who resided in Portland Square, Plymouth, in 1846, and received a Doctorate of Law in 1850. Harris himself was an excellent scholar and possessed a large Hebrew bible from which he was able to translate freely. His opinion on the Word was highly respected by students and he held weekly readings of the bible at Plymouth, which were well attended. He was also a Plymouth Brethren preacher, alternating with B.W. Newton. Unfortunately, the two did not quite see eye to eye on all matters of religion, resulting in the Newton controversy. [2]

Henry Bulteel caused a sensation when he preached 'A Sermon on I Corinthians, 11.'[12] before the University of Oxford at St Mary's on Sunday 6 February 1831, which included much plain speaking about the state of the universities and the Church of England. This controversial sermon was printed, the demand for copies being so great that it ran to six editions. Because of this sermon and Bulteel's preaching out of doors and in dissenting chapels, the Bishop of Oxford revoked his licence and, in August 1831, his connection with the Church of England ended. His followers, known as 'Bulteelers', built him a chapel at the rear of Pembroke College, where he conducted services on the principles advocated by the Plymouth Brethren. [3]

The magazine *The Christian Witness* was started under Harris's editorship in 1834, and it has been said that the *Witness* of today follows more on the lines of the original than any other magazine, and regularly inserts valuable papers written in these early days.

Harris was a deep, prophetic student and took a leading part in the meeting held in the Freemasons' Hall at London in May 1864. He was also the author of several books on religion, to name but two; *Law and Grace* and *The Priesthood and the Cross of Christ*.

Bulteel was also a prolific writer and the author of a book entitled *The Doctrine of the Miraculous Interference of Jesus on behalf of Believers*, in which he narrated how, by means of prayer and intercession, he had cured and restored to health three women. He also became a believer in the doctrine of universal redemption and a denier of the doctrine that Christ died for the elect only. In agreement with the views of his cousin James, Henry entered into the Newton controversy in 1845, issuing an anonymous denunciation of the Puseyite party and of John Henry Newman in particular. [4]

Harris was married twice, his first wife being Sophia Robertson, whose sister Louisa was married to his brother Christopher. His second wife was Mrs Frances Farish, daughter of the celebrated author, Legh Richmond. They lived in a house called Mount Pleasant,[5] later moving to Billacombe Villas, and then to Plympton. Finally, they lived at Weston-super-Mare with an old friend, Captain Percy Hall, where Harris died on 9 October 1877. His widow, Frances, died in 1886. A portrait shows Harris as kindly in appearance, white-haired with a bald pate and a full beard.

Bulteel married Eleanor, sister of Alderman C. J. Sadler of Oxford. He lived with his wife and family at The Crescent, Plymouth, where he died on 28 December 1866. [6]

Edward Francis Coke

The Rev. Edward Francis Coke M.A. came to Plymstock in 1843, with his wife Fanny and baby daughter Frances. Three more daughters, Juliana,

Amy and Charlotte, and a son, Edward Francis, were all born at Plymstock.[1] In 1845 he was the first incumbent to occupy the newly-built parsonage in Church Road on land given by the Duke of Bedford.[2] This was the site of the former tenement known as 'Candishes tenement at Tree', the tree being situated at the junction of Church Road with Burrow Hill. Before the parsonage was built it was usual for the incumbents to occupy one or other of the tenements belonging to the manor. A Survey dated 1755 shows the Rev. William Cookson as occupying this tenement.[3]

It was unfortunate for Coke that he arrived to take up his incumbency in the midst of what might be termed an ecclesiastical row which began in January 1831, with the appointment of Bishop Henry Phillpotts, a 'high' churchman, who soon began to tighten up the rules and bring a stronger sense of discipline into a diocese which was considered to have become very lax. His pastoral letter setting out guidelines succeeded only in antagonising some of the clergy, who resisted the new orders, and upsetting many parishioners who saw these as 'Romish innovations'. One of the points at issue was his examination of ecclesiastical law regarding the wearing of the surplice for certain church services. He decided to resolve the doubt by requiring that the surplice be always used.[4] A spate of parish meetings ensued and placards appeared everywhere reviling the bishop.

Plymstock ministers were obviously divided on the question of the surplice, the Rev. Coke obeying the order, whilst the Rev. Babb, minister of the Chapel of Ease at Turnchapel resisted, informing his congregation that they would imperil their souls if they attended ritualistic services in Plymouth. When the bishop heard of this he deprived him of his licence and refused a Prayer from the Three Towns that he be reinstated.[5]

A Plymouth solicitor, Mr J. E. Elworthy, who lived at Stentaway House, Plymstock, was one of the speakers at a Church meeting in Plymouth, in December 1844. After criticising the bishop he turned his attention to Plymstock, 'the tithes of which', he said:

amounting to £1300 or £1400 a year were received by the Dean and Chapter of Windsor, by whom the present incumbent, the Rev. E.F. Coke who, he understood, wore the surplice in the pulpit, was appointed. And yet, notwithstanding the revenue derived from this parish was so large, the benighted, miserable and spiritually destitute parish of Plymstock was about to be blessed with the service of an additional minister of the Church of England, to be provided by some charitable institution.

A full report of this meeting appeared in the *Plymouth Herald* and on 4 January 1845 a letter from the Rev. Edward Coke was published. (See Chapter 10).

Asking to be allowed to 'unravel this tissue of misconceptions' he outlined the facts concerning the Plymstock tithes and continued:

If he (Mr Elworthy) considers it prostitution for ecclesiastical bodies to take great tithes for keeping up daily services in the cathedral, he must call it something worse for gentlemen to take tithes for doing nothing and ride about in their carriages.[6]

This last comment, although true, was unfortunate, as it was a criticism of the Harris family of Radford, who held a lease of the tithes, worth at that time £781, per annum.

At last, Bishop Phillpotts bowed to the storm of protest and withdrew his previous orders, leaving the clergy 'to continue the service in their churches as they have hitherto done'. Despite the extremely conciliatory tone of his letter it was not the end of the matter at Plymstock, for it seemd the Rev. Coke was a strong supporter of the Tractarian Movement and he endeavoured to pursue his belief that more attention should be given to the rubrical directions in the book of common prayer.

So much feeling was aroused by the Rev. Coke's reforming zeal that a parish meeting was held on 28 January 1845, when Colonel H.B. Harris was elected to the chair. This resulted in four unanimous resolutions: the first 'viewed with alarm the attempts now making to revive certain forms and ordinations which have long been suffered to be dormant and which if carried out would have the effect of approximating our Protestant establishment to the rites and ceremonies of the Church of Rome'. The second mentioned violent attempts by the present incumbent to effect certain alterations in the interior of the church. Resolution four was that copies of the resolutions be sent to the Bishop and to the Rev. Coke.[7]

The Rev. Coke's outspoken attitude was taken note of by the Dean when he visited Plymstock in 1847 and made his report on the condition of the church, for he wrote:

The incumbent is Mr. Coke, a young man said to be active, but it is to be proved, not very judicious'.

The Dean also noted:

'Church in good repair but considerably disfigured by modern improvements.'[8]

This must refer to the replacing of the original pews in 1828 with plain ones made of deal. (See above). The Dean and Canons were well aware of this local dispute, for preserved in their archives at St George's Chapel at Windsor is a copy of the newspaper carrying the Rev. Coke's letter.

Despite the controversial start to his incumbency the Rev. Coke conducted the Church Grammar School in the new parsonage, which was described in 1850 as 'a highly respectable academy to which a library and reading-room was attached.'[9] This appears to be the only mention of this school, which probably ceased in 1852 when Edward Coke was succeeded by William James.

NOTES AND REFERENCES
SOME WELL KNOWN PLYMSTOCK MINISTERS

Robert Forster
1. Plymstock Parish Register, West Devon Record Office.
2. Dictionary of National Biography.
3. St Andrew's Parish Register, Plymouth, W.D.R.O.

James Lampen Harris and Henry Bellenden Bulteel
1. Plymstock Parish Register, W.D.R.O.
2. H. Pickering, '*Chief Men among the Brethren*'.
3. Dictionary of National Biography.
4. D.N.B.
5. Census returns for Plymstock, 1861.
6. D.N.B.

Edward Francis Coke
1. Plymstock Parish Register, W.R.D.O.
2. *London Gazette*, 19 May 1846.
3. Plymstock Manor Survey, 1755, *Bedford Records*, Devon Record Office.
4. Rev. R.J.E. Boggis, M.A. '*History of the Diocese of Exeter*', 498-501.
5. H.J. Whitfeld, '*Plymouth & Devonport in Times of War and Peace*', 506.
6. *Plymouth, Devonport & Stonehouse Herald*, 4 Jan. 1845.
7. Ibid, 29 Jan. 1845.
8. St George's Chapel, Windsor, The Aerary, Visitation, 1847, *III J.10*.
9. White's Directory of Devonshire, 1850.

Chapter Ten
THE PLYMSTOCK TITHES

The earliest concept of tithe, formerly called church-scot, also a payment in kind, has an ancient and worthy foundation, for Theodore, Archbishop of Canterbury AD 669-690, ruled that tithe could lawfully be given only to the poor, to pilgrims and by laymen to their churches;[1] although it was considered that a lord who built a church should assign at least a part of the tithe to the support of the priest. By the tenth century, tithe, originally a voluntary contribution, had become a legal obligation and there were stringent conditions for the enforcement of payment. Under the Ecclesiastical Laws of King Edgar tithe was reserved to the use of parish churches only; the poor and the pilgrims have faded from the picture.[2] In those days the parish church was the priory church of St Peter and St Paul at Plympton; Plymstock being an appendant chapel. Although collected at Plymstock; the corn in the tithe barn, the animals in the parish pounds, and the ducks and geese in the prior's pond, the revenue belonged to the prior.

The action of John Howe, the last prior of Plympton, in granting a lease of the Plymstock tithes to Walter Shere and Christopher Hornbrook in 1538,[3] was to have far-reaching and long-lasting consequences, for it seems that following Edward VI's grant of the Plymstock chapel to them, the dean and canons of Windsor were quite content to be relieved not only of the burden of receiving and disposing of tithe produce, but also of appointing the incumbent.

After the dissolution of the monasteries the new leaseholders, called 'lay impropriators' were under no obligation to relieve the poor; in fact the charitable and pious use to which tithes were first appropriated was completely lost sight of in the new Statutes.[4] Tithes, ostensibly paid to the church as hitherto, now served only to supplement the income of the new leaseholders.

The manuscripts of St George's Chapel at Windsor give details of the following leases:[5]

> 20 June 1548. *from William Frankleyn, Clerk, Dean and the Canons of the King's Free Chapel of St George, Windsor, to John Wright, Gentyllman, of the Chapel of Plymstok, in the county of Devon, being a Chapel annexed unto the parsonage of Plympton, late in the holding of Walter Shere and Christopher Hornbrook, for forty–one years at a rental of sixty–two pounds, the said John to admit and appoint a priest the said Dean and Canons to find the stipend.*

By 1587 Anthony Rous* and his two sons, Arthur and Anthony, having obtained a surrender of the unexpired portion of the lease granted to John Wright, were themselves granted a further lease at a rental of £62; i.e. £54 to the dean and canons and £8 to the curate.

On 30 September 1606 Sir Anthony Rous and his surviving son Arthur sold the remainder of their lease to John Harris of Lanrest. The following day,

---

* Of Halton, on the Cornish bank of the River Tamar

1 October 1606, a lease was granted to Christopher Harris of Radford, Esq., and John Harris of Lanrest, for 21 years at a rental of £64; i.e. £54 to the dean and canons and £10 to the curate.

John Harris of Lanrest was the nephew and heir of Christopher Harris of Radford (knighted 1607) in the parish of Plymstock. In the event, both he and his eldest son Christopher predeceased Sir Christopher. John's second son, another John, succeeded to the Radford estate and to the lease of the Plymstock tithes. The Harris family continued to hold the lease of the Plymstock chapel and tithes until well into the nineteenth century, when the Tithe Commutation Act of 1836 commuted payment to a rent-charge instead of payment in kind. In 1842 The Plymstock Tithe Apportionment shows Harry Bulteel Harris as holding a lease of the tithes, the total amount of the rent-charge payable to him being £781.3s.6d. [6] When Colonel H.B. Harris died in 1863 his only son, John Crichton Harris, did not take up residence at Radford, the family's long lease of the tithes coming to a close. In any case the end was in sight, for an Order in Council promulgated on 28 June 1867 transferred the estates of the dean and canons of Windsor to the Ecclesiastical Commissioners, the patronage remaining undisturbed.

During the 1930s the general depression in agriculture led to agitation against the payment of tithe rent-charge and, in brief, a Royal Commission, followed by the Tithe Act of 1936, finally extinguished rent-charge and brought in payment by annuity. A later Act made these annuities redeemable at the payer's request for a lump sum. [7]

NOTES AND REFERENCES
THE PLYMSTOCK TITHES

1.   English Historical Documents, 2nd ed. V. I, 75.
2.   Eng. Hist. Doc., *King Edgar's code at Andover*, 959-963, V. I, 40.
3.   Joyce Youings, *Devon Monastic Lands*, 99.
4.   George Oliver, *Monasticon*, Preface, X.
5.   J.M. Dalton, *The Manuscripts of St George's Chapel*, Windsor, 55 & 442.
6.   Plymstock Tithe Apportionment, preamble.
7.   Church Commissioners, *Notes on Tithe and Tithe Rentcharge*, 1966.

Chapter Eleven
THE PURITAN REVOLUTION

During the Commonwealth period, 1649-1660, the Church of England was disestablished and its ruling structure of bishops, and deans and chapters was destroyed.[1] Presbyterians, baptists and independents were recognised by the Commonwealth as the three religious bodies forming the 'Protectorate Church'. Episcopalian and Roman Catholic worship was prohibited and the use of the prayer-book was forbidden. The efficiency of the clergy was secured by the establishment of committees to remove those who did not conform from their livings, and the institution of a central board of triers to examine the fitness of all new candidates for benefices.[2]

One consequence of these revolutionary measures was that the committee for Devon:

> demized (transferred) *ye chappell of Plymstock, being a chappell annexed unto the parsonage of Plymton.*

A surveyor was appointed to deal with the property of the dissolved Chapter of Windsor and this particular transference was registered with him on 2 July 1650.[3]

The committee who carried out an examination of the administration of Plymstock church, also in 1650, reported the following:

> *they say upon their oaths that in the parish of Plymstock the Sheafe and Tithe are impropriated and are worth by the year one hundred and twenty pounds, to witt, the Sheafe one hundred pounds yearly and for priory's Tithe twenty pounds yearly or thereaboute And that Jonathan Rashley Esq. is ye present propriator by order of a Lease from the Dean and Canons of Windsor, the yearly rent being fifty pounds or thereabouts. And the incumbent there is Mr John Bishop placed in by the election of the parishioners and approbation of the honourable committee of Devon, to whom there is allowed yearly for his salary by the said Jonathan Rashley Esq. the small tithe in the parish of Plymstock And ten pounds per annum as a free gift from the feoffees of Elize Hele Esq. late of Fardel, Cornwood, And that there is a very painful* (painstaking) *minister and a very populous congregation.*[4]

A large number of ministers who were loyal to the Established Church were ejected from their churches. Even some of the rectors and vicars who were not wholly dispossessed were harassed and ill-used. This persecution reached a climax in 1655 when Cromwell, then Lord Protector, issued a proclamation which forbade any ejected clergyman to keep a school or any gentleman to keep such a clergyman in his house as chaplain or tutor.[5] As a result, Thomas Hake, who kept a school at Plymstock, was visited by men from the Plymouth Garrison, who confiscated his books and took him into Plymouth where he was imprisoned and almost starved.

During this time many hundreds of clergymen were driven to destitution. Many died from their privations, especially those confined in the hideous prisons of that time, and those whom the Protector sent into slavery in the West Indies. These were kept under hatches and most died on their way, their families suffering extremes of poverty. Although Thomas Hake escaped at last, he and his wife were forced to live miserably without any safe or settled home.[6]

The restoration of the monarchy in 1660, followed by the Act of Uniformity in 1662, brought back the prayer-book and completely restored the Church of England. In 1662 Thomas Hake was presented to the vicarage of Walkhampton, but was not to enjoy his new position for long, for it seems the dreadful privations he had undergone had taken their toll and he died in 1666, being buried on 12 June at Plymstock Church.[7]

In 1662 Joan Hake was granted the *Corte House* at Plymstock for her use for life. This lease was for 99 years on the lives of their sons, Thomas Hake and Richard Hake. This indicates that she was the wife of Thomas Hake, for an account of his sufferings mentions that he had an estate there by his wife, so it could be assumed they lived there when Thomas was taken into Plymouth in 1655. The Hake family had occupied the *Corte House* since 1582, when Humphrey Hake and his wife Elizabeth were granted a lease of this property.[8]

When a Catalogue of the depressed clergy, with particulars of their sufferings, appeared in folio form in 1714 and was published in 1727, the list of names added up to 3334. The removal of the Puritans from the churches after the Restoration was considered to be a just reprisal for their harsh actions when in power.

NOTES AND REFERENCES
THE PURITAN REVOLUTION

1. Catalogue of *Ecclesiastical Records of the Commonwealth*, 1643-1660, *Introduction*, Lambeth Palace Library.
2. Dict. of Nat. Biog., *Oliver Cromwell.*
3. *Commonwealth Surveys*, 1650, No. 16, 154, Lambeth Palace Library.
4. *Commonwealth Surveys*, XII/5, 169-71.
5. A.D. Greenwood, *History of the People of England*, V. II, 349.
6. Dr John Walker DD, 1714, *An Attempt towards recovering an Account of the Numbers and Sufferings of the Clergy of the Church of England.*
7. Walker, *Account of the Clergy of the C. of E.*, An Appendix, 417. Plymstock Parish Register.
8. *Bedford Records*, L1258, Devon Record Office.

Chapter Twelve

THE CIVIL PARISH OF PLYMSTOCK

There is no evidence that civil parishes were created either by Act of Parliament or by Royal Charter. Their existence depended upon ancient tradition and immemorial custom, and their acceptance by parliament as units of local government sprang from a growing need during the sixteenth century to fill the gap left by the Dissolution of the Monasteries, notably with regard to the poor. Efforts by the government to provide for the relief of genuine poverty took the form of various enactments to raise money by voluntary contributions to relief funds. The inadequacy of these measures led ultimately to the Poor Relief Act of 1601, which empowered the levying of a poor rate.[1]

At the time of the Reformation the parish already had officers such as churchwardens, who were elected by the parishioners, and the petty constable, sometimes called warden or tithingman. Originally an officer of the manor, he was directly responsible to the high constable of the Hundred Court which was held at Plympton. To these offices were added by statute, the Overseers of the Poor, 1536 & 1553, and the Surveyor of the Highways, 1555, often called the Waywarden. These officers were appointed by the Justices of the Peace to whom they were required to submit their annual accounts. In addition to the unpaid officers with their independent powers, there were paid servants such as the parish clerk, who could be elected by the parishioners, the sexton and the bell–ringer, etc. These parish officers formed the nucleus of committees known as 'Vestries', so called because their meetings were usually held in the church vestry. Legislation also gave these bodies powers over burial grounds and allotments.[2]

The growth of parish responsibility during the sixteenth and seventeenth centuries shows that parliament had come to regard the civil parish as a legal entity, the long-established geographical bounds of the older ecclesiastical parish remaining unchanged. In fact, a prominent churchman, Bishop Edward Stillingfleet considered it necessary in 1698 that these boundaries should be carefully preserved by annual perambulations.[3]

Once again the Plymstock Rate Book gives an illuminating insight into parish life during this period. The signatures of several of the local gentry appear frequently and include in the year 1611 Sir Ferdinando Gorges, Governor of the Fort of Plymouth, and Sir Christopher Harris of Radford, Customer (Customs Officer) of Plymouth. Other names which appear are Thomas Barkley of Downhorne, George Blake of Coombe Farm, Elburton; Thomas Hake of Court House; John Candish of Candishes Tenement in Church Road, now the Plymstock Inn; and Thomas Riche, who was granted a lease of 'Down Horne' in 1655.

The rate levied on various properties is also recorded, the list being headed by Radford with an annual payment of 13s.4d. As a comparison,

Pomphlett Mill was assessed at 2s., and at 'Oarston' the occupant of the 'Passing Boat' at £1.6s.0d. There were of course variations in the rate levied according to the expenses the parish had to meet. The following are examples: in 1694 a rate was made by the constables:

for ye paying of Golie Hospitall, Bridge-money and other charges and impositions in the parish of Plymstock during their office.

An exceptionally high rate was levied for that year, for John Harris of the Barton of Radford was to pay £6.8s. and the occupant at West Hooe was assessed at £10. Several items of payment are worth noting; one in 1570 shows that parishioners at Plymstoke gave a payment towards the restoration of the bridge at Feringdon,* and another in 1573 records the purchase of gunpowder. Among the disbursements of Thomas Hake and Richard Pike, churchwardens for the year 1655, is an item paid to:

* This was almost certainly the bridge at Farringdon near Exeter.

Robert ?, constable of ye Hundred, for and towards the repairing of the houses and places of judicature within the Castle of Exon.

An interesting entry for 1657 shows that 14s.1d. was paid to the constable for the repairing of Hebrew and Roman bridges. These payments of bridge-money are a reminder of the *Om Homme* (South Hams) charter of AD 847:

that this land is to be exempt from every secular burden except military service and the building of bridges. [n.1]

During the 1650s the parish was divided into three areas for rating purposes, Radford heading the list for the South Division, Coombe Farm, Elburton, for the East Division, and Downhorn Farm for the Plymstock Division. [4]

Dean School. The first National School for Plymstock, built in 1827. This print was taken from a plan attached to an Agreement dated 1896. Dean School was then a boy's school, the room on the right being used as a Sunday School for girls.

The Dean School was the first National School for the parish, being erected in 1827 at a cost of £400 on a site sold to the minister and churchwardens by the Duke of Bedford. The cost was met by contributions and payments of the children. Mr Martin Jenkins was the Master and Miss Mary Lexton was the Mistress. The original school building was surveyed in 1970 when it remained intact at the heart of a rather confused group of buildings, mostly of relatively recent date. In the old building a stone plaque inscribed NATIONAL SCHOOL 1827 could be seen inserted over the fireplace. The whole of the buildings on this site have since been demolished. [5]

The controversial Local Government Act of 1894, involving over 800 amendments, created the Parish Council and the Parish Meeting. This Act came into force on 5 March 1894 and on 4 December, at a public meeting convened by the Overseers and held in the Dean schoolroom, the Plymstock Parish Council was formed, the new council taking over the civil functions of the Vestry. From forty candidates 13 councillors were elected. This civil parish of Plymstock became one of the largest in the country, a considerable increase in population resulting in the number of councillors being raised to the maximum of 21. [6]

As with the old rate book, the minutes of the parish council provide many details of life in the parish during a period of great change and rapid development. Parishioners were entitled to attend council meetings, but were not permitted to speak. Notices of all meetings had to be displayed at the church entrance and at other prominent places. [7]

The parish meeting, which was held annually in March, was an opportunity for parishioners to speak and to vote on any resolution. No land owned by a parish council could be sold without the consent of the parish meeting. [8] The parish council could acquire land for allotments, recreation and open spaces. Plymstock Parish Council became the Burial Authority for the Ecclesiastical Parish and on Thursday 30 October 1947 the consecration ceremony and official opening took place at Ridge Cross cemetery on the Wembury Road.

In 1954 the chairman of the Plymstock Parish Council was presented with a distinguishing badge of office. This was a silver medallion which was worn suspended from the neck by a wide blue ribbon.

Under the provisions of The Plymouth Order 1966, which came into force on 1 April 1967, the Plymstock Parish Council was dissolved and the greater part of the old civil parish was amalgamated with the city of Plymouth, the outer fringe being incorporated with the adjoining parishes of Brixton and Wembury. [9] Plymouth's added area was divided into two wards; Plymstock Radford and Plymstock Dunstone, three councillors for each ward being elected to serve as members of the Plymouth City Council.

Plymstock schools

For many years Dean School was the only National School for the parish, until schools commenced at Oreston (1873), Goosewell (1883), Hooe (see Chapter 18), and an infants' school on the waterfront at Turnchapel. Dean became a boys' school at least by 1883, continuing until 1911 when it was closed, the pupils being transferred to Plymstock School at Church Road. This school was enlarged in 1938, when it became the senior school of the district. After being again enlarged in the 1960s it became Plymstock Comprehensive School.

The old school at Goosewell became an infants school when a new junior school was opened nearby.

Also, during the 1960s primary schools were opened at Pomphlett, Dunstone and Elburton, followed by Coombe Dean,* a comprehensive school for the Goosewell, part of Elburton, and Wembury areas.

* Opened in January 1976.

NOTES AND REFERENCES
THE CIVIL PARISH OF PLYMSTOCK

1. Sidney and Beatrice Webb, *English Local Government*, Vol. I, *The Parish*, 1906, 5 & 9.
2. Webb, *Eng. Local Gou.*, 25–30.
3. Edward Stillingfleet, *Ecclesiastical Cases relative to duties and rights of parochial clergy*, part I, 348.
4. *Plymstock Rate Book*, West Devon Record Office.
5. J. Barber and I.M. Langdon, *Buildings of architectural or historic interest in the parish of Plymstock, 1970*.
6. Minutes of Plymstock parish council and parish meetings, W.D.R.O.
7. Charles Arnold–Baker, *Parish Administration*, 1958, 47–8.
8. Arnold–Baker, *Parish Admin.*, 106.
9. *The Plymouth Order, 1966*; Plymouth Central Library, Local History Department.

n.1. See above, *Saxon Settlement at Plymstock*.

Chapter Thirteen

RADFORD: A FEUDAL ESTATE

Long before the Norman Conquest the Saxon settlements at Plymstock and Hooe were linked by an old road with two notable landmarks; Barrow Hill, with its Bronze Age burial mounds, and *Raedford*, an ancient ford over the brook which flowed into a tidal creek of the Cattewater. It is probable this brook was forded when the Romans traded at Mount Batten.[1]

The name *Radeford*, a variation of the Old English name, is older than the family who settled there during the thirteenth century, for they took their name from the place. Historians have considered the name to be derived from the reddish colour of the soil and the ford over the brook.[2] This interpretation could be extended to the colour of the ford, which may have been constructed of local limestone which is a reddish colour. The nearby Radford Caves, surveyed in 1962 and 1963, include such names as 'Red Curtain' and 'Red Corridor'.[3]

At the time of the Domesday Survey, 1086, one hundred acres of land at Radeford still belonged to the king as part of his manor of Plympton. When Henry I succeeded to the throne in 1100 he granted this manor to Richard de Redvers, son of Baldwin, sheriff of Devon. Richard also became first earl of Devon after the Conquest. [4] Although there had been military service of a sort under the Saxons, the imposition of knight service by the Normans placed a far heavier burden on the holders of large estates, who found it difficult to supply the service required of

them by the king. Because of this a system of infeudation was introduced, which put estates in fee and commuted knight service into monetary payments, one fee being equal to a knight's service, and two men-at-arms were reckoned as equal to one knight. Also, by subinfeudation land could be sublet to an undertenant who would then be liable for part of the fee. The manor of Plympton was assessed at $2^1/_2$ fees and the honour, which comprised many manors scattered throughout Devon, was assessed at 89 fees.[5]

Arising from this requirement a military estate was created at Radford and in 1243 William le Abbé of Loughtor, the Domesday manor of *Lochetora* – adjoining Newnham at Plympton – was the tenant. [6] By 1284 William had been succeeded by Henry le Abbé at Loughtor, Radford being held under him by Walter de Radeford for services and two shillings per annum. [7]

William le Abbé must have been a prominent figure during the thirteenth century, for he was one of the witnesses when, some time after 1262, Isabel de Fortibus, Countess of Devon, to whom the manor and honour of Plympton had descended, confirmed the charter of her father, Baldwin, to the burgesses of Plympton. William's signature appeared as *Willo le Abbé de Radeford aliis*. [8]

Early attempts to unravel the pedigree of this family are often contradictory, the most recent and reliable being *A Survey at the Hall, Weare Giffard, Devon*, which shows that William le Abbé was married to Cecily

Giffard, sister of the last Sir Walter Giffard. When Sir Walter's grand-daughter, Emma, wife of Robert de Dinham, died childless in 1291, her Giffard inheritance reverted to the descendants of her great-aunts, Cecily and Rohesia, Weare falling to Cecily's share. [9]

William and Cecily had two children, Walter de Radford and Emma de Radford. As Henry le Abbé inherited William's estates at Loughtor and Radford he may have been William's son by a first marriage.

In addition to other holdings William le Abbé was tenant in fee of the manor of Alfameston* – otherwise Treawen – now Traine Farm in the parish of Wembury.[10] Alfameston was held of him by William who adopted the name *atte Treawen*. Emma de Radford married William atte Treawen and they had a daughter, Joan. In 1284 Emma held Alfameston in succession to her father. When William atte Treawen died Walter de Radford became the guardian of his niece Joan, holding Alfameston for her in 1303. By 1310 Joan held Weare Giffard in right of her grandmother, Cecily.

Walter de Radford's son, Walter, married secondly his cousin, Joan, changing his name to Treawen. Walter and Joan Treawen appear in the Weare Giffard chart which shows their grandson as William Weare – alias Treawen. [11]

Henry le Abbé, still at Loughtor in 1303, was succeeded by his great-nephew, Walter de Radford, elder son of Walter de Radford alias Treawen, by his first marriage to Mabel Treverbyn, who divorced him. He held Loughtor and Radford in 1346. [12]

All these name changes have added considerably to the confusion surrounding the le Abbé descent.

The last of the le Abbé alias de Radford male heirs died without issue, leaving his estates of Loughtor and Radford to his sister Alice, wife of Henry Beauchamp.[13] The ancestor of John Harris, Esquire, seated at Radford in the time of Henry V (1413-1422) is said to have obtained the same by his marriage with the heiress of Radford. [14]

The first known John Harris had a son John, who married the heiress of Hansford. He died in 1430 leaving two sons, both named John – not at all unusual at that time – the elder John inheriting the Radford estate (see Chapter 7, Plymstock's Medieval Chapel) and the younger John marrying the heiress of Stone of Lifton. This branch of the family became known as Harris of Hayne in the parish of Stowford. [15]

An Inquisition held in 1485 after the death of John Harris of Radford showed that he had a son Francis, born 1475, and a daughter Elizabeth. This inquiry into his lands revealed that in addition to a *messuage* and one hundred acres of land at Radford he also possessed forty acres of land and ten cottages at Esthoo, held of the king as of the honour of Plympton Earl by knight service. Esthoo was the small manor of East Hooe, now Higher Hooe, formerly in the possession of Ralph Giffard.[16]

During the minority of Francis, the king, Henry VII, gave custody of Radford to Roger Holand. When Francis claimed his inheritance in 1496 the writ reciting the evidence showed that David, the prior of the House and Church of Plympton, and his fellow monk, David Blackhede, were godfathers at his christening at Plymstock Church. [17] On 28 May 1498 the escheator in Devon was ordered to take fealty of Francis, son of John Harrys Esquire, who held of the king and to give him seisin of his father's lands since on 26 October 1485, the king granted the said honour to his kinsman, Edward, Earl of Devonshire. [18]

* There are many variations in the spelling of this name, but Alfameston is the form used in a deed which is in Barnstaple Athenaeum.

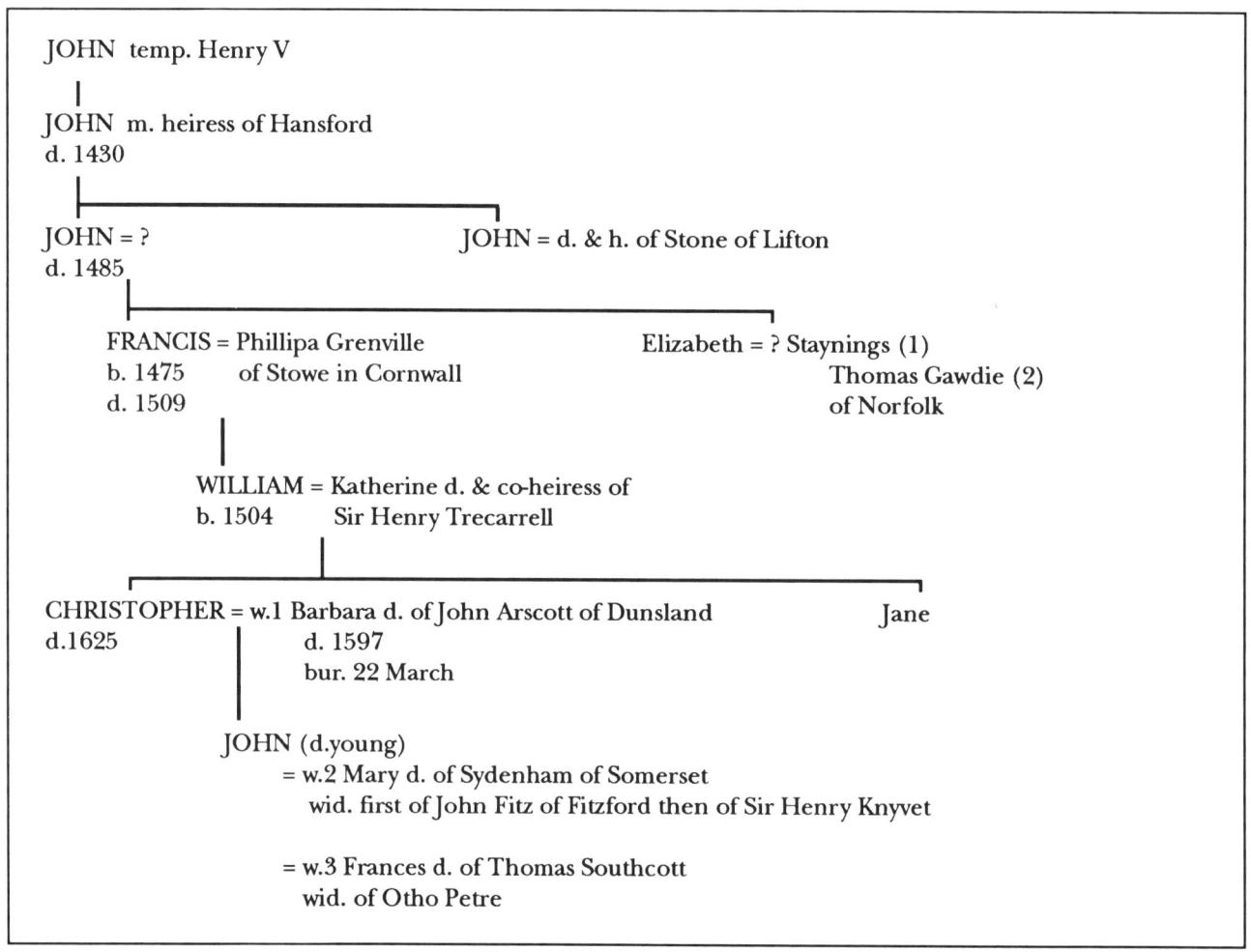

JOHN temp. Henry V

JOHN m. heiress of Hansford
d. 1430

JOHN = ?   JOHN = d. & h. of Stone of Lifton
d. 1485

FRANCIS = Phillipa Grenville   Elizabeth = ? Staynings (1)
b. 1475   of Stowe in Cornwall   Thomas Gawdie (2)
d. 1509   of Norfolk

WILLIAM = Katherine d. & co-heiress of
b. 1504   Sir Henry Trecarrell

CHRISTOPHER = w.1 Barbara d. of John Arscott of Dunsland   Jane
d.1625   d. 1597
                   bur. 22 March

JOHN (d.young)
  = w.2 Mary d. of Sydenham of Somerset
    wid. first of John Fitz of Fitzford then of Sir Henry Knyvet

  = w.3 Frances d. of Thomas Southcott
    wid. of Otho Petre

Pedigree – Harris of Radford.

Francis married Phillipa, daughter of Sir Thomas Grenville of Stowe in the parish of Kilkhampton, their only son being William, born in 1504. Francis died in 1509, his widow Phillipa marrying secondly Humphrey Arundell of Lanherne, who took over the management of the Radford estates. His name heads the Subsidy Rolls of 1524-27 for the parish of Plymstock, which was the first taxation list giving the names of

Devon inhabitants since the subsidy of 1332.[19] Phillipa died in June 1524, her son William coming of age the following year.

William married Katharine, daughter and co–heiress with her sisters of Sir Henry Trecarrell of Launceston. William was one of the leaders of The Western Rebellion in 1549, when the men of Devon and Cornwall protested against the new prayer book which had been introduced at Whitsuntide by Edward VI. The rising was finally overcome in August when William, together with other insurgents, was taken to London and imprisoned in the Fleet. He was released on 1 November by order of privy council, but was probably fined. [20]

William and Katharine's children, Christopher and Jane, lived in Cornwall during the lifetime of their father, probably at Trecarrell in the parish of Lezant, Christopher becoming one of the resident justices and a deputy lieutenant of that county. We first learn of him at Radford in 1580 in association with his kinsman, Edmund Tremayne, of Collacombe, Lamerton, who was clerk of the privy council at Westminster, for during that year Francis Drake had returned to Plymouth with great treasure. On 24 October Queen Elizabeth wrote to Edmund Tremayne from Richmond commanding him to assist Francis Drake in sending to London bullion brought into the realm by Drake, but to leave £10 000 worth in Drake's hands. This last instruction 'to be kept most secret to himself alone'.[21] On 8 November Edmund Tremayne wrote to Sir Francis Walsingham, Queen Elizabeth's Secretary of State, expressing his great satisfaction in having Mr Christopher Harris associated with him in charge of the treasure brought home by Francis Drake. It is no secret that Drake's share of the treasure was stored at Radford.[22] State Papers dated 24 December 1580 give a detailed account by Alderman Richard Martyn, Francis Drake and Christopher Harris of the amount of gold and silver bullion in ingots brought from Sion and laid up in a vault in the Jewel House, the silver bullion weighing 22 899 lbs, the coarse silver 512 lbs 6 oz and the gold bullion 101 lbs 10 oz . (Indorsed by Burghley *The quantity of bullion brought into ye Tower by Fr. Drake.)*[23]

Edmund Tremayne's sister, Katharine, was the first wife of John Harris of Lanrest, near Liskeard. The exact relationship of Edmund to Christopher Harris, who was the brother of Jane Harris, second wife of John Harris is not too clear. It was obviously a close personal relationship, for Edmund looked on him as a son. Edmund Tremayne, d. 1582, was the eldest son of Phillipa Grenville, daughter of Sir Roger Grenville, d. 1523, of Stowe in Cornwall, whose grandson Roger commanded and was lost in the *Mary Rose* in 1545. Roger's son, Sir Richard Grenville, then became heir to his grandfather, Sir Richard Grenville, and purchased from the Crown the former Cistercian Abbey of Buckland. In 1581 he conveyed this estate to Christopher Harris and Sir John Hele for £3400. It seems certain they were only acting for Drake, to whom they reconveyed the property.[24]

In 1584 Christopher Harris was member of parliament for Plymouth and, with Drake, member for Bosinney in Cornwall, pushed the Water Bill through parliament to bring water to the town of Plymouth. In 1585 Harris represented Drake at the funeral of his godfather, Francis Russell, Earl of Bedford. He was also executor of Drake's will when he died at sea in 1596. [25]

When Spain's massive preparations for the invasion of England became known Sir Richard Grenville prepared a plan for the defence of Plymouth. Once

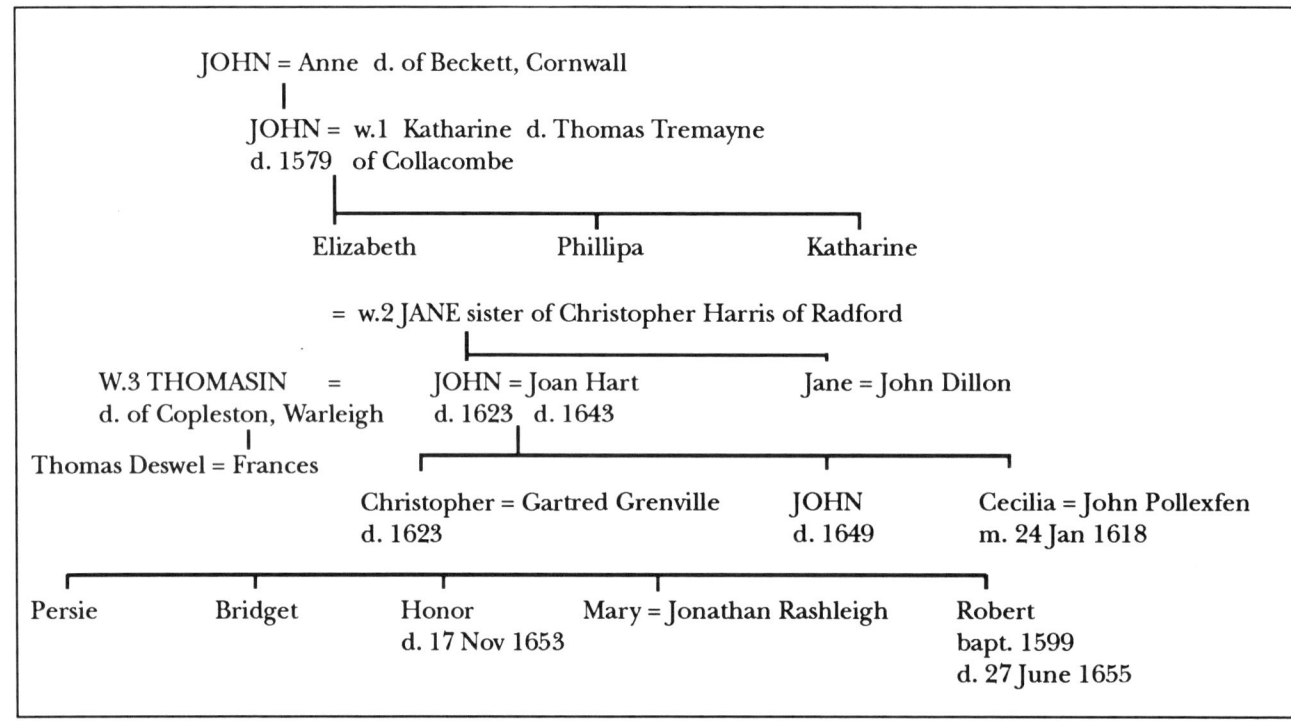

JOHN = Anne d. of Beckett, Cornwall

JOHN = w.1 Katharine d. Thomas Tremayne
d. 1579   of Collacombe

Elizabeth   Phillipa   Katharine

= w.2 JANE sister of Christopher Harris of Radford

W.3 THOMASIN   =   JOHN = Joan Hart   Jane = John Dillon
d. of Copleston, Warleigh   d. 1623 d. 1643

Thomas Deswel = Frances

Christopher = Gartred Grenville   JOHN   Cecilia = John Pollexfen
d. 1623   d. 1649   m. 24 Jan 1618

Persie   Bridget   Honor   Mary = Jonathan Rashleigh   Robert
                             d. 17 Nov 1653   bapt. 1599
                                                                         d. 27 June 1655

Pedigree – Harris of Lanrest.

again the military nature of the Radford estate was emphasized when Christopher Harris was considered to be:

a sufficient gentleman to take charge to defend this quarter with the inhabitants of Plympton Hundred.

This plan, dated 1586-8, shows the various gun emplacements around the Sound and on St Nicholas (Drake's) Island, with the direction and range of their fire. Seven or eight batteries of guns were needed to cover the waters of the Sound and 21 companies of troops would have to be stationed at various landing places. One example is that 200 soldiers were required to defend Oreston Passage. [26]

In 1600 Christopher Harris, then vice-admiral of Devon, was appointed temporary governor of the Hoe Fort in place of Sir Ferdinando Gorges, whose implication in the Essex plot resulted in his dismissal. Harris was followed by Sir John Gilbert, who remained governor until 1603. On the accession of James I, Sir Ferdinando Gorges was re-appointed. [27] Harris was also Customer (Customs Officer) for Plymouth and it is recorded that calicoes, spices, sugars etc. and captured goods were taken to Radford and stored in the cellars. [28]

During the municipal year 1600-1601 Christopher Harris entertained Sir Walter Ralegh, who was Lord Warden of the Stannaries, when the corporation of Plymouth hired 'a greate bote' to convey them to Radford. [29] At that time there was no bar and boats could go right up to the quay wall by the boat-house. In July 1618, in less happy circumstances, Harris held Ralegh under house arrest at Radford, before he was taken to London where, on 29 October, he was executed in Old Palace Yard. While Ralegh was at Radford he was persuaded to escape. An account written by Captain Samuel King, who returned to Plymouth with Ralegh in *The Destiny*, tells us that a barque was engaged which would carry Ralegh to France and:

On the first night at about one of the clock they secretly took boat to have gone aboard but before they reached the barque which was moored beyond command of the fort, Ralegh changed his mind and returned to Radford unsuspected by anyone. [30]

In 1606 Christopher Harris obtained a Lease of the Chapel of Plymstock, which included the tithes of the parish (see Chapter 8), which Edward VI had given to the dean and canons of Windsor. The following year he was knighted by James I. Although he was married three times he had no direct heir. His first wife was Barbara Arscott by whom he had a son, John, who died at an early age. Secondly, he married Mary, a daughter of Sydenham of Somerset and widow of Sir John Fitz of Tavistock. His third wife was Frances, daughter of Thomas Southcott and widow of Thomas Petre.

In 1617 Sir Christopher Harris, Knight, erected houses for five poor people at Goosewell with plots and lawns, together with a charge of £10 per annum on the manor of Goosewell. This property was granted to Thomas Barkley, Esq. (of Downhorn) and others as Trustees. Subsequent nominations were to be with Sir Christopher Harris and his heirs. In February 1934 the Alms Houses at Goosewell were sold and the money invested, which brought in sufficient income to give to six old couples in the parish not in receipt of Poor Relief 7s.6d. per month. In the 1960s these cottages were demolished and a row of modern terraced houses built on the site. [31]

An Inquisition taken after the death of Sir Christopher Harris shows him as military tenant of the manor of East Hooe and the capital *messuage* at Radford. He was also a military tenant in fee of the manor of Staddiscombe and possessed the manor of Goosewell. [32] Much land is mentioned, some of it intermixed with the lands of the Plymstock manor, then in the possession of Edward, 3rd Earl of Bedford. These named fields had originally been given in frankalmoign (a free and charitable gift to the church). [33]

Sir Christopher's estates descended to the heirs of his sister Jane, who was married in 1562 to John Harris of Lanrest. By him she had two children, John and Jane. John married Joan Hart and they had several children. John and his eldest son, Christopher, who was married to Gertrude Grenville, both died at Radford in 1623 when a smallpox epidemic was sweeping the West Country. John, the second son, inherited the mansion and estate at Lanrest. He was recorder for the borough and member of parliament for Liskeard. [34] When his great-uncle, Sir Christopher Harris, died in January 1624-25 he also succeeded to the Radford and Goosewell estates. John's younger brother, Robert, became the military tenant in fee of the holding at Staddiscombe. The mansion at Lanrest continued as the family home of John's mother, Mrs John Harris, his brother, Persie, and his sisters, Mary, Honor and Bridget.

John Harris married Elizabeth Johnson of Bonham in Wiltshire and they resided at Radford where a son, John, was born in July 1631.

Elizabeth died in childbirth and was buried at Plymstock Church. [35] This unhappy situation may have lead to the leasing in 1633 of the mansion and estate at Radford to George Trosse; [36] John probably returning with his infant son to Lanrest. John also assigned the lease of the Plymstock tithes to Jonathan

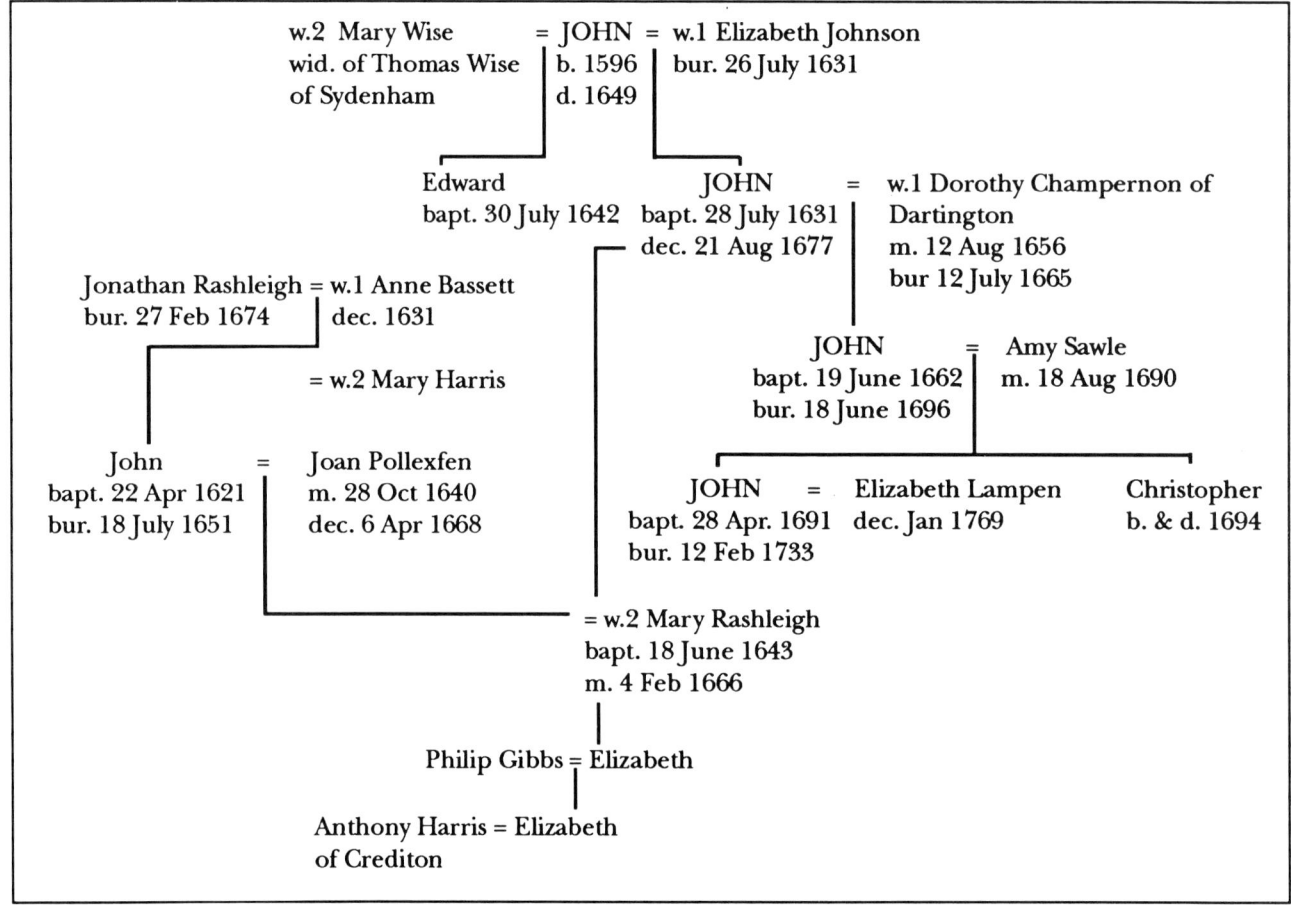

Pedigree – Harris of Lanrest and Radford.

Rashleigh of Menabilly, who had married his sister Mary. [37]

In 1641 John Harris remarried; his second wife, Mary, was the daughter of Edward Lord Chichester, and the widow of Thomas Wyse, elder son of Sir Thomas Wyse of Sydenham. On 12 October, prior to their marriage, John Harris settled on Mary and their future children the manors of Maders and Cartuther, near Liskeard. [58] John and Mary's son, Edward, was born at Radford and baptised at Plymstock Church on 30 July 1642.

Early pedigrees of the Harris family are incorrect, including the *Visitation of the Heralds*, for they omit the birth of John Harris in 1631, and refer to the death in 1637 – again in error for 1631 – of Elizabeth, wife of John Harris, as being a daughter of Champernon. This is erroneous, for the pedigree of the Champernons shows no such union at that time. John's second marriage to Mary Wyse and the birth of a second son has also been overlooked.

John's troubles were not at an end, for in August 1642 the serious differences between the king and parliament came to a head, with Charles setting up his standard at Nottingham. John, as a member of parliament, at first subscribed to the solemn league and covenant, but afterwards joined the king at Oxford. His name appears among the list of members who were 'disabled' by parliament in 1644 for deserting the service of the House and adhering to the royalist cause. A committee for dealing with 'Delinquents' was set up by parliament (1643-1653), the sole object of which was the seizure and confiscation of their estates. Those appointed to deal with the disposal of these estates were known as Treason Trustees. [39]

John Harris's brother, Robert, who became Major-General of His Majesty's Infantry before Plymouth, is noted during the royalist retreat from Cornwall in January 1646, when he refused to obey an order of Sir Richard Grenville to guard a bridge over the River Tamar, asserting he would take orders only from General Digby. In mitigation of his action, Sir Richard Grenville had been behaving in an arbitrary way and was soon afterwards confined in Launceston prison. [40] Robert's loyalty to the royalist cause was proved beyond doubt on 11 April 1646 when the Council of War at Pendennis Castle, the royalists' last hold on the county of Cornwall, sent a letter to the prince, who had repaired to Jersey, appealing for provisions. This letter was signed by John Arundell of Trerice, John Digby and Robert Harris. In Pendennis the situation of the garrison was so desperate that on 27 June they sent a last appeal to the prince, when Robert Harris's signature again appears among those of other royalist officers. This letter, written in cipher, reached Jersey safely, but only after the prince had left for France. The appeal from Pendennis was forwarded to him and was followed up by letters dated 22 July from Sir Henry Killigrew and Joseph Jane of Liskeard, begging for a speedy dispatch of provisions. No relief arrived and finally, on 15 August, Sir John Arundell and his brave garrison knew themselves beaten and agreed to treat for their surrender. The fall of Pendennis marked the end of the Civil War in Cornwall. [41]

With his Staddiscombe holding confiscated (see Chapter 19) Robert Harris subsequently lived with his sister Honor at Tywardreath in Cornwall, where he died in 1655, being buried there in St Andrew's Church on 29 June. Honor Harris, known to many as the heroine in Daphne du Maurier's book *The King's General*, predeceased him and was also buried in this church on 17 November 1653.

The defeat of the royalists and the execution of Charles I in 1649 left England with a Commonwealth government. Branded a delinquent, John Harris's Lanrest estate, together with his holding in the castle at Liskeard and other Duchy lands in Cornwall, were seized, Lanrest being sold in 1650 by order of the parliament. [42]

On 24 March 1647 John Harris of Radford, 'being sick in body but perfect of remembrance' made his will. This document gives us an insight into the plight of the family at that time. Despite his reduced circumstances he left monetary bequests of forty shillings to the Governor and Overseers of Liskeard to be distributed to the poor and a similar sum to the Overseers at Plymstock for distribution to the poor of the parish.

Thereafter he makes particular mention of his dear and loving wife Mary, whom he prays the Lord to comfort and protect and leaves her his personal and household effects, all carefully listed. Furniture, bed-linen, table-linen, kitchen utensils and items of silverware are all described. He then appoints his son John his first and sole executor, whom he requests to pay his debts and:

that his plate not hereby bequeathed shall be speedily disposed for the payment of a debt of two hundred pounds unto one Mr John Brigham of London, which he the said John Brigham standeth engaged hereunto. (see below).

This loan may have been for the payment of a fine imposed by the Commonwealth government, for a royalist normally had to pay a fine of one–tenth to one–third of the value of his estate. Finally, he instructs:

Jonathan Rashleigh Esq., John Pollexfen Esq. and John Rashleigh Esq. to be Administrators and Assigns unto his Executor and to be Overseers of the same.

John Harris's will was proved in the Prerogative Court of Canterbury on 3 November 1649 by Uncle John Pollexfen, son John renouncing. [43]

It is not known whether John Harris was buried at Plymstock Church as no entry has been found in the Parish Register. Certainly no burial service would have taken place, for the use of the Prayer Book was forbidden. As a delinquent it is possible he was buried at Plymstock in an unmarked grave and that no record of his burial was permitted. Even King Charles I, after his execution on 30 January 1649, was denied the burial service when he was laid in the vault of St George's Chapel at Windsor. The omission of John Harris's burial from the Plymstock Register has led to some historians confusing his death with that of his son John, who died in 1677.

In 1653 Mary Harris married a third time, becoming the second wife of Sir Henry Cary, another royalist, whose home, Cockington Court, was sequestered and sold by the Commonwealth government about a year later. Lady Mary retired to the Wyse's family home of Sydenham. A marble slab in the chancel of Marystow Church records her death on 27 May 1657. [44]

John Harris's second son, Edward, is mentioned on 20 November 1653, when Mary Cary, on behalf of her son, Edward Harris, begs discharge of Cartuther, near Liskeard, Maders and other lands in Cornwall, settled on her and her issue male by her late husband, but sequestered for his recusancy. The Committee for Compounding the Estates of Delinquents decided to inquire and certify. It is probable these lands would have been released, for the law decreed that one-fifth of delinquents' estates was to be allowed for the maintenance of their children. [45]

A sequel to the mention of silver plate in John Harris's will came on 6 December 1827, when a man engaged in ploughing a field at Brixton found twenty-three pieces of silver plate which bore the Harris Arms. The legal ownership was settled by a jury specially empanelled to decide the matter. At that time it was considered the plate had been hidden by a steward during the Civil War and the secret of its hiding place had been subsequently lost. There being no doubt as to its ownership it was assigned to John Harris Esq. of Radford, descendant of the former owner. The plate was sold for £1255 and was later disposed of to Mr Albemarle Cator of Woodbastwich, Norfolk, who had married into the Mohum Harris family. [46] (See below).

After the installation of Oliver Cromwell as Lord Protector of the Commonwealth in December 1653, the young John Harris was faced with a permanent ten per cent fine, which was levied on all royalist and political opponents.

Some of these fines ranged upwards to £6000, but those who supported the government had their fines reduced and in some cases taken off for their services. [46]

The discontent aroused by these harsh measures was so great that an uprising was planned, which disturbed the exiled king, who did not wish his subjects to enter upon any rash or sudden insurrections 'which could only contribute to their own ruin without the least benefit to his service'. He sent the Earl of Rochester over with power to postpone or authorize an insurrection. Misled as to the strength of support Rochester sanctioned the rising and took charge of the North. On 8 March 1654/55* at the rendezvous at Marston Moor, the intention being to possess York, he found himself with only about one hundred followers and decided to abandon the hopeless enterprise. He escaped and returned to the Continent early in June. [47]

Sir Joseph Wagstaffe, who had been sent over at the request of the Western royalists, joined with Colonel John Penruddock and with about two hundred followers they entered Salisbury on 12 March, where they proclaimed Charles II as king. Leaving Salisbury with about four hundred men they marched into Dorset, but gained few recruits on their way. When they entered Somerset their numbers began to diminish and the few who remained were either taken or dispersed on 14 March at South Molton in Devon, being surprised at night by Captain Unton Croke. Wagstaffe escaped and returned to the court of the exiled king, Penruddock being captured. The intention had been to link up with royalist supporters in Cornwall, most of whom were assembled at Trerice, the home of Colonel Richard Arundell. It is probable the young John Harris was with them. [48]

The royalists were concerned that their most secret plans became known to the government. The reason was that Cromwell had an excellent system of intelligence which kept him well-informed. This was under the command of Secretary of State John Thurloe, whose control of the post office enabled him to intercept correspondence; the spies he kept at the court of the exiled king and the plotters whom he corrupted or intimidated into supplying him with each new movement of the royalists. [49]

On 23 March President Lawrence wrote to the Attorney-General that his Highness (Cromwell) had decided to issue commissions for bringing to trial

* At that time the year commenced on 25 March.

persons engaged in the late rebellious insurrections. Then, on 10 April Colonel John Copleston, Sheriff of Devon, wrote from Plymouth to Captain Henry Hatsell at Exeter:

intreating him to do his utmost to get as many honest petty jurymen as he could as there would be a gaol delivery at the Castle on the 19th.

A most shocking aspect of this affair was that in order to convict the royalists Copleston sent a warrant:

that such (jurymen) *shall appear as will not favour the interest.* They were to be told that *the sheriff would only want them for this time, and that it shall be no prejudice to them.* Copleston ends; *I will pay your charges for warning the men.* A clear case of bribery! [50]

The first to be tried was John Penruddock, who challenged 22 jurymen before 12 could be sworn. It was realised that as most of the prisoners might do the same the trials would be long, but it was the law and must be allowed.[51] John Harris was almost certainly confined for a time in the dungeons of Plymouth Castle, along with other Stuart sympathisers, but was freed later. The town receiving no money for their maintenance, the mayor released several cavaliers, for which he was soundly rebuked by the Protector, the town then being allowed 8d. per day, to be deducted from captured cargoes.

With his trial imminent and his future uncertain, John Harris endeavoured to protect his lands by a Deed of Entail. This Indenture, made on 25 November 1655, between himself and Samuel Bury, gentleman, and Anthony Williamson, yeoman, both of Plymstock, conveyed his manors of East Hooe, Goosewell, Whitchurch and the capital *messuage*, barton and lands known as Radford, to them to hold

in trust for his brothers, Edward and Christopher Harris, the sons of his father, John Harris and Mary Wise Harris. Both brothers were minors, Edward, the eldest, being 13 years of age. [52]

John Harris's trial took place at London in April 1656, when he was sentenced to be outlawed. By virtue of his outlawry an Inquisition into his possessions was taken at Plymouth on 9 October by Sir John Copleston, Sheriff of Devon. His lands were then seized and in December 1657 Cromwell, for the sum of thirty pounds and an annual rent of 8s.4d., granted and farm-let the barton of Radford to George Johnson. [53]

The Dartington Parish Register records John Harris's marriage to Dorothy (wrongly entered as Elizabeth) Champernowne (Champernon) on 12 July 1656. Under the Commonwealth government marriages were in the form of a civil contract. If, as often happened, a marriage service was performed secretly this would have taken place in the old church in the grounds of Dartington Hall, only the tower of which now remains.

When the monarchy was restored in 1660 John Harris's outlawry ended and his lands were restored to him. Also, the Tenures Abolition Act 1660 meant that the old feudal services and obligations were done away with. Formerly a freehold held in socage, Radford now became a freehold in the true sense of the word.

A son, John, was born to John and Dorothy Harris in 1662, his baptism on 19 June being recorded in both the Plymstock and Dartington parish registers.

When Dorothy's brother, Arthur Champernowne, died in April 1664 the entail of the Dartington estate arranged by him in 1657 was suspended until the Trustees had raised a sum of £5000 for Dorothy. [54] She died the following year and was buried at Dartington on 12 July 1665, leaving this sum to her husband (see below).

On 4 February 1666 John Harris of Radford married Mary Rashleigh, [55] daughter of John Rashleigh and his wife Joan (formerly Pollexfen) who were married at Plymstock in 1640. To celebrate this occasion a beautifully carved pulpit and sounding-board were provided for Plymstock church, the latter bearing the inscription M.H. 1666. On 30 July 1667 John Harris revoked and made void his Deed of Conveyance of his lands in Devonshire unto his brothers, Edward and Christopher Harris. This Memorandum was written on the back of the original Deed of Entail.

John Harris was a contemporary of the Plymouth surgeon, James Yonge of Puslinch, who recorded in his *Journal*:

> *In August 1677 died my honourable friend, the famous Mr John Harris of Radford, who I had three years before cured of an old fistula in his fundament.*

The use of the word 'famous' must surely refer to John Harris's support of the royalist cause and his subsequent outlawry. An imposing memorial was erected in the north-west corner of the Harris (now Lady) Chapel in Plymstock Church, with an effigy of a kneeling figure, bewigged and clad in armour, behind which is an inscription. Centrally placed in the pediment is the Harris Coat of Arms in colour, quartered with the Arms of Champernowne and Rashleigh.

Mary Harris was the Executor of her husband's will and a much-damaged Deed is an undertaking by her to the Trustees of the Dartington Estate to secure the sum of £5000 to the use of her stepson, John Harris of Radford.[56] It is probable that Mary Harris took over the management of the Radford Estate during the minority of her stepson John, for her name appears in the Plymstock Rate Book for this period.[57]

The Harris Plate

The Harris Plate was again put up for sale in 1911 by Christies, being purchased for £11 000 by Mr Crichton. This name suggests a connection with the Harris family. (See the Harris of Radford pedigrees page 101 and 103).

Up-to-date information is that in 1992 a collection of 26 parcel gilt dishes engraved with the Harris of Radford Arms was purchased by the British Museum with the aid of £900 000 from the National Heritage Memorial Fund. Known as 'The Armada Service' these deep bowl–like dishes are typical of a design in vogue during the late sixteenth century and bear hallmarks which cover the period 1581 to 1601.[58]

Formerly to be seen at the British Museum, this unique collection of Elizabethan dining silver was loaned to the Plymouth City Museum and Art Gallery from May until October 1993.

NOTES AND REFERENCES
RADFORD: A FEUDAL ESTATE

1.   a. Aerial Photograph, 623315. b. Devon Place Names c. E. Ekwall, *The Concise Oxford Dictionary of Place Names*, 1959.
2.   Sir William Pole, dec. 1625. *The Description of Devonshire*, pub. 1791. Tristram Risdon, *Survey of Devon*, work completed 1630, pub. 1811.
3.   Sutton Caving Group, Plymouth.
4.   Dictionary of National Biography.
5.   J. Brooking Rowe, *History of Plympton, 1906*.
6.   Pole, *Devonshire*.
7.   *Feudal Aids, Devon, 1284–6*, 335.
8.   J. Brooking Rowe, *Plympton Erle*, 82–3.
9.   A.W.B. Messenger, LRIBA, *A Survey of the Heraldry at the Hall, Weare Giffard, Devon*. Trans. Devonshire Assoc., LXXV, Pedigree I.

10. *Testa de Nevill,* 1242–3.
11. Trans. D.A. 1943, LXXV, 198–9, Pedigree I.
12. Trans. D.A., 199.
13. John Stevens, *Early Plympton History,* MS, 21.
14. a. D. Gilbert, *History of Cornwall* b. John Prince, *Worthies of Devon.*
15. *Visitation of Devon,* ed. Vivian.
16. *Calendar of Inquisitions Post Mortem,* 1 Henry VII, Vol. VI, 34, No. 78, (12 January 1485).
17. *Cal. I.P.M.,* 22 Hen. VII, Vol. XII, 32, No. 31, (12 April 1497).
18. *Calendar of Close Rolls,* Memb. 12, No. 1012, 300, (28 May 1498).
19. *The Devon Muster Roll,1569,* ed. A.J. Howard & T.L. Stoate, pub.1977
20. Frances Rose-Troup, *The Western Rebellion,1549,* Chap.22, 340–6.
21. *Calendar of State Papers, Domestic,* October 1580, 682.
22. *Cal. S.P., Dom.,* 1547-80, No. 17, (8 November 1580).
23. *Cal. S.P., Dom.,* 1547-80, No. 60, (24 December 1580).
24. J. Youings BA, *Drake, Grenville & Buckland Abbey,* Trans. D.A., Vol. 112, 91-9.
25. Dict. Nat. Biog.
26. Public Record Office, MPF6, S.P. 46/36/4, Elizabeth I.
27. Richard A. Preston, *Gorges of Plymouth Fort,* Pt. VI, 116-7.
28. *Hatfield Records,* Historical Manuscripts Commission, Guildhall Library, London.
29. *Widey Court Book,* Plymouth Municipal Records, 142, West Devon Record Office.
30. William Oldys, Preface to Sir Walter Ralegh's *History of the World.*
31. Charity Commissioners, *Ecclesiastical Charities*
32. *Cal. I.P.M.,* C/142/688/38. 1625. P.R.O.
33. *Concealed Lands, Devon.* P.R.O.
34. John Allen, *History of the Borough of Liskeard,* ed. William H. Paynter.
35. Plymstock Parish Register.
36. Counterpart Lease, 1633, P.R.O., E/367/400.
37. *Commonwealth Surveys, 1650,* Lambeth Palace Library.
38. Lady C. Radford, *The Wyses and Tremaynes of Sydenham,* T.D.A., Vol. XLI, 133-45. Hugh R. Watkin, *Cary of Cockington,* 1920, 14-15.
39. a. *Calendar of Committee for Sequestration of Delinquents' Estates;* b. *Commonwealth Exchequer Papers,* 1643-60; c. *State Papers, Domestic, 1646, No. 20, G1-269.*
40. Edward Earl of Clarendon, *History of the Rebellion,* 1643–53.
41. Clarendon, *Hist. of Reb.,* June 1646.
42. Allen, *Hist. of Liskeard.*
43. Fairfax, 175, & *Prerogative Court of Canterbury,* 3 Nov. 1649, P.R.O.
44. Watkin, *Cary of Cockington.*
45. *Calendar of the Committee for Compounding Delinquents' Estates; State Papers, Domestic,* 1643-60, Pt. IV, 3150, 20 Oct. 1653. *S.P., Dom.,*1643-60, Pt. IV, 71, 1655.
46. H. Whitfeld, *Plymouth & Devonport in Times of War and Peace,* Appendix, Radford House.
47. Oxford History of England, *The Early Stuarts,* 1603-60, 271. A.D. Greenwood, *History of the People of England,* Vol. II, 323.
48. *S.P., Dom.,* Pt. IV, 237–8, July 1655.
49. Dict. of Nat. Biog. (Thurloe).
50. *S.P., Dom.,* 91, 10 April 1655.
51. *S.P., Dom.,* 91, 19 April 1655.
52. Deed of Entail, 20 Nov. 1655; W.D.R.O. 74/671/3.
53. *Pipe Rolls,* P.R.O., E367, & Crown Leases.
54. *The Champernowne Family,* MS, 264; Plymouth Central Library, Local History Dept.
55. *Visitation of Cornwall,* ed. Vivian. *St Breock Parish Register,* Cornwall.
56. Deed, *Mary Harris widow, 1678;* W.D.R.O. Z15/30/29.
57. Plymstock Parish Rate Book, W.D.R.O.
58. Dora Thornton, *Apollo,* The International Magazine of the Arts, January 1993, 49.

Chapter Fourteen

RADFORD: THE HARRIS FAMILY
AND THE NAVAL BANK

Finally freed from the traumatic events preceding the restoration of the monarchy, everyday matters once again claimed the attention of Plymstock inhabitants, the first being the Hearth Tax, introduced in 1662, in order to make up a deficiency in the annual revenue granted to the king by parliament. This first in a series of hearth taxes demanded an annual payment of two shillings for each hearth, the occupier being required to make a written statement to the parish constable, who later collected the money, which was payable half–yearly. The Plymstock return, dated 30 July 1662, has four divisions: Plymstock, Elburton, Plymstock South and Oreston.

Heading the Plymstock South division is:

Anthonie Williamson, who is to pay for nine hearths being the occupier of the barton of Radford for John Harris Esq. Also, *William Staple is to pay for two fire hearths which are in Radford Mill.* [1]

This ancient mill, mentioned in 1303, when it belonged to the manor of East Hooe,[2] was visited by the Rev. John Swete, who toured Devon in 1794. His *Journals* include a watercolour of Radford Mill.[3] Ann Hugill, believed to be the last occupant of the mill, died in January 1820, at the age of 84 years.[4]

In 1690 John Harris of Radford, son of John and Dorothy Harris, married Amy Sawle of Penrice near St Austell and a son, John, was born in 1691. Another son, Christopher, born in 1694, died the same year.

John Harris Esq. died in 1696. It is not known who managed his estate during the minority of his son and heir. In 1725 this John Harris married Elizabeth Lampen of Holwell, Stoke Climsland. They had four children; John b. 1726, Lampen b. 1727, Christopher b. 1729 and Elizabeth b. 1731.

John Harris died in 1733, killed, it was said, while riding his horse on Hooe Hill, known locally as 'Murder Hill'. His eldest son, John, who would have taken over the Radford Estate when he came of age, was one of the founders of the Naval Bank, which opened its first premises at Market Place, Plymouth in 1773, trading under the name of Harris, Turner & Herbert and, in 1783, as Harris, Harris & Scott. This was one of the few banks authorized to issue their own currency, which was in the form of a promissory note, payable on demand.

The Naval Bank was still at Market Place in 1814, its trade name then being Harris, Rosdew & Co. In 1823 the bank moved to imposing new premises, built in the Italian style, situated at the corner of Whimple Street and Kinterbury Street, trading as Harris, Rosdew, Harris & Co.[5]

A house near to the Naval Bank in Kinterbury Street was once occupied by William Hawkins, mayor of Plymouth 1538-9, who, in 1537, obtained a conveyance of a property in this street from Margaret Pyne, widow. Here he lived with his two sons, William and John (later Sir John).[6] In the heart of the old town of

Radford Mill. From a watercolour by John Swete, 1794.
(By permission of the Devon Record Office and Mrs V. Swete. D564 V.7 p.49).

Plymouth, the Naval Bank and new properties in Whimple Street and on the east side of the adjoining St Andrew's Street, were a complete contrast to nearby Elizabethan houses, such as Sir Francis Drake's town residence at the top of Looe Street and the Merchants House (now restored) on the west side of St Andrew's Street. At the east end of Whimple Street was the *old* Guildhall, built in 1800 to replace the Jacobean Hall. With the re-planning of the city following the Second World War, the cobbled Kinterbury Street disappeared.

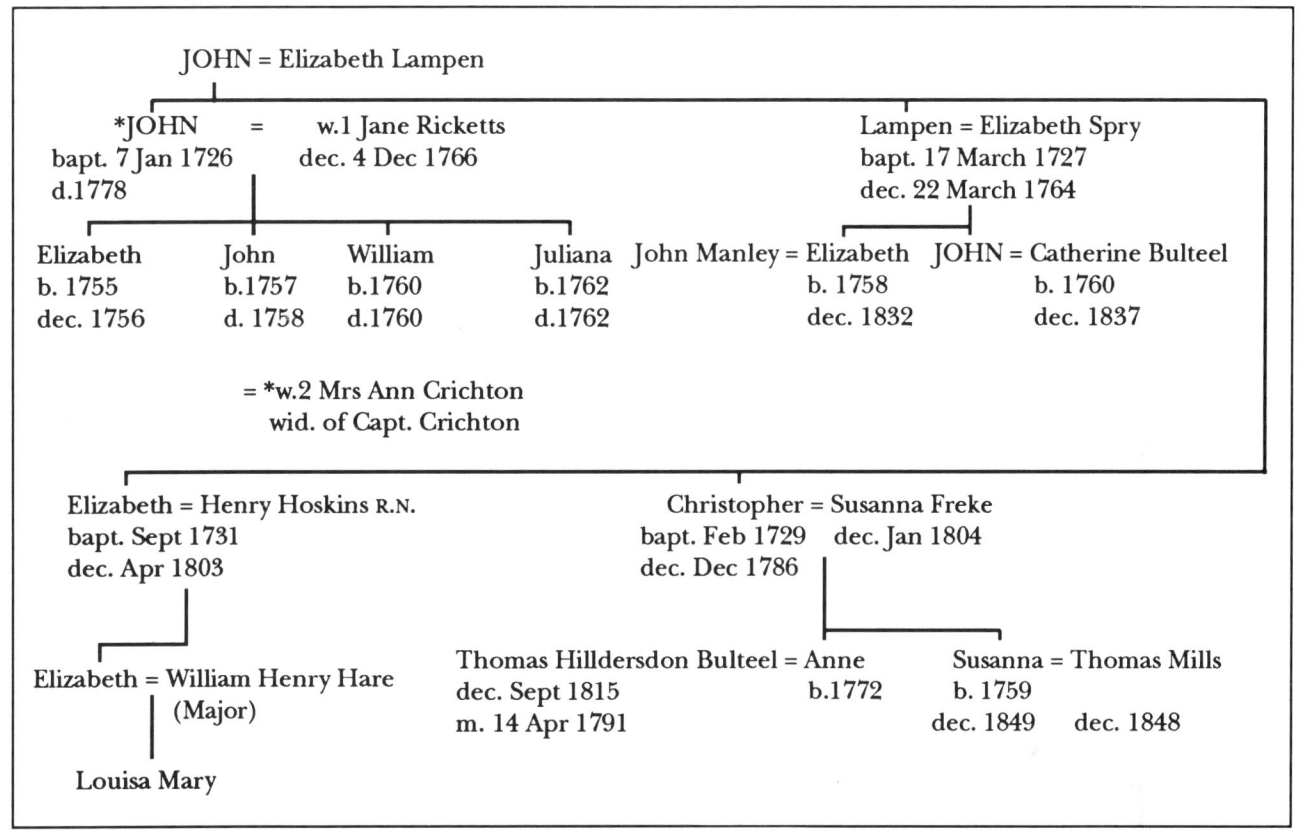

JOHN = Elizabeth Lampen

*JOHN = w.1 Jane Ricketts
bapt. 7 Jan 1726   dec. 4 Dec 1766
d.1778

Lampen = Elizabeth Spry
bapt. 17 March 1727
dec. 22 March 1764

Elizabeth
b. 1755
dec. 1756

John
b.1757
d. 1758

William
b.1760
d.1760

Juliana
b.1762
d.1762

John Manley = Elizabeth
b. 1758
dec. 1832

JOHN = Catherine Bulteel
b. 1760
dec. 1837

= *w.2 Mrs Ann Crichton
wid. of Capt. Crichton

Elizabeth = Henry Hoskins R.N.
bapt. Sept 1731
dec. Apr 1803

Christopher = Susanna Freke
bapt. Feb 1729   dec. Jan 1804
dec. Dec 1786

Elizabeth = William Henry Hare
(Major)

Louisa Mary

Thomas Hilldersdon Bulteel = Anne
dec. Sept 1815   b.1772
m. 14 Apr 1791

Susanna = Thomas Mills
b. 1759
dec. 1849   dec. 1848

Pedigree – Harris of Radford

The towns of Plymouth and Dock (later Devonport) had a thriving mercantile trade which no doubt contributed to this bank's early success. Probably because of his association with merchants engaged in the slave trade, John Harris acquired an African slave. An entry in the Plymstock parish register reads:

Bapt. Thomas Radford a Negro belonging to Mr Harris Apr. 3 1774.

The Rev. Vincent Warren of Pomphlett Farm was vicar of Plymstock at that time. This is the only record in the registers of a black slave and nothing more is known about the fate of Thomas. This iniquitous trade was abolished in 1807.

John Harris was married twice, first to Jane Ricketts, by whom he had four children, all of whom died in infancy. After Jane's death in 1766 he married Ann, widow of Captain Crichton and elder daughter of

The Naval Bank (top left) in Whimple Street, Plymouth.

Francis Freke of Hannington Hall, Wiltshire. John died in 1778, his widow marrying Griffith Williams. Ann died in 1833 at the great age of 98 years. [7]

John Harris's will, dated 30 September 1778, bequeathed his capital *messuage* and barton farm called Radford and his several manors of Radford, otherwise East Hooe, Goosewell and Whitchurch, and all his manors and lands in Devon and Cornwall, to his nephew John Harris, the son of his late brother Lampen, for his life:

And then to the first and all and every the sons of the said John Harris successively in tail male.

This will was proved on 2 January 1779 in Doctors' Commons by John Harris the nephew, sole executor of the said will.

Another brother, Christopher, a Justice of the Peace and Freeman of the Borough of Plymouth, was married to Susanna Freke, sister of Ann. Christopher built the large house Belle-Vue (now known as Hooe Manor) in 1777. He died in 1786 and one of his daughters, Anne, who married Thomas Hillersdon Bulteel of Flete House in 1791, lived in this house, where their ten children were born. Another large family house, The Retreat was built nearby in 1775.

John Harris, the nephew who succeeded to Radford, married Catharine Bulteel of Flete in 1783, and there were 14 children of this marriage. During

Hooe Manor, formerly Belle-Vue.

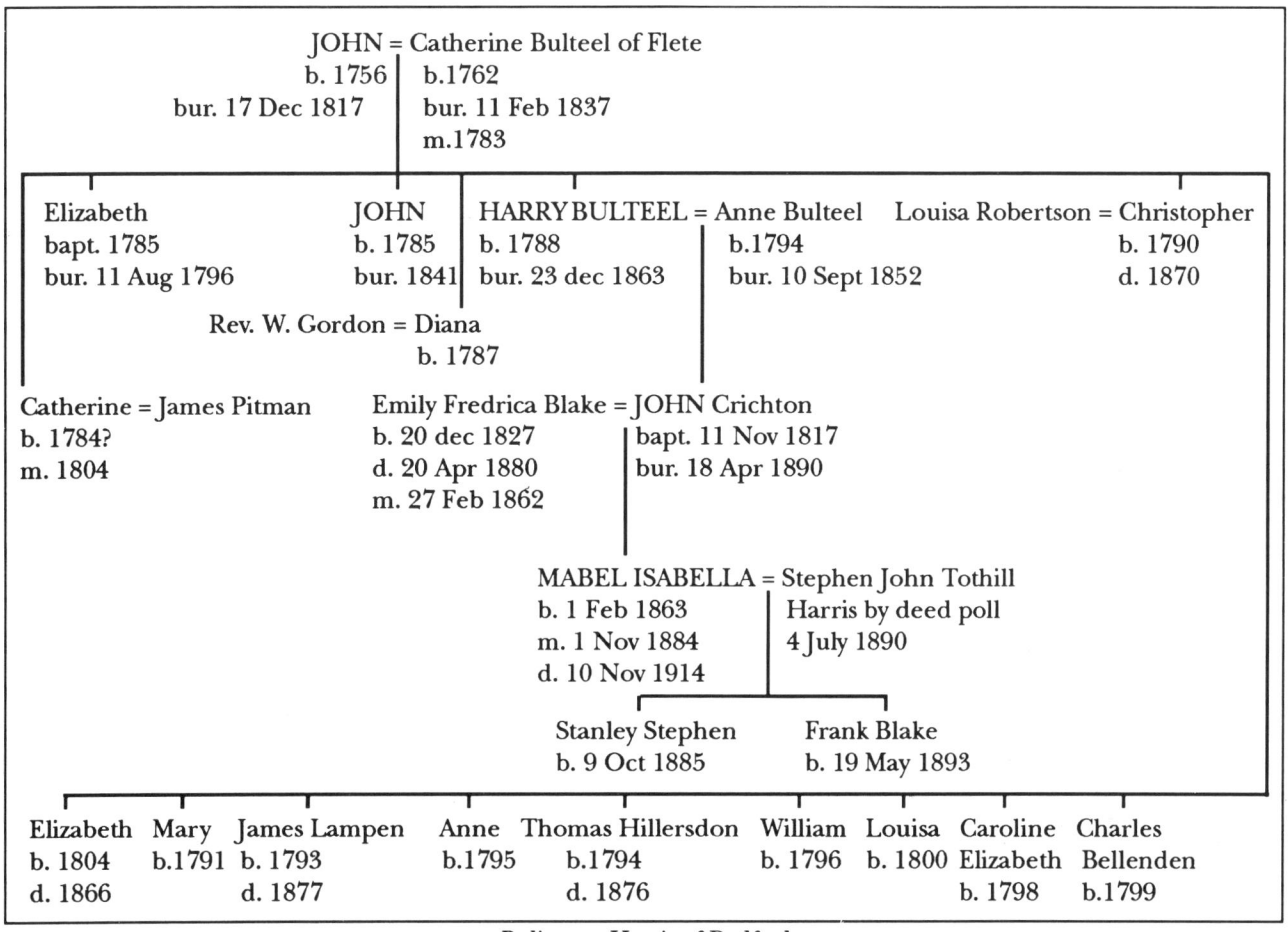

Pedigree – Harris of Radford.

his lifetime, with the co-operation of his eldest son, John, the Radford Estate was extended and embellished, land being obtained from the Duke of Bedford in an exchange agreement. This was a tidying-up of the duke's Plymstock manor, whereby he obtained possession of certain fields within his manor which belonged to the Harris family. In return, the duke conveyed land on the north side of the creek to John Harris. [8]

As a result of this transaction an embankment with sluice was constructed over the tidal creek, creating a freshwater lake. A pseudo castle built on the causeway

Radford Castle. From a watercolour by J. Cocks, 1891
(courtesy of Mr D.G. Spear).

provided a home for workmen on the estate. At least two children were born there during the late nineteenth century. A carriage-drive was laid out through the newly-acquired land and ornamental ponds and waterfalls – known as the duck ponds – were constructed at the head of the creek. Radford

The ornamental ponds at Radford.
From the sale catalogue of 1917.

Lodge was built at the west entrance to the estate, replacing Borough Lodge which stood near to the original entrance.

Radford House is said to have been renovated at this time under the supervision of a celebrated architect, and it is also considered that Armour Cottage, with its massive fireplace dated 1640, and the boathouse named St Keverne were built using surplus worked granite stone from the mansion. Both of these are now picturesque ruins, while, to the regret of many, the Radford mansion was demolished in 1937. Radford Lodge, a Grade II listed building, still survives as part of a modern dwelling and stands at the entrance to Radford Park Arboretum, a project of the Plymstock & District Civic Society and its Radford Heritage Group.

During the Napoleonic Wars a great tragedy befell Thomas and Anne Bulteel of Belle-Vue when their two eldest sons, John 21 years and Christopher 18 years, both died on 8 March 1814, during an attack on Bergen, a town on the Zoom River in the Netherlands, which had been taken by the French in 1795 and successfully held by them against the British, who tried to drive them out in 1814. Their father heard the news while visiting the post office at Plymouth. He immediately removed his third son, Thomas Hillersdon, from the Royal Navy and entered him in the Naval Bank. He never recovered from the shock of his loss and died the following year, aged 49 years. [9]

John Harris of Radford died in 1817, his eldest son inheriting the Plymstock estates as well as landed property in other places. His will made a particular request to his son John to help his brother, Thomas Hillersdon Harris, then a student in the Temple, London, by giving him an allowance if 'from want of success in his legal pursuits, he should happen to require such financial aid'. Thomas qualified as a

St Keverne boathouse, Radford. From a watercolour by J. Cocks, 1891. (Courtesy of Mr D.G. Spear).

barrister and lived in one of the newly-built villas at Billacombe. He was unmarried and nothing else is known about him. [10]

John was also a bachelor and Plymouth records show that on 29 September 1810 he was elected and sworn in as a burgess or Freeman of the Borough, having been nominated by Joseph Pridham, mayor of Plymouth 1809-10. John died in 1841 while in Germany and was buried in the Lutheran Church at Ems in the duchy of Nassau. His will shows that he was head of a banking firm carried on in the borough of Plymouth under the name of the Naval Bank by himself and his brother Christopher Harris. He confirms his responsibility to make good any deficiency in the English Staff Account of the Naval Bank and charged his will to raise the same by sale or mortgage of all or any part of his real estate. This indicates that some difficulty relating to the bank's finances already existed.[11] This provision may have resulted from the banking crisis of 1825, when another prominent Plymouth bank failed and those who possessed bank notes were clamouring for payment. The Naval Bank issued a reassuring notice that their customers need not feel the least apprehension regarding their stability

Armour Cottage and St Keverne boathouse ruins,
with the lime kiln in the background.

and that they were perfectly able to liquidate every demand without selling an acre of their landed property 'which is entirely unentailed'.[12]

John Harris was succeeded by his brother, Harry Bulteel Harris. Born at Radford in 1788, Harry entered the army in 1804, became a lieutenant the same year and rose to the rank of major in 1814. In 1808-9 he saw active service at Corunna during the Peninsular War, when he served with Sir David Baird's Division under Sir John Moore. In 1815 he was with the Duke of Wellington at Waterloo. Harry's distinguished service was recognised in 1833 by King William IV, who created him a Knight Companion of the Royal Guelphic Order of Hanover, which had been instituted by George III to mark the occasion of the elevation of Hanover into a kingdom and to commemorate the bravery of Hanoverian troops at Waterloo.[13] In 1837 Harry was promoted to the rank of colonel. He married his cousin, Anne, daughter of Thomas and Anne Bulteel of Belle-Vue, and they had one son, John Crichton Harris, born in 1817.

When Harry inherited the family estates he became a senior partner in the Naval Bank. During his lifetime the lease of the Plymstock tithes, which he held of the dean and canons of Windsor, was commuted to a rent-charge by the Tithe Act, 1836. The Plymstock Tithe Apportionment Book, 1842, states the annual sum due to the lessee, Harry Bulteel Harris, to be £781.3s.6d.[14]

Harry's son, John, was a captain in the First Devon Militia in 1846, from which he resigned in 1852. Following his marriage to Emily Frederica, daughter of George Hans Blake of Mutley, Plymouth, he lived for a short time at Thorncot, East Hooe, where his only child, Mabel Isabella, was born in 1863. The marriage soon ended in separation and in 1866 John was living at Yealmpton, probably at the residence of his uncle, Captain William Harris.[15]

His father, Colonel Harry Bulteel Harris, who died in 1863, was buried at Plymstock Parish Church on 23 December. His coffin, made by workers on the estate from a piece of chestnut wood grown at Radford, was conveyed by them to the grave.[16]

Harry's will makes it clear that his only son, John Crichton Harris, did not wish to enter the Naval Bank of which his father and Uncle Christopher were partners, preferring instead to live as a gentleman on his own private means and expectations, irrespective of the entire benefit which he might derive from the landed property which had come to them under the will of Harry's late brother, John. He agreed with his father that Emily Hoskins Hare, a grand-daughter of John Harris and Elizabeth Lampen, should occupy The Retreat for her life and that Caroline Emily, wife of Francis Freke Bulteel, then residing at Furzehats (Furzehatt House), should occupy Thorncot for her life. His father devised to him his personal estate which comprised Radford House, Belle-Vue, The Retreat, Thorncot and all premises situated within the manor of Radford, otherwise known as East Hooe in Plymstock, together with family portraits, plate and household effects. [17]

The bare facts of history do not tell us of the internal problems which must have beset this family as well as any other. There may have been good and valid reasons for John Crichton Harris's attitude towards the family business. Was he aware that the Naval Bank was already in financial difficulties? And was this in part due to neglect on the part of his father who was a professional soldier, and his Uncle John, who is said to have spent much time in Germany? Whatever the reasons for his desertion of the family home and business it certainly opened the door to the Bulteels who, after his death in 1890, not only obtained possession of the Radford Estate, but also gained complete control of the Naval Bank.

According to Harry's will, his nephew, William Harris, subject to his continuing partnership in the Naval Bank, was to inherit:

all the rest and residue of the real estates including the rent-charge in lieu of tithes of certain lands within the parish of Liskeard.

This condition would appear to confirm that lands other than those at Plymstock were tied to the Naval Bank as collateral security. Harry Bulteel Harris was also lord of the manor of Whitchurch, near Tavistock, and this manor would have formed part of the real estate inherited by William. It seems a pity that money was not raised either by sale or mortgage of these assets to put the Naval bank, already showing signs of insolvency, on a firm financial basis.

William Harris of Yealmpton, b. 1796, was the sixth son of John and Catherine Harris. He entered the Army and served with the 16th Lancers, rising to the rank of captain. He married Jane Diana, youngest daughter of John Bulteel of Flete and Lyneham. They lived first at Brixton, later moving to The Lodge, a commodious and attractive Georgian style residence in the village of Yealmpton. Their eldest son, William, b.1832, entered the Naval Bank as a clerk and was later taken into partnership. Little is known of a younger son, John, b. 1833, except that in 1861 he was living with his parents and a sister, Louisa, b. 1843. John died in December 1865 and Louisa died in September, 1875. [18]

On 21 January 1861 William married Jane Christian, daughter of William Chapell Hodge, head of the Devonport Bank, who lived at Pounds House, Pennycross. They had three sons, William Hubert Gage, b. 1862 at Yealmpton, John Harry de Burgh, b. 1863 at Pennycross and Ronald Bellenden, b. 1865 at Plymstock. After the death of his uncle William lived at Radford House. His marriage appears to have failed, for in 1870 William is again residing at The Lodge, Yealmpton, and in 1871 his wife Jane and their three sons are living at Pounds House with her widowed father. Nothing more has come to light of her whereabouts, for in 1881 Pounds House was occupied by her brother, Chapell William Hodge, banker, his wife and six young daughters.

William Harris, banker, continued living at The Lodge, Yealmpton, until 1881, during which time he shared the house with his parents, although keeping his own apartment and servants. By 1883 his name has disappeared from the directories, so it may be assumed either that he had died or had moved away. In 1885 Captain William Harris is still living at Yealmpton with his wife Jane, but has moved to another older house nearby called The Retreat. By

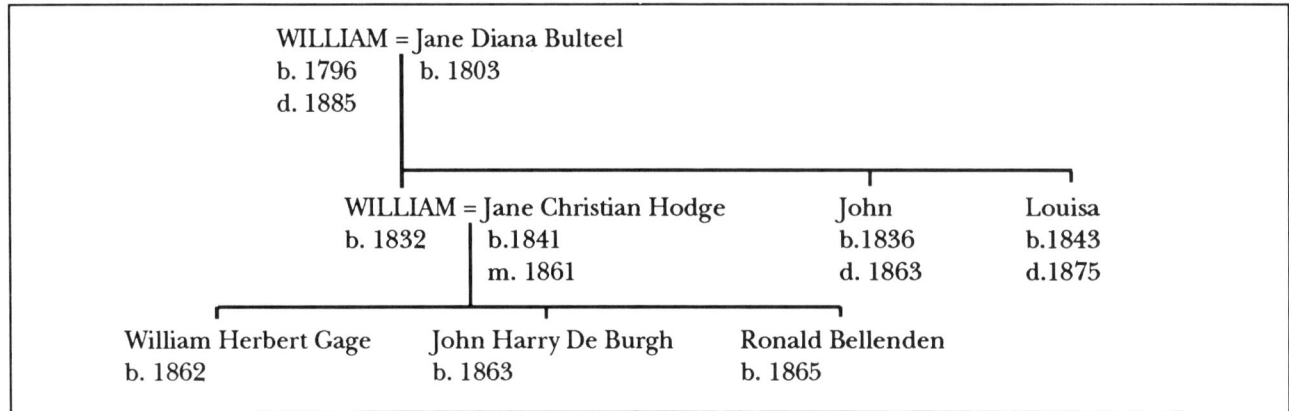

WILLIAM = Jane Diana Bulteel			
b. 1796 b. 1803			
d. 1885			

WILLIAM = Jane Christian Hodge   John   Louisa
b. 1832   b.1841   b.1836   b.1843
       m. 1861   d. 1863   d.1875

William Herbert Gage   John Harry De Burgh   Ronald Bellenden
b. 1862   b. 1863   b. 1865

Pedigree – Harris of Radford.

1889 he must have died, for only his wife's name appears in the Directory, and by 1893 her name has also disappeared.

In 1871 Radford House was occupied by a family of five sisters, daughters of a Scottish baronet. The eldest, Louisa A. Edmondstone, aged 26 years. A lady's maid, housemaid, under-housemaid and a footman are also listed in the census return for this year. By 1878 they have gone and the Misses Surgisson are living there.

Christopher Harris, b.1790, third son of John and Catherine, was a senior partner in the Naval Bank. He died in 1870, having been retired for some time due to failing health. Christopher's eldest daughter, Louisa, married her cousin Thomas Hillersdon Bulteel of Belle-Vue, who was entered into the Naval Bank by his father in 1814. Their son was Thomas Bulteel, who later came into possession of the Naval Bank and also of Radford.

Thomas Bulteel, banker, lived with his wife Margaret, at Thorncot, Higher Hooe, but in 1862 moved to a villa at Billacombe. By 1881 he and his growing family were in residence at Radford House,

where four of their ten children were born. The Bulteels lived in considerable style and to all outward appearance Thomas was a pillar of society.

A former resident, Mrs Kate Tucker, now deceased, who lived with her husband and family in Borough Lodge, which stood near to the original entrance to Radford House, remembered the balls held at the mansion and that her children used to open the gates for the carriages bringing the guests to these functions, sometimes being rewarded with a penny. Mrs Tucker was well-known at Plymstock and lived to the great age of 92 years. The story is also told that Thomas Bulteel in his top hat and tails would feed the birds in the duck ponds on his way to the train – the Turnchapel branch line – which would take him in to Plymouth. A public footpath from Radford to Oreston crossed the track, so it is possible the driver stopped the train at this point to pick him up. The census returns for 1881 show that there were seven servants in residence at Radford House. The sole job of one maid was to keep the numerous oil lamps trimmed.

Thomas Bulteel's eldest son, Percy Francis, b. 1864,

Radford Lodge. Taken from the sale catalogue of 1917.

lived with his wife Julia and their five children at The Retreat, Higher Hooe. He was taken into partnership at the Naval Bank by his father.

John Crichton Harris, the lineal descendant of the Harris family left Devon in the 1860s and lived at Wootton-under-Edge in Gloucestershire until his death in April 1890. His daughter, Mabel Isabella, married Stephen John Tothill, who changed his name to Harris by Deed Poll in July 1890. Her father's will, obviously made some years before his death, appointed George Pridham and Glenie Pridham, Gentlemen, both of Plymouth, trustees and executors of his will and Guardians of the person and estate of his daughter, Mabel Isabella Harris. They must have both died, for Administration was granted to Mabel Isabella (wife of Stephen John Harris) of Bridgetown, Totnes, the Residuary Legatee for life. Although his father had bequeathed Radford House and other properties situated within the manor of Radford, otherwise known as East Hooe, together with family and household effects to him, these were not specified

in his will which, after making several small bequests to friends, left the bulk of his fortune, which in monetary terms was not large, to his only child. [19] It is clear that Mabel Isabella did not obtain possession of these properties, for an Abstract of the Title of the Radford Estate recites a series of Indentures, the first being dated 12 June 1899, which show that the Radford Estate was conveyed 'to the use of Thomas Bulteel in fee simple'.

Mabel and Stephen Harris had two sons, Stanley Stephen b. 1885 and Frank Blake b. 1893. Both saw active service in the First World War and were both wounded, being demobilised in 1919.[20] Mabel Isabella and her husband moved to Paignton, where they lived in a house called Dromore in Cleveland Road. She died there on 10 November 1914, shortly after the failure of the Naval Bank. Her husband remained at this address for several years, but after 1926 his name disappears from the directories. In 1930, Frank Harris lived at Craithie in Dendy Road, Paignton, and a Christopher Harris, almost certainly a grandson of Mabel and Stephen, lived in a house called St Keverne, obviously named after the Radford boathouse. No further information has come to light regarding this branch of the family.

When Percy Francis Bulteel died in 1907, Thomas brought in his younger son, Frederick Thomas, and a friend, Mackworth Praed Parker, as partners. Thomas Bulteel died in 1908, leaving the two remaining partners to face the fact that the Naval Bank was in serious financial difficulties.

An important and revealing clause in the Abstract of Title of the Radford Estate in the Parish of Plymstock, showed that at the date of Thomas Bulteel's will (17 October 1907) and thence to the date of his death (24 November 1908) this estate was vested in the said

Thomas Bulteel in fee simple in possession, but as trustee for and as part of the assets of a partnership business of bankers subsisting at the date of his death between himself, Mackworth Praed Parker and Frederick Thomas Bulteel under the firm name of Harris Bulteel & Co. (Naval Bank) at Plymouth and elsewhere.

The two remaining partners tried to restore the situation and on 29 April 1912 Frederick Bulteel mortgaged lands and premises at Radford for the sum of £25 000. The partners also gambled on the Stock Exchange, but without success and on 22 August 1914 the Naval Bank closed its doors for the last time. The tragedy was that many people lost their life savings as a result.

On 9 April 1915 an examination in bankruptcy of Mackworth Praed Parker and Frederick Thomas Bulteel was heard at the Western Law Courts before Mr Registrar McCrea, the trustee for the estate being Mr Percy T. Pearce. The Official Receiver explained there had been exhaustive examination relative to the Radford Estate and other properties connected with the Naval Bank. During questioning by Mr Pearce, Bulteel stated that his partnership with his father and Mr Parker commenced in 1907 when an agreement was entered into and signed. According to that document the capital of the partnership, the whole of which belonged to Mr Thomas Bulteel, should consist of the capital contained in the private ledger of the bank. Mr Bulteel later admitted that Radford, Preston and Stobbiscombe was his father's capital in the bank and explained that they were inherited by his father from his grandfather. 'Who told you that Radford was inherited property', said Mr Pearce, 'I tell you at once you are absolutely wrong'. Debtor was under the impression that the properties had come to the family through marriage with the Harris's, but he realised now that his opinion was inconsistent with a declaration his father had made. [21]

Public examination was closed on 26 June 1915 and the partners were sent to the Assizes for trial on 30 November. On 17 December the trial was removed to London where, in March 1916, the case came before Mr Justice Avery at the Old Bailey. The Prosecuting Counsel (Mr Foote) in concluding his case added that it was quite true he had commented seriously upon the conveyance to Mr Bulteel of the Radford property. 'It was grossly improper that Mr Bulteel should have taken that conveyance'.

The judge in his summing up said:

The outstanding fact of this case about which there can be no dispute is that this Naval Bank has been insolvent since, and probably some time before, the year 1858. There was a deficiency of £133,000 in the year 1859.

The jury brought in a verdict of guilty, with a recommendation to deal as leniently as possible with the prisoners. They were both sentenced to six months imprisonment in the Second Division. [22]

The attractively produced catalogue with plans and photographs, announcing the Sale in Bankruptcy of the Radford Estate by Public Auction at the Royal Hotel, Plymouth, on 28 June 1917, contains the following graphic description of the house and its surroundings:

The Mansion House known as Radford, Conveniently placed in the well-timbered Park-like lawns with charming Pleasure Grounds and Terraced Walks, Ornamental Ponds, Miniature Lake, Entrance Lodge, and well-timbered Woodlands with excellent Sporting attractions. Charming Walks, symmetrical flower beds, excellent Fruit Gardens, ample Glass-houses, Vegetable gardens, three ornamental ponds connected with each other by Water-Falls and Sluices, and a Beautiful Lake about seven acres in extent, separated from Hooe Lake, which is an arm of the Cattewater, by a Dam over which there is a roadway which passes under a Castellated building known as Radford Castle.

A watercolour picture of Radford House, painted by Philip Hutchings Rogers, probably during the first quarter of the nineteenth century, shows the entrance to the house midway between the east and west wings, facing south. The photograph in the sale catalogue of 1917 shows the entrance on the east wall of the west wing.

The west wing was the newest and most important, for it contained the large drawing-room, beautifully decorated and fitted with mahogany doors. Adjoining it was the billiard-room. Both had bow windows overlooking the pleasure grounds on the western side. The dining hall at the front, facing south, was

Radford House and grounds. From a watercolour by Philip Hutchings Rogers.

surrounded with moulded oak or chestnut panelling up as far as the plaster frieze. On the first floor of the west wing were two bedrooms with bow windows and communicating dressing-rooms. On the half-landing was the blue bedchamber, the pink bedchamber with dressing-room adjoining and two bathrooms. The older east wing contained the schoolroom, night nursery and maids' bedroom, three servants' bedrooms, four secondary bedrooms, bathroom and five attics. All bathrooms were supplied with hot and cold water. [23]

The auctioneers, Messrs Andrew & Son, estimated that in Radford Woods alone there were 3000 trees worth not less than thirty shillings each. Radford House, gardens, woodlands, 263 acres; Barn Farm 84 acres; rough pasture 16 acres; woodlands 71 acres. Total 434 acres.

The bidding commenced at £8000 and at £11 000 the hammer fell to William A. Mitchell, Rockville, Plymstock.[24] Lower Goosewell Farm, Higher Goosewell Farm and Jews Wood were sold as separate lots (see Chapter 15).

For a time Radford House was let to tenants, but, inevitably, during the periods when it fell vacant the fabric deteriorated, no doubt helped on by vandals and so it was decided the mansion should be demolished and the interior fittings sold. This final act of desecration was carried out in 1937. A sad end to a house that had been the pivot of family life for over seven centuries, much of it happy with children at play and some of it sad when tragedy struck.

Radford was a silent witness to many events of national significance; the storage of fabulous treasure in the cellars – Francis Drake's share of the plunder brought home from his epic voyage round the world; the excitement of preparation against invasion when Spain's great Armada approached England's shores; the imprisonment and attempted escape of the famous Sir Walter Ralegh, brought low by the enmity of King James and a disastrous voyage to Guiana; and the Civil War, when Englishmen fought and killed each other.

Hooe Manor (Belle-Vue) was purchased by the Plympton St Mary Rural District Council in 1947 and Radford Lodge with the adjoining parkland and Radford Woods were purchased in 1962, being designated Public Open Spaces in the Plympton/Plymstock Town Map. When the Plymouth Order came into force on 1 April 1967 all these properties passed to Plymouth City Council. Hooe Manor, divided into flats, is let to tenants, and Radford Woods and Radford Park, now an Arboretum, are popular open spaces.

Radford Lodge was occupied by Mr & Mrs Redpath until the 1960s, Armour Cottage was the home of a workman on the estate and St Keverne's boathouse was also a family home until it was irretrievably damaged by fire. The Castle, now restored, occupies a central position on the causeway which separates Radford and Hooe Lakes. The Retreat, privately owned, is now a nursing home and Thorncot is still an attractive residence in private occupation.

The famous strawberry fruit gardens at Higher Hooe, which was a favourite resort for parties to enjoy strawberry and cream teas, are long gone and with them the simple pleasures of bygone days.

NOTES AND REFERENCES
RADFORD: THE HARRIS FAMILY
AND THE NAVAL BANK

1. *Devon Hearth Tax 1674*, ed. and pub. by T.L. Stoate, 1982.
2. *Devon Feet of Fines*, No. 1342, Esthoo held by Ralf Giffard.

3. J. Swete, Journals 1794; Devon Record Office.
4. *Plymstock Parish Register.*
5. *Bailey's Western and Midland Directory 1783; Universal British Directory 1798; Brindley's Directory 1830; Flintoff's Directory 1844.*
6. C.W. Bracken, *A History of Plymouth and her Neighbours, 1931*, 75, 58-9.
7. *Plymstock Parish Register; The Family of Pitman*; West Devon Record Office, Stapleton Accession 381.
8. *Bedford Records,* D.R.O. Bundle 1, Title Deeds 1812 & 1819.
9. Stapleton Deposit, W.D.R.O.
10. Somerset House, Wills.
11. Somerset House, Wills.
12. *Naval Bank Notice, Nov 26, 1825*, Trans. of Devon Assoc. V. LXXXI, 290.
13. *The Family of Pitman*, 105-6, W.D.R.O.
14. *The Plymstock Tithe Map and Apportionment,* D.R.O.
15. *The Family of Pitman,* 104.
16. *Western Morning News,* report.
17. Somerset House, Wills.
18. *Yealmpton Parish Register,* W.D.R.O. & *Yealmpton Census Returns,* Plymouth Central Library, Reference Dept.
19. Somerset House, Wills.
20. *The Family of Pitman.*
21. *Western Morning News,* 9 April 1915.
22. *Western Morning News,* 22 March 1916.
23. *The Radford Sale Catalogue,* 1917, Plymouth Central Library, Local History Dept.
24. *Western Morning News,* 29 June 1917.

Chapter Fifteen

GOOSEWELL

The Domesday Survey of 1084-6 shows that in 1066 the manor of *Gosewella* was held by the Saxon Heche when it paid geld for half a hide and could be ploughed by two ploughs. By 1086 the manor had been given to one of William's knights, William de Poillei. Robert, who held the manor under him, had in demesne one virgate, three bordars, one cow, thirty sheep, five swine and two acres of wood. Altogether there were 162 acres of land and it was worth five shillings a year. [1]

With feudal tenure well-established, Nicholas le Bastard held Goosewell in 1241 for half a knight's fee of the honour of Plympton. Then in 1285, and again in 1303, Baldwin le Bastard was in possession. Some time before 1346 Goosewell passed with Baldwin's daughter and heiress to Roger de Whytleye and in 1377 John Whytleye also held Goosewell for half a knight's fee. He was succeeded by Walter Whytleye who became lord of the manor of Goosewell, the freeholders being Henry Martin and John Forster. [2]

It was quite usual for manors to be leased to tenants who could then let property within the manor to undertenants. Goosewell changed hands three times more, passing to Grenville, then to Halse of Efford and finally to Christopher Harris of Radford. [3]

Goosewell's name is obviously derived from the keeping of geese and the proximity of a well. J. Brooking Rowe, writing in 1875, tells of an old building on the site of the present Beanhay,* which had several carved panellings in it of quaint design in bas-relief, three being preserved:

> *One of these represents a figure holding, encircled by one arm, a well or fountain and with the other pulling forth from it a goose by the neck.* He queries: *how did the goose and the well become associated?*[4]

The boundary of the Goosewell manor adjoined the Radford estate on the west, stretching eastward through the valley to the Wembury Road at Elburton. There was once a carriage-drive from Radford House which skirted Buddle Wood, crossing a stream which flowed down from Basinghall Plantation by a small bridge, and then across a field to Goosewell Farm. From there it proceeded via Goosewell Plantation and then diagonally across a field to an entrance at Wembury Road. An attractive lodge, Elizabethan in character, at this entrance is still in an excellent state of preservation. Goosewell Plantation became known as Jew's Wood after Little Isaacs, a travelling salesman, was murdered there in 1760 by a soldier who stole his goods and then attempted to sell them in Plymouth. When questioned he confessed to the crime and was executed at Exeter. [5]

A ditch and stream marked the boundary between the manor of Goosewell and the manor of Plymstock..

---

* This was *Woods Cottage*. The present house called Benhay is a property of Regency character, built in 1810-1820, taking its name from the Bean Hay, an enclosure of land behind the older house.

A little to the south of this boundary stood Lower Goosewell Farmhouse – almost certainly on the site of the old manor house. This was a vernacular building of sixteenth or seventeenth century date, which was demolished in the 1960s to make way for housing development. A short distance to the north of the boundary was the large tenement holding known as Higher Goosewell, which belonged to the manor of Plymstock. In common with other Plymstock properties Higher Goosewell was leased to tenants and in 1755 the lessee was Elizabeth Neal. In March 1815 John Harris of Radford applied to the Duke of Bedford to purchase *Gooswills* tenement. The sale was agreed, the purchase price being £9412.17s.6d., less the several leasehold interests of £1362.11s.5d., leaving a total payable of £8050.6s.1d. [6] The old Higher Goosewell farmhouse was replaced by an attractive late Georgian building, now a residential home for the elderly.

Both the Higher and Lower Goosewell Farms continued to be leased to tenants and in 1891 Higher

Goosewell Farmhouse was occupied by Charles Blatchford, farmer, and Lower Goosewell Farmhouse by Walter Wyatt, farmer. [7] In 1917 both farms suffered the fate of all Radford Estate properties, being sold by public auction. Eventually the farm lands were acquired for housing development and none of the land now remains in agricultural use. Combe Dean School stands on former farm land in the valley to the east and Jew's Wood has been preserved. Parts of the old carriage-drive which bordered this wood and Buddle Wood are now used as public footpaths. The Radford Sale Catalogue shows the total area of Lower Goosewell Farm as 147 acres and Jew's Wood as 8 acres. Higher Goosewell Farm was 74 acres, 3 rods, 28 poles.

The old almshouses at Goosewell, erected at the expense of Sir Christopher Harris in 1617, having become a burden for the Trustees, were sold into private ownership by public auction on 16 June 1933, the net proceeds of the sale amounting to £657.18s.10d. The five cottages were demolished in

Goosewell Almshouses.

Goosewell Farmhouse.

the 1960s and a row of modern terraced houses have been built on the site.

Undoubtedly, the rambling Lower Goosewell Farmhouse and the almshouses were the most ancient and attractive buildings in this area and it is unfortunate they were not listed as Buildings of Architectural or Historic Interest.

The subject of a sepia water-colour painted in 1922 by Hubert Harris, is a picturesque cottage at the top of Goosewell Road, formerly Stokenway. The cottage in the painting resembles Furzehatt House on Goosewell Corner, which was sold in 1917. Goosewell Infants School has been built nearby. The sixteen 'newly-erected' Goosewell cottages, now Goosewell Terrace, were also sold, the rent for each being at that time £10 per annum. [8]

NOTES AND REFERENCES
GOOSEWELL

1. Devonshire Domesday.
2. Rev. O. Reichel, *Hundreds of Devon.*
3. J. Brooking Rowe, MS, *History of Plymstock,* D.R.O. Sir William Pole, *The Description of Devonshire.*
4. Rowe, *Hist. of Plymstock,* D.R.O.
5. H.F. Whitfeld, *Plymouth & Devonport in Times of War and Peace,* pub. 1900.
6. Morley Records, F8, D.R.O.
7. Census Returns, 1891.
8. *Radford Sale Catalogue,* 1917.

Believed to be Furzehatt House.

116

Chapter Sixteen

PLYMSTOCK DURING THE CIVIL WAR 1642-1646

The serious dispute between Charles I and parliament came to a head in August 1642, when Charles's standard was raised at Nottingham. From that time England was divided into two factions; the royalists and the parliamentarians.

Plymouth, as a naval port, was well aware that Charles had used English ships to carry Spanish troops to the Netherlands, although England was supposedly neutral in Spain's war with the Dutch. In fact, on 9 January 1642, 2000 mariners marched on the Guildhall in London to present a Protestation which set out the reason for their coming, which, briefly, was their concern at the trend of events and their old fear of Spain and Popery. This document offered their services for the defence of parliament and the protestant religion. Therefore, it is not surprising that by July 1642, before hostilities actually commenced, the navy was in the hands of parliament and it was on the navy that Plymouth was to depend for supplies during the siege which was to last until January 1646.

When the Governor of Plymouth, Sir Jacob Astley, left to join Charles as his major-general of foot, Plymouth declared its support for parliament; the mayor, Thomas Ceely, taking charge of the Hoe Fort and the Island. Soon afterwards, parliament appointed Colonel Ruthven as Commander of the Fort and Island, and Philip Francis, mayor, to the command of Plymouth Castle and the town.

Plymstock is first mentioned in January 1643 when the parliamentarian commander, the Earl of Stamford,

spent some time at Plymouth organising the town's defences. One of these was a fortified work on a hill to the south-west of Turnchapel, which was named Mount Stamford.

During August 1643 Colonel John Digby, with a royalist force of 600 horse troops and 300 foot soldiers, was stationed at Plymstock with a guard at Hooe and cannon at Oreston. Digby scoured the countryside with his horse troops, keeping a close watch on all roads and river crossings in order to prevent supplies being taken into Plymouth. [1]

By the end of September Plymouth received reinforcements from Portsmouth by sea; two first-class commanders, Colonel Wardlaw and Colonel Gould, and 500 men. On 8 October Wardlaw carried out a surprise attack on the royalist guard at Hooe, taking over fifty prisoners and some ammunition. [2]

During October, Prince Maurice, a nephew of the king, came westward with an army of five horse regiments and nine foot regiments. Deploying his forces around Plymouth, he set up his headquarters at Widey House, Crownhill. Reinforcing the garrison at Plymstock, Pomphlett Mills was commandeered and troops encamped on a nearby hill which was named Orden Hill, but later renamed Pleasure Hill. It is probable that Pomphlett Farm was also occupied.

William, 5th earl of Bedford, and lord of the Plymstock manor, supported parliament, and there can be no doubt his tenants' farms were raided for livestock and produce to support the royalist troops. Also, trade of produce with Plymouth being prevented, one can only guess at the hardship suffered by the inhabitants.

A remarkable achievement of the royalist army was the transporting of 13 fishing vessels overland from the River Yealm to Plunket Mills bay (Pomphlett Creek). The narrator of the *Siege of Plymouth* described this undertaking as 'being accomplished with great labour'.

Watchers at Prince Rock seeing all the activity in the creek opposite considered that an attack on Cattedown was imminent and the little redoubts and breastworks there were strengthened. Instead, on 21 October, the royalists made a landing by night at Hooe, where they built a square work on the hillside within pistol shot of the fortification at Mount Stamford. [3] From this point they attempted to surround the fort in order to prevent supplies being taken in. This move forced the soldiers in the fort to come out and attack the new work. After three hours fierce fighting the parliamentarians overcame the royalists, taking Captain White and fifty other prisoners, together with the new work.

Leaving a guard of thirty musketeers under the command of an ensign, this victory was set at naught only a few hours later by the ensign's negligence, for either by treachery or cowardice he not only neglected to give the alarm to the fort when the royalists attacked during the night, but abandoned his post, thus exposing the troops in the fort to greater danger than before. [4]

The royalists brought up reinforcements and the following morning saw a continuation of the struggle when the royalist position was retaken by the parliamentarians. This time is was destroyed and Mount Stamford strengthened by slight outworks – a breastwork on each side, terminated by a half-moon along the ridge – which were manned as well as the smallness of the force at hand permitted. Each day there were assaults and skirmishes and on 3 November the royalists raised batteries within pistol-shot of the fort, which on the 5th began to fire, discharging upwards of 200 demi-cannon and whole culverin shot, besides the shot of smaller guns. On the first day several breaches were made in the fort and the lieutenant and some gunners were killed.

The royalists, with reserve troops and supplies at Plymstock, had all the advantage, for, despite a signal of distress being made, no supplies came by sea to the isolated fort at Stamford. At last, with only seven men left out of the original 36 and ammunition and supplies running out, the parliamentarian captain surrendered the fort on condition he and his men should march out with colours flying and their best demi-culverine gun and to an exchange of prisoners. These terms were accepted by the royalist captain, who accorded the full honours of war to the soldiers who had fought so bravely. Altogether this action covered a period of 22 days. [5]

The defeated parliamentarians retired to Haw Stert where they commenced the erection of a work, but from tiredness and lack of support from Plymouth they were forced to abandon this also. The royalists then built a fort on this peninsula with batteries to cover the town and Sutton Pool. This was a square erection with ordnance and smaller forts below at the water's edge. Already, ships had been driven out of Cattewater by the royalist cannon at Oreston and on the west side of Plymouth Sound a royalist battery under Mount Edgcumbe at Barn Pool prevented ships from sailing into Stonehouse Creek, so that Mill Bay became the only sanctuary for ships bringing supplies into the beleaguered town.

Philosophically, Plymouth considered the loss of Mount Stamford to be advantageous as a means of uniting their small strength for the defence of the town. Conversely, the royalists found the possession of Mount Stamford no great advantage and in July 1644, when Essex the parliamentary general, advanced into the west they abandoned it, together with their fort on Haw Stert. Plymouth did not re-occupy Mount Stamford, but settled a small garrison on the abandoned fort on Haw Stert.

On the 21 April 1644 a surprise attack was made from Prince Rock on the royalists at Pomphlett Mill, when prisoners were taken and provisions brought in to the town.

In September King Charles arrived at Widey with his main army which was launched against Pennycomequick fort, when sailors from the naval ships anchored in the Sound helped soldiers from the garrison to defend the town. The battle lasted all day, when the royalists withdrew after failing to penetrate the Plymouth defence. About this time Vice–Admiral William Batten, who was a good friend to Plymouth, fortified the tip of Haw Stert, which was renamed Fort Batten after him.

The following year, during the night of 17 February 1645, Sir Richard (Skellum) Grenville sent a large force of royalists to re-occupy Mount Stamford, where a breastwork of faggots at least 12 feet thick was constructed, which they intended to complete the following night. The Plymouth garrison was taken by surprise, but plans to combat this move were soon put in hand. The little force at Fort Batten was strengthened at noon on 18 February by a party of horse and foot brought over by boat, the latter mostly

seamen under Captain Swamley. Then under cover of the fire from sixty guns from the ships and forts the new Fort Stamford was attacked and carried, the royalists being driven from the field and pursued for two miles. Many prisoners were taken, among them Lieutenant-Colonel Mohun, Sergeant-Major Richard Hele, four lieutenants, two ensigns and 92 soldiers. [6]

The last item in Plymouth's Siege Accounts refers to Fort Arundell, a work of the enemy which is mentioned in association with a work at Plymstock. January 5th 1646:

> *Item. Paid to Major Barnes 16s.8d., and 1s. for payment of the like summe unto 25 soldiers ymployed in ye raissinge of fortifications against Forte Arundell on yssuinge forth of ye fources of ye garrison on Saturday last.*

It is possible that Fort Arundell was one of the three royalist works at Oreston. [7]

The Siege of Plymouth was finally raised by General Fairfax on 18 January.

N.B.   The year then commencing on March 25th, all the dates have been adjusted to conform to present-day computation.

NOTES AND REFERENCES
PLYMSTOCK DURING THE CIVIL WAR 1642–1646

1.   Llewellyn Jewitt, *The History of the Borough of Plymouth*, 182.
2.   Siege Pamphlets.
3.   John White, *A True Narration of the Siege of Plymouth*, 2.
4.   R.N. Worth, *The Siege of Plymouth*, T.P.I., Vol. V, 265.
5.   Worth, *Siege of Plymouth*, 266.
6.   *A True Relation of a Brave Defeat given by the Forces in Plymouth to Skellum Grenville, on Tuesday, 18th February, 1646.* Worth, *Siege of Plymouth*, 293-4.
7.   Worth, *Siege of Plymouth*, 297.

Chapter Seventeen

TURNCHAPEL AND MOUNT BATTEN

Mount Batten, formerly Haw Stert, meaning *high finger of land*, is the peninsula which juts out into Cattewater and The Sound.[n.1] Tucked into its north-facing shore against a background of limestone cliff is the village of Turnchapel, its name previously thought to be a natural transition from St Anne's Chapel to the abbreviated Tan Chapel, which appeared on maps until the late eighteenth century. However, Tan is the earlier name, the Chapel being added in order to Christianise its pagan origin. There are numerous instances of places in southern Britain with two such names; a pagan one, Tan Hill, and a Christian one, St Anne's Hill. [1]

The name Tan is interesting, for Tin or Tan means *fire. San Tan* is the Breton name for *holy fire*, also the Gaelic for fire is *teine*. There is considerable evidence that places formerly called *Tan* were in pagan times connected with fire-worship. Dr T.F.G. Dexter, an authority on the subject, considered that Tin or Tan was a fire-god.

It seems that in pre-Christian times the Plymstock *Tan* may have been one of the places where fire-festivals were celebrated, and also that a beacon fire was kept alight as a guide to ancient mariners. [2] The high land above Turnchapel overlooks the Cattewater and the sheltered Hooe Lake where, it is thought, much of the commerce was carried on in early days.

Turnchapel, an attractive mixture of late Georgian and early Victorian buildings, grew and prospered when shipbuilding yards were established along the waterfront to the east and west of the village. The most striking feature in the village is a terrace of fifteen fine late -eighteenth-century houses running west from the Mansion House along Boringdon Road, parallel with the waterfront. These were built by Mr John Cater, a shipbuilder, and were known locally as The Barracks. The largest of these, the Mansion House, was once a private art gallery.

In 1677 there was an establishment at Turnchapel, in the Cattewater, for 'breaming and repairing' the king's ships, but the increased dimensions of ships required the provision of suitable slips and dry docks for such work to be carried out.

During the eighteenth century there were two shipbuilding and repair yards, their owners being Mr John Cater and Mr Silas Frost, who leased their land from Lord Boringdon of Saltram. In 1797 the first wet dock was constructed at Turnchapel at the expense of Lord Boringdon, several Royal Navy frigates being repaired at this yard. Then between 1800 and 1804 Lord Boringdon enclosed a dry dock, the construction of which proved to be a long, arduous and costly undertaking. In 1801, when the dock gates were closed for the first time, the apron blew up and the dock filled with water. Although strengthening work was carried out another disaster occurred in September 1802, 'on a morning of an equinoxial spring tide when being charged it gave way at high water'. It was not until the end of 1804 that this work was completed and dock finally made watertight. [3] The first naval vessel to be built in this dry dock was the *Derwent*, an 18 gun sloop, rigged as a brig. Work on her began in December 1806 and she was launched on 23 May 1807. [4]

Turnchapel possessed the only private shipbuilding yard in Devon which was adapted for the construction of line-of-battle ships, this shipyard being owned at that time by Mr Isaac Blackburn, who also held his land on lease from Lord Boringdon. The *Armada*, a 74 gun third rate ship was begun in February 1807; the largest vessel of war ever built in a local merchant's yard. She was launched on Thursday 22 March 1810, the naming ceremony being performed by Mrs Pridham, wife of the Mayor of Plymouth, Mr Joseph Pridham. The next morning the *Armada* went up the Hamoaze to be docked and coppered, and to be commissioned. [5]

The *Clarence*, a third rate ship with 74 guns, was also built in Mr Blackburn's yard. Work on her began in November 1807 and she was launched on 11 April 1812. [6] An oil painting by John Rogers of the launch of the *Clarence* at Turnchapel is on view at the Plymouth City Museum and Art Gallery.

In 1813, the *Diana*, of 38 guns, underwent a thorough repair in Mr Blackburn's yard. [7] This was the last major work to be carried out by him, for in April 1814 the Sheriff's officer ordered that all the property of Mr Blackburn should be consigned to the Broker for sale by auction. [8] In 1826 this shipyard was purchased from the Earl of Morley (formerly Lord Boringdon) by Mr Pope, a shipbuilder and merchant of Plymouth. It remained in his possession until it was offered for sale by auction in May 1859, when it was purchased by Mr Nicholas Were for £4274. [9]

The only record of work carried out at Mr Pope's yard appears to be the launch of a schooner of 300 tons, the *Arthur Parsen*, in May 1855, and two small vessels in December 1860. *[10]

On 10 May 1849 a schooner, the 200 tons *Countess of Morley*, owned by Mr Charles Williams, and named by his wife, was launched from Mr Routleff's shipbuilding yard at Mount Batten. The same year Lord Morley obtained permission to construct a patent slip at this yard, capable of taking vessels of 600 tons burthen, which was then being manufactured by Mr J. Mace of Plymouth Foundry. [11] The position of this slip is shown a little to the west of Turnchapel on an Ordnance Survey Map of 1888.

A Saltash steam barge, designed and built by Mr Mace at his Plymouth Foundry was then taken apart in large pieces and conveyed to Mr Routleff's yard for convenience of launching in September 1851. The hull of the vessel was of iron, the deck and upper part being wood, the latter having been furnished by Mr Routleff. [12] In 1882 Mr W.S. Kelly took over Mr Routleff's yard.

The *Directory of Devonshire* for 1878-9 records that Mr Fred Darton was a yacht, steam launch and boat builder at Turnchapel, and Mr Isaac Brace Darton was a boat builder at Mount Batten.

During the nineteenth century extensive mineral working took place along this coastline from the tip of Mount Batten to West Hooe. This was for limestone and during quarrying operations a seam of nodular iron ore was revealed at the angle of coast forming the west end of the village. [13] Deserted shafts in this area indicate that this seam of iron was worked out.

The Turnchapel railway branch line from Plymouth was opened in January 1897, with a half-mile extension beyond Turnchapel station which passed

*These were in fufilment of a contract with the government entered into by Mr Pope.

121

The launch of the Clarence '74' *at Turnchapel. A painting by John Rogers.*

through a tunnel under Boringdon Road to Turnchapel Wharves. This branch line finally closed to passengers on 10 September 1851. [14] The swing bridge which carried this line over the entrance to Hooe Lake has been demolished, leaving only the unsightly iron and wood piers.

The Oreston & Turnchapel Steamboat Company was formed in 1871 by Henry E. Elford in order to run a ferry from both these villages to the Barbican at Plymouth. After Phoenix Wharf was opened in 1895 the Barbican landing was discontinued and the new, more commodious and convenient Phoenix Wharf

122

was established as a permanent place for the landing and embarking of passengers. In addition to the Turnchapel pier there was a landing place at Mount Batten which the company leased from the Earl of Morley. In May 1908 the company ordered a pontoon for this landing and also a bridge to connect with the landing. This improvement, which enabled steamers to land at the lowest tides, proved to be very satisfactory. However, when in February 1917 the government took possession of the field and cottages at Batten for a flying station, the continued use of this landing was threatened. By April 1917, the pontoon and bridge at Batten having been much damaged by rough weather through the winter, it was decided to have it repaired and replaced, but after repair work the authorities at the seaplane station which was being developed there, refused to allow the steamers to land passengers, except those engaged on the works. Because of this the company decided not to replace the pontoon bridge until they were allowed to land passengers there as before. [15]

In 1901 the steamer *Express* was sold for £300, and in 1902 the company approved the building of another boat at Turnchapel. On 8 May the new steamboat appropriately named *May Queen*, was successfully launched. A larger boat, *Countess of Morley*, purchased by the company in 1895, was sold in 1903 for £2650. [16]

In February 1911 the Plymstock Parish Council entered into an agreement with the Admiralty, which had taken over the large shipbuilding yard, that a public right of way leading to the 'old landing place' on the east side of this yard should be stopped up, and in exchange the Admiralty would provide a new public landing at the west end of their coaling depot. [17]

In 1953 this war-damaged pier was in such a poor condition that the parish council called in a consulting engineer to advise on rebuilding. However, when the War Damage Commission agreed to consider only the proper cost of removing debris from the damaged pier, the council reluctantly agreed to its demolition. A petition was received protesting against the proposed demolition of the pier and a matter arising from this was that apparently, in 1943, a naval vessel had collided with the pier causing further considerable damage. The council then wrote to the Admiralty regarding this alleged collision, requesting investigation and compensation. When the Admiralty required further information, the organiser of the petition was requested to obtain written statements from any witnesses of the incident to enable the matter to be further pursued by the Admiralty. After a further letter from the petitioner stating the Admiralty vessel to be the *Barnstone*, but, it seems, no written statements from eyewitnesses, it was considered whether it was advisable to proceed with the proposed claim against the Admiralty. [18]

Eventually, with the consent of a parish meeting held in March 1955, the council resolved that Turnchapel pier be demolished. The war damage value payment amounted to £778.19s.3d. and the actual demolition which took place in 1956 cost the parish council £940. A small portion of this pier still remains, but serves no useful purpose. The council retained the right of way from Boringdon Road down to low water mark. [19] 'A Public Landing Place' metal sign is still on the wall at the entrance to this pathway.

During the late nineteenth and early twentieth centuries boat builders were still active at Turnchapel and Mount Batten, the following being recorded in 1895: Alfred Borlace, boat builder, Turnchapel; Isaac Brace Darton and Henry Darton, boat builders,

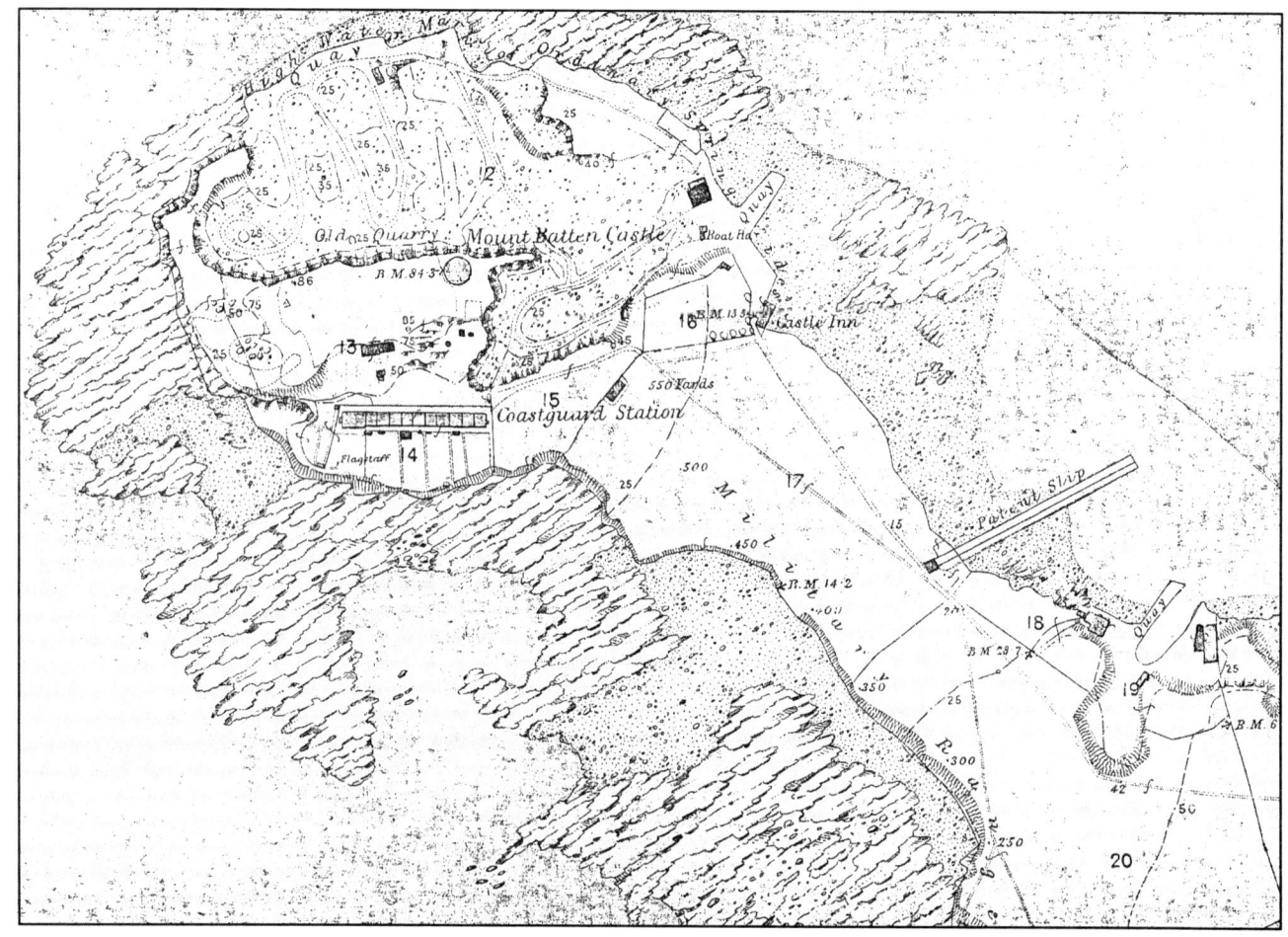

Mount Batten – taken from the 1888 Ordnance Survey map.

Mount Batten and William S. Kelly, ship and yacht builder at Mount Batten. Alfred Borlace and Isaac B. Darton are still in business in 1904, but William Kelly's yard at Mount Batten does not appear in the directory for this year. This was obviously a declining industry,

for no boat builders are mentioned in the directory for 1939.

There was a flourishing coal trade at Turnchapel, which for upwards of thirty years was run by the Westlake family of Staddon Farm. Other merchants

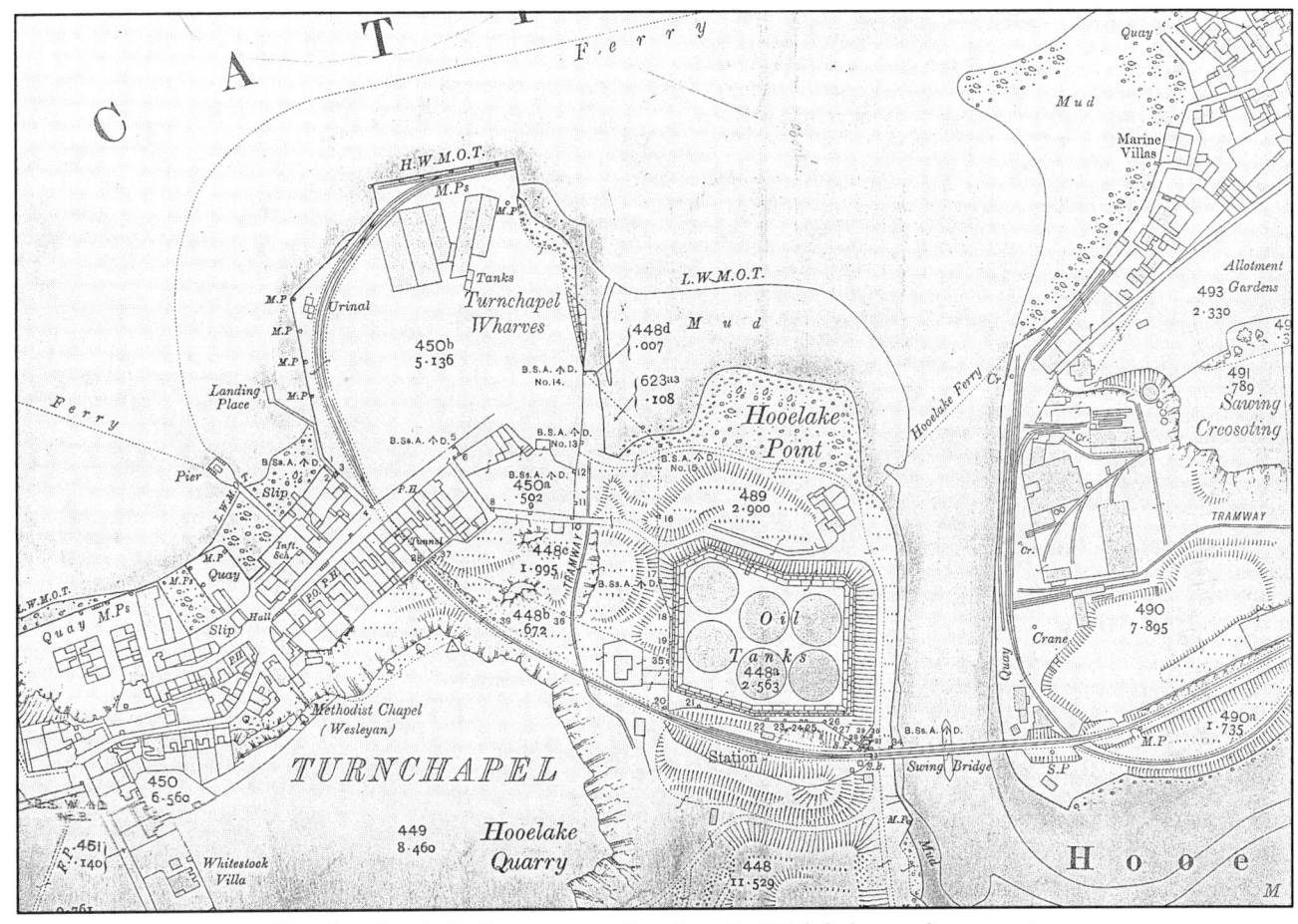

Turnchapel and the Cattewater – taken from the 1914 Ordnance Survey map.
Between 1888 and 1914 the shipyard disappeared and the Turnchapel Branch Railway was
built under the Boringdon Road to the Admirality Coaling Depot at Turnchapel Wharves.

were Philip Ellis; and William Hart, whose name appears in 1857 as a coal and lime merchant, and again – possibly a descendant – in 1923 as limestone quarry owner. Billy Hart's quay is near the remains of the railway bridge at Hooe Lake, and eighteenth century limekilns alongside the nearby road were listed as Ancient Monuments Grade II in December 1989. Other industries included Moore and Babb,

The foreshore at Mount Batten and the Cattewater, with the Royal Citadel and Plymouth in the background.

ochre and brick manufacturers, and J.H. Bennett, stone and marble mason, both recorded in a directory for 1870. [20]

As evidence of a thriving locality Turnchapel possessed nine shops in 1895, but with the gradual loss of its former trades this number was reduced to five in

1939 and today only one tiny shop on the steep hill leading to Mount Batten remains. The Boringdon Arms and the New Inn, both busy and attractive public houses, provide focal points in the life of the village, but the Shipwrights Arms, which adjoined the Mansion House, closed some while ago. The Castle

The Cattewater with Turnchapel in the background.

Inn at Mount Batten was closed when the peninsula west of Turnchapel was taken over by the Royal Air Force. A plaque on the wall opposite the entrance to R.A.F. Mount Batten, records the following:

LAWRENCE OF ARABIA 1888 – 1935
On his return from India in 1929 T.E. Lawrence, under the assumed name of Shaw, was posted to a Flying Boat Squadron at R.A.F. Mount Batten.

He remained in the marine craft section until his discharge in February 1935.

The Continental Oil Company occupied one of the large quarries between Turnchapel and Hooe. There were six large oil tanks and in April 1970 there was a petroleum explosion and fire which necessitated the evacuation of families living nearby to Plymstock School. This was followed by a second explosion, when the flames from the burning tanks could be seen from a great distance. Public protest led to the closure of this depot.

In the centre of Turnchapel was the former Methodist Chapel, now a private residence. Nearby was the Jubilee Hall, erected in 1897 to celebrate Queen Victoria's Diamond Jubilee. The building has gone and on the site is a paved garden. To commemorate Queen Elizabeth's Silver Jubilee in 1977 a seat was presented to the Turnchapel Conservation Area.

Mount Batten Castle

Mount Batten Castle, now protected as an Ancient Monument, is a symbol of the role this peninsula has played over many centuries in the defence of the harbour and town of Plymouth. This circular tower of limestone, built sometime after the construction of the Royal Citadel to help command the narrow entry to the Cattewater and Sutton Pool, has two floors, the upper having a vaulted roof. There are embrasures for ten guns and over the entry is a coat of arms carved from Portland stone, which is so badly weathered that identification is not possible. No record of this has been found.

The strategic importance of Haw Stert, alias Mount Batten, was recognised by Sir Richard Grenville in 1586-8, when he prepared his hand-drawn plan for fortifying Plymouth. On the point of the peninsula is a 'new bulwark – 3 new peice to be plased', and nearby are encampments at Turnchapel and Jennycliffe which would require 400 soldiers:

to keepe and defende this place being now easie for the enemie to take and bie nature verye strong & doth commande the town of Plymouth & all this part of the harbour.

The direction and extent of fire from the guns on Haw Stert is towards the Sound, being criss-crossed by those from other batteries. [21]

Despite the defeat of the Armada the Spanish threat did not disappear and in the 1590s the Hoe Fort was being built under the supervision of the Queen's military engineer Robert Adams. Also, Plymouth's Municipal Records for the year 1598-9 show that Sir Richard (Champernowne) was to pay the town 54s. 'for bordes to sett fourth Sr Champernowne's barracathes on Hoe Stert'. Queen Elizabeth expected the gentlemen of the county to contribute towards the defence of the town.

When Cosmo de Medici, Grand Duke of Tuscany, came to Plymouth in March 1669, on his way to the Court of Charles II, Count Lorenzo Magalotti recorded his impressions of the area. Mount Batten appeared as an island on the Plym and the Batten Siege Fort could still be seen (see Chapter 16). The knoll of this promontory may well have appeared as an island at that time, for in 1663-4 the low-lying ground behind this hillock was partly breached on either side by the sea.[n.2] Over the years this erosion increased to a point where it was feared the sea would break through.

After the Cattewater Harbour Commissioners were incorporated in 1874 plans were put in hand for the construction of a breakwater at Batten. This 915 feet long pier halted the erosion and considerably increased the protection afforded to ships sheltering in Cattewater. [22]

A clue to the date of the construction of the round tower might be an entry in Plymouth's Receiver's Book for the year 1689-90, which shows that £88.18s.1d. was spent in raising fortifications on Piggs Point (later known as Queen Anne's Battery) and

Batten, 'when the French fleet was on the coast with ammunition and utensills of war'.

Mount Batten Castle was under threat in 1962 when the Air Ministry said there was no alternative to the tower being demolished, as the cost of preservation was too heavy. [23] Fortunately, Sir Henry Studholme, M.P. for the area, and Mr J. Paton Watson, Plymouth City Engineer and Surveyor, opposed demolition and were successful in having the building protected as an Ancient Monument.

In 1975 two seventeenth century cast-iron cannons were hoisted to the top of the 40 feet high tower by the crew of H.M. Air Force vessel, *Sea Otter*. The seven-pounder and the nine-pounder were refurbished at Totnes by the Ordnance Workshop of the Historical Manuscripts Department of the Department of the Environment, as part of a plan to restore the tower to its original condition. [24]

Although Mount Batten Castle has been saved, the future of the land adjoining the hillock on which it stands is less certain, for the Ministry of Defence is to close R.A.F. Mount Batten, when it is likely that Plymouth City Council will decide its future use.

N.B. Since this chapter was completed the Royal Air Force have vacated Mount Batten and in 1993 the Plymouth Development Corporation took over the site. Now, in Spring of 1995, plans have been published for the development of this peninsula. These promise an exciting future for Mount Batten when it will once more be open to the public, the 274m long breakwater, recently restored, becoming an attractive promenade and a major feature of the Corporation's regeneration programme.

The entire headland area is to be retained as a landscaped open space with room for leisure opportunities. The potential for a water transport service between Mount Batten and Plymouth is also being investigated.

NOTES AND REFERENCES
TURNCHAPEL AND MOUNT BATTEN

1. T.F.G. Dexter Ph.D., B.Sc., B.A., *Fire Worship in Britain*, 52.
2. Dexter, *Fire Worship in Britain*, 51.
3. R.H.C. Fice, *South Devon Times*, 22 April 1960, (quoting from a MS by J.B. John Lord Boringdon ?).
4. K.V. Burns, Lt-Cdr, D.S.M., R.N. *Plymouth's Ships of War*, 49-50.
5. Burns, *Plymouth's Ships of War*, 31.
6. Burns, *Plymouth's Ships of War*, 42.
7. *Naval Chronicle*, v. 29, 1813, 246.
8. John Harris, *History of Plymouth*, MSS, 77-8.
9. Burns, *Plymouth's Ships of War*, Introduction.
10. *Plymouth, Devonport and Stonehouse Herald*, 3 May 1855.
11. *P.D. & S. Herald*, 2 June 1849.
12. *P.D. & S. Herald*, 20 September 1851.
13. J.C. Bellamy, *Pilim–stoc and its Church*, P.D. & S. Herald, 2 July 1853.
14. D. St John Thomas, *A Regional History of the Railways of the Westcountry*, App. 11, 189.
15. *Oreston & Turnchapel Steamboat Company Ltd*, Minutes of Shareholders' Meetings, April 1917.
16. *O. & T. S. Co. Ltd*, Minutes, May 1902.
17. *Agreement with plans*, Plymstock Parish Council with the Admiralty, 1911.
18. Minutes of the Plymstock Parish Council, W.D.R.O.
19. Minutes of Plymstock Parish Meeting.
20. Plymouth Directories, Central Library, Local Studies.
21. Public Record Office, *Map; MPF 6*, 1586-8.
22. C.W. Bracken, *A History of Plymouth and her Neighbours*, 243.
23. *Western Morning News*, 28 April 1962 & 17 May 1962.
24. *Western Evening Herald*, 28 February 1975.

n.1. Excavations by Professor B. Cunliffe of the University of Oxford in 1983-4 revealed that the area next to Clovelly Bay northeast of the limestone bluff was first used intensively by people engaged in metal working and long-distance trade around 1000 BC. Successive buildings and paved areas were then constructed here, and a midden developed on the isthmus. During the Iron Age, trading links were maintained with southwest France and perhaps further afield. In the later Iron Age, c.100 BC – AD 100, connections appear to have been strongest with Britanny and with Hampshire and Dorset. Pre-Roman coinage from all thses areas has been found at Mount Batten, and bronze fibulae (safety pins) and fine pottery also attest such links. The finds from the Mount Batten settlement are at this time complemented by discoveries made at Mount Stamford in the 1850s, of finely decorated bronze mirrors, rare pottery vessels, glassware and further fibulae associated with an extensive cemetery. Investigations in 1993-4 have shown that the settlement at Mount Batten continued on into the Romano-British period with no appreciable break in activity. At this time, settlement also extended to areas in Plymstock such as Lower Hooe and Elburton (see Chapter 20). *Note contributed by Dr. Keith Ray, City Archaeological Officer, Plymouth City Council.*

n.2.   Mr R.N. Worth, who gave a lecture at Oreston in March 1888, said: *Every lighter trading there had to take a load of rubble once a year from the Cattewater and deposit it upon the isthmus.* This order was made during the reign of Henry VIII.   Ref. Western Daily Mercury, *The History of Mount Batten.*

Chapter Eighteen
WEST HOOE

Although West Hooe has always been closely associated with Plymstock, being part of the ancient parish, it once had a distinct and separate life of its own, the group of buildings at the head of the lake being the focal point of the little agricultural and maritime community which grew up on the east side of Hooe Lake to become the village of Lower Hooe. As early as 1281 there was a ferry between Hooe and Sutton worked by a barge belonging to John Beaupré, the bailiff of Trematon, the toll being a halfpenny per horse or man. [1]

The Domesday Survey records under *Ho* that this manor was held by Alebric before the Conquest and that it had been granted to Judhel of Totnes, who also held Staddon and Staddiscombe. Judhel became the greatest magnate in South Devon, whose lands owed the king the service of seventy knights. There was land in Ho for two ploughs, with five acres of pasture and it was worth by the year twenty shillings. Of this, Stephen, who held the land under Judhel, had in demesne half a virgate and one plough. He had there six villeins, two bordars and one serf. Also, four head of cattle, forty sheep and five acres of pasture. The provision of fully armoured and mounted knights or regular payments of fixed sums was also demanded, for William held England under an iron grip of military service. [2]

Because of this requirement the comparatively small manor of Hooe became linked with the manor of Egg Buckland. This became apparent when, on 1 July 1166, Wido de Bocland, to whom both manors had descended, made them over to the prior of Plympton, receiving them back as a perpetual tenant at a rental of 12 shillings a year and military service, the manors being jointly assessed at two knights' fees, Hooe contributing one quarter and Egg Buckland one and three-quarters fee. [3]

On 1 July 1201 Wido's successor, Alan de Bocland, appeared as plaintiff before a court of Justices at Exeter concerning his right to the tenancy. After Alan acknowledged both manors to be the right of the prior and his church at Plympton, the prior granted them to Alan on the same terms as before. Trouble flared up again after Alan's death, when the tenancy descended to his daughter Isabella, and on 25 June 1238 Isabella complained to a court at Exeter that Robert, prior of Plympton, did not honour an agreement made between her father Alan and Joel, predecessor of the present prior. When Isabella also acknowledged the right of the prior he agreed that she and her heirs should hold these manors for ever. In addition he gave Isabella five marks of silver. It seems the priors had no intention of letting their tenants forget their suzerainty. [4]

Following Isabella's marriage to Osbert Giffard the tenancy continued in the Giffard family without a break until 1306, when, during the tenancy of Ralph Giffard, the two manors were divided; Egg Buckland being settled on John and Eva Giffard and their heirs. In the same year a serious dispute arose between Ralph and Osbert, another member of the Giffard family who claimed the manor of Hooe. This matter was taken before the High Court at Westminster where, after warranty of charter was summoned, Osbert acknowledged the right of Ralph, who agreed that Osbert should have possession of the manor on condition that it should revert to Ralph after Osbert's death and not descend to the heirs of Osbert. In 1346 John Bernard was tenant of Hooe from Ralph Giffard, late tenant of Plympton Priory. [5]

About this time West was added to the name of Hooe to distinguish the manor by the lake-side from another manor at the top of the hill to the east, which became known as 'Esthoo' and is now known as Higher Hooe. Formerly in the possession of Ralph Giffard in 1428, this forty acre manor with its ten cottages came into the possession of the Harris family of Radford, who held it in 1472. This manor also had a *messuage*, a mill, one plough-land and five acres of meadow and it paid a quarter part of one fee. [6]

The Giffard's tenancy of West Hooe must have lapsed during the fourteenth century, the tenancy changing hands many times and more legal battles being fought for possession; the only difference being that these later disputes were caused by the subletting of the manor to various people. These did not involve the priors of Plympton, who still remained the undisputed overlords.

During the fourteenth century a chapel was built adjoining the *messuage* at West Hooe and on 4 August 1387 Bishop Brantyngham licensed to prior John of Plympton Priory and his canons the right to celebrate divine service in the chapel of St Laurence within their manor of West Hooe. John Brackley (Member of Parliament for Plympton in 1384), who resided at Plympton, was tenant of West Hooe in 1403, when he and his family were granted a licence to have divine service performed 'within their mansions of Plympton and Westhoobray'. [7]

It was recorded in 1875 that a farmhouse called Palace Court at the head of a creek called Hooe Lake has remains of ancient buildings. A chapel with 'two trefoils with eight windows and the remains of a door may still be seen'. The upper part of the lake is also called Palace Lake. [8] Only an arched doorway, together with a barn, survive to mark the site of the chapel and the once-extensive group of buildings. Both have been listed as Buildings of Architectural or Historic Interest.

Later in the fifteenth century West Hooe came into the possession of Sir William Paulet, and on 12 September 1488 he and his wife gave it, together with other lands, to their nephew Amyas Paulet. After Sir William's death in 1500 an Inquisition into his former possessions showed that he had been in possession of land at West Hooe which he held of the prior of

The ancient archway at West Hooe Farm, 1965.

Plympton at an annual rent of 6s.8d., the services which belonged to the manor being at that time unknown. After the dissolution of Plympton Priory in 1539 West Hooe came into the possession of the Crown. It was kept in hand for a time and let out on a tenancy for a rental of 8s. per annum. For administrative purposes it was attached to the Buckfast Abbey roll. [9]

The next known tenant was Thomas Forde, a Plymouth merchant who was mayor of Plymouth 1585–6. It seems likely that during his mayoralty the courtyard was paved with pebbles arranged so as to form devices, one of these representing the Plymouth Coat of Arms, a saltire between four castles. Some years later in 1621 lands in Plymouth were sold subject to leases made by Thomas Forde of 'Westhowe in Plymstocke'. [10]

An Indenture dated February 1631 records the sale of Westhoo in the parish of Plymstock to Richard Forde by the Court of Augmentations, a body set up to deal with the disposal of former monastic lands. [11] Judith Forde of West Hooe married Captain Ralph Burrow of London on 16 January 1691. Burrow Lodge in Church Road takes its name from this family.

The Civil War was in progress when Richard Forde died in April 1643. West Hooe was soon in the front line, for when the royalists occupied Plymstock in August of that year they set up a guard at Hooe, almost certainly commandeering the manor house for this purpose. When, on 8 October, a force of parliament-arians from Plymouth landed and attacked their quarters, the old buildings would have been much damaged during this assault. Also, the battle of Fort Stamford would have inflicted further damage (see Chapter 16).

West Hooe never regained its former status, a farmhouse being built on a part of the site of the former mansion. Also, during the Commonwealth government the little chapel would have been deliberately destroyed.

The estate at West Hooe later came into the possession of the Rogers family, who were leading merchants in the days of Plymouth's great colonial trade. An earlier member of this family, John Rogers, was the first martyr of Queen Mary's reign. For his forthright Protestant views and his refusal to conform to the restored Catholic faith he was sent to Newgate prison and on 4 February 1555 he was taken from his cell and burnt alive at Smithfield. [12]

A descendant, John Rogers, was a Member of Parliament for Plymouth in 1698 and was created a baronet by William III. During this time the seat of the family was at Wisdom, but in later years the family lived at Blachford, also in the parish of Cornwood. In 1777, Sir Frederick Leman Rogers was elected Recorder for Plymouth, and a later descendant, Sir Frederick Rogers, a brilliant scholar and barrister, was appointed Permanent Under-Secretary of State for the Colonies in 1860, and was raised to the peerage in 1871, when he became Lord Blachford.

Another distinguished member of this family was Dame Hannah Rogers, who founded a school at Plymouth for mentally handicapped children. This school was later moved to Ivybridge.

There is no record of the Rogers family having lived at West Hooe and the manor was divided into holdings and let to tenants. The Tithe Map of 1842 shows the barton farm, then comprising 242 acres in the tenancy of John Hart. During the twentieth century housing development has covered most of the former agricultural land and, latterly, the

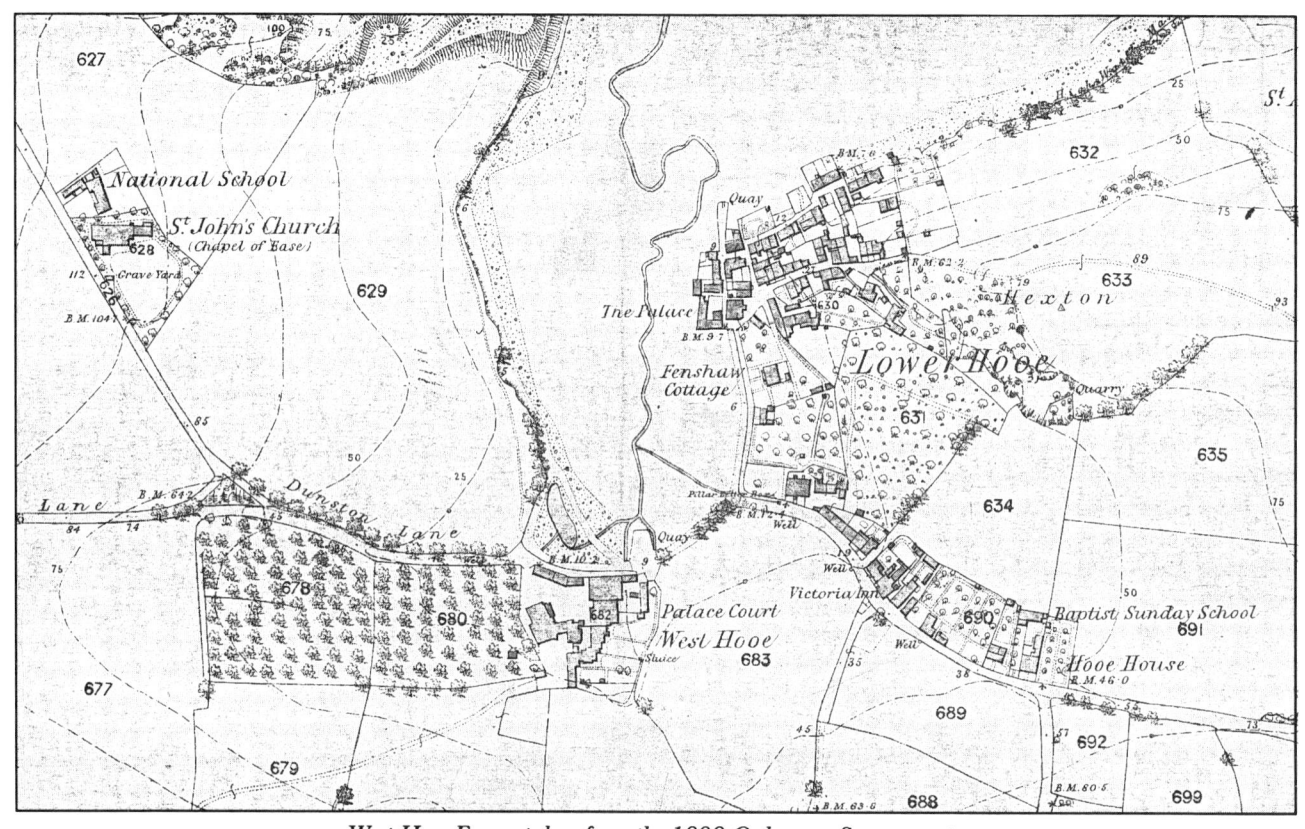

West Hooe Farm: taken from the 1888 Ordnance Survey map.

farmhouse has been demolished to make way for a shopping precinct.

A Plymouth artist, Samuel Prout, who was distinguished for his portrayal of picturesque subjects, captures the quiet charm of West Hooe as it appeared in 1810, with its pastoral fields stretching up the hillside and the little village of Hooe overlooking the placid waters of the lake. For many years Hooe was famous for its strawberry tea-gardens, which attracted many visitors, and an early nineteenth century guide book describes the view from the hills above the village 'as exceedingly extensive and grand'.

During the nineteenth century a new enterprise also extolled the attractions of Plymstock's coastal areas, for on 3 May 1869 the Oreston Steamboat Company commenced running their new steamboat *Little Pet* from Oreston to the Barbican Pier, Plymouth, calling at Turnchapel each way. The leaflet

Hooe Lake with Radford Castle in the background. From a watercolour by J. Cocks. (courtesy of Mr D.G. Spear).

The village of Lower Hooe and West Hooe Farm, with Hooe Lake in the foreground. From a watercolour by J. Cocks. (Courtesy of Mr D.G. Spear).

announcing this service pointed out that the inhabitants of Plymouth would find this a favourable opportunity for visiting the beautiful scenery at Radford, Hooe, Staddon Heights, etc.; the modest charge for this trip being one penny each way.

Before the days of mains water supply, Hooe relied on a spring which, rising in Furze Wood, flowed down the hillside through the grounds of the manor house, where a supply was piped to the buildings. The surplus emptied through a conduit into the lake. A trough can still be seen by the side of the road. Water from this spring was also stored in a reservoir on the hillside and piped to some of the properties in the village. In addition there were wells for those who were not connected to this system.

The new church of Saint John the Evangelist was completed in 1855 and a National School was built alongside for the children of Hooe and Turnchapel. Hooe Ecclesiastical Parish was created on 9 May 1856; the ancient public footpath from Radford Dip to Radford Woods, known locally as 'Stippy-Steppy', forming part of the boundary dividing the new parish from the old.

A junior school at Lower Hooe was officially opened on 12 October 1931. It has since been extended to include a physical education hall and a swimming pool.

NOTES AND REFERENCES
WEST HOOE

1. C.W. Bracken, *A History of Plymouth and her Neighbours*, 18.
2. *Exeter Domesday*.
3. Rev. O. Reichel, *The Hundred of Plympton in Early Times*, 275. Devon Fine No. 45.
4. Devon and Cornwall Record Society, *Devon Feet of Fines*, V. 1, 1196-1272, No. 274.
5. *Feudal Aids*, No. 401.
6. *Calendar of Inq. Post Mortem*, 34, No. 78, 12 January 1485.
7. *Register, Bishop Stafford*, A.D. 1403, Licence to celebrate.
8. J. Brooking Rowe, *History of Plymstock*, MS, 1875, D.R.O.
9. Public Record Office.
10. Rowe, *History of Plymstock*, MS.
11. P.R.O., L.R. 1/17.
12. *Dict. Nat. Biog.*

Chapter Nineteen
STADDISCOMBE

Staddiscombe, an attractive rural village on the southern fringe of the former parish of Plymstock, has evidence of habitation covering a period of two thousand years. During the mid nineteenth century a visiting archaeologist, Mr J.B. Davidson, discovered and examined an earthen bank in a field a short distance to the north of Court Gates Farm. His article, 'Pre-Conquest Devon', which appeared in *Trewman's Exeter Post* on 3 April 1861 included the following:

> *Staddiscombe Castle is an entrenchment close to a hamlet of the same name. It is also called Castle Borough. This camp is nearly circular and about seventy yards in diameter. It is formed by a single rampart from twenty to thirty feet in height.*

Much of the bank, Mr Davidson saw, has disappeared but sufficient remains to identify this ancient site.

This pre-Conquest manor, held in 1066 by the Saxon Aluric, paid geld for one virgate. There was enough land for two ploughs, but when the Domesday Survey was taken there was only one plough, with one villein and one bordar. Also recorded are two heads of cattle, one swine, 12 sheep, half an acre of meadow, twenty acres of pasture and a wood two furlongs in length and one furlong in breadth. This mention of a wood is interesting, for an ancient wood still survives in a steep-sided combe to the north of the village.[1]

This manor, comprising 200 acres, was granted to Judhel and held in conjunction with Staddon by William, Staddiscombe developing as the principal manor. During the twelfth century both manors passed to the Stoddon, alias Britt family, who held both manors until the 1370s, when they passed to the Wyse family of Sydenham (see below).

The Britt family produced some notable personalities, among whom were: Sir Richard Brito, recorded during the reign of Henry II; Ralph Britt, high sheriff of Devon in 1348; and Walter Britte, a famous scholar of Merton College, Oxford, who became a follower of John Wycliffe, the religious reformer. After Wycliffe's death in 1384 Walter maintained the principles of his great master, professing poverty, going barefoot and poorly clad in russet. [2]

Staddiscombe was held by Guy de Britt (1284-6), being successively held by three others of the same name, then by Ralph Britt, who was followed by Guy Britt, who married Isabell, daughter of Adam Branscombe.

Their son Robert had a daughter and heiress, Margaret, who married Thomas Wyse of Sydenham, and their son John married Thomasin, daughter of Baldwin Fulford of Dunsford. [3] Alicia, daughter of John and Thomasin Wyse, married James Russell, their son becoming John, Lord Russell, first Earl of Bedford. [3a]

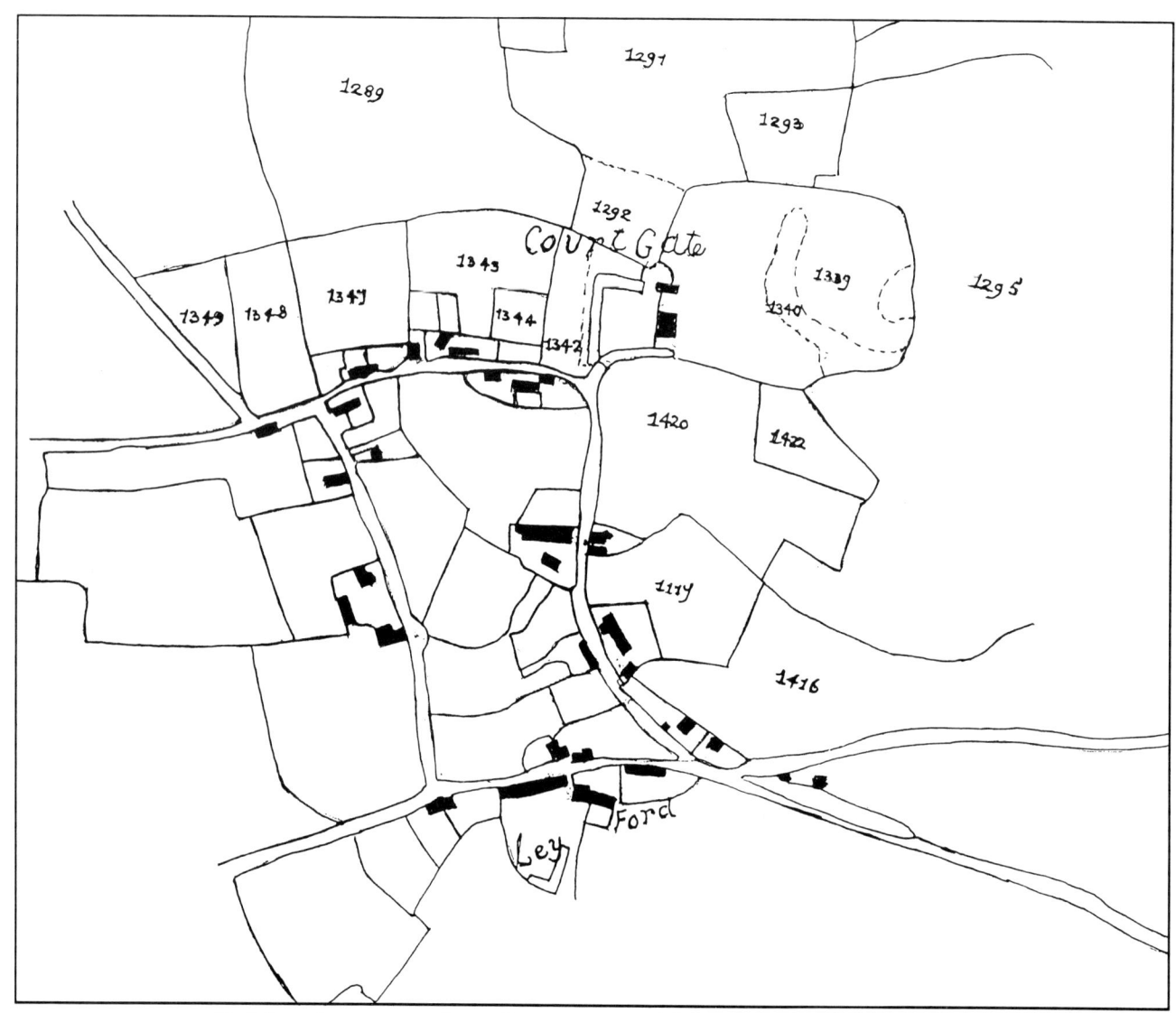

Staddiscombe – a map redrawn from an extract of the Plymstock Tithe Map of 1842.

138

An Inquisition taken after the death of John Harris of Radford in 1485 showed that in addition to his estates of Radford and East Hooe he held two acres of land in *Stetyscombe* worth 4s. held of the heirs of Thomas Wyse by fealty and 4d. rent. A later Inquisition taken in 1625 after the death of Sir Christopher Harris of Radford showed that he also was a military tenant in fee of Staddiscombe. [4] When his great-nephew, John Harris of Lanrest in Cornwall, inherited the Radford Estate John's younger brother, Robert, was given the holding at Staddiscombe. This military obligation he fulfilled when he was appointed Major-General of His Majesty's forces before Plymouth during the Civil War, 1642–1646. [5]

Robert Harris was declared a Delinquent by the Commonwealth government for his support for the royalist cause and, as a result, his military estate at Staddiscombe, worth £45 a year, was confiscated. Then, in 1650, Richard Candish of Plymstock applied to the Committee for the Compounding of Delinquent's Estates for this land because, he said, Robert Harris owed him £100. [6] No order was made in favour of Candish, but Robert Harris's connection with Staddiscombe was not renewed and he lived with his unmarried sister, Honor Harris, at Tywardreath in Cornwall, where he died in 1655. (See Chapter 13.).

The Wyse family continued to hold the manor of Staddiscombe for some time until, during the mid seventeenth century, the manor was acquired by Sir William Morice, remaining in the possession of this family until the latter part of the eighteenth century, when it came into the possession of John Pollexfen Bastard of Kitley in the parish of Yealmpton, who greatly increased the family estates. [7]

Court Gates was the principal farm of the manor and it was there the manor courts were held. A lease dated 1824 was granted by Edmund Rodney Pollexfen Bastard to William Pearse of Court Gates Farm and Burches Tenement for six to twelve years at the option of either party, Burches Tenement being in the occupation of Ephraim Dodridge. [8] In 1868 a member of this family, also named Ephraim Dodridge, while working at Rocky Park, Plymstock, came across a cache of Bronze Age implements, which became known as 'The Plymstock Hoard'. (See Chapter 1.).

According to the Census Returns, Jane Pearse held Court Gates in 1841, and by 1891 Philip Hine was in occupation. Court Gates Farm is now in the possession of Edward Hendy, whose family have farmed at Plymstock and Elburton for many centuries.

Although a great deal of land to the east is now covered by housing development, the village of Staddiscombe remains practically unspoilt and Court Gates is still a viable farming unit.

Staddon

Staddon occupies a high ridge of land which lies within the south-west corner of Plymstock, the seaward boundary of the ancient parish following the coastline to join the landward boundary at Bovisand beach. From Jennycliffe Bay to Staddon Point the rocky shoreline rises with dramatic effect to the plateau of Staddon Heights, now a popular golf course. It was here that artefacts dated to the Mesolithic period were found in 1885. (See Chapter 1.).

This was the Domesday manor of *Stotdone*, which was farmed in 1066 by the Saxon, Alwin, when it paid geld for one virgate and there was sufficient land for two ploughs. This manor of 185 acres was part of the vast area of land in Devon awarded to Judhel of Totnes by the Conqueror. It was held under him by William, who had in demesne half a virgate and the villeins half a virgate. William had one bordar, a wood one furlong in length and half in breadth, and 20 acres of pasture, worth by the year five shillings. [1]

Wederige, situated between Staddon Heights and Haw Stert (Mount Batten), was held by the Saxon, Otrus, when it paid geld for one furlong. Owned by the Earl of Mortain, brother of the Conqueror, this 48 acre manor, worth three shillings, was held by Rainald. [2]

During the twelfth century Stoddon was held by Hugh Stoddon, [3] and in the late thirteenth century by William Stoddon, knight, sometimes called Britt. [4] According to John Prince (1643-1723), who wrote *Worthies of Devon*, the Britts were a family of great antiquity, supposed to have proceeded from the British race. William was followed by Gwydo le Brit, who held Staddon and Staddiscombe, the Britt family continuing to hold both manors until the latter end of the reign of Edward III (1327-1377), when Margaret, daughter and heiress of Robert Britt brought these manors by marriage to Thomas Wyse of Sydenham in Marystow. [5]

During the seventeenth century Sir William Morice, high sheriff of Devonshire in 1651, acquired much land at Plymouth, including Staddon, Staddiscombe and Wederige, becoming known jointly as the manor of Staddiscombe. Sir William was made governor, with his son William, of the Hoe Fort and St Nicholas (Drake's) Island, and in 1660 was also keeper of the Port of Plymouth. [6]

Staddon once had a beacon, which probably dated from the thirteenth or fourteenth century. At that time a Keeper of the Coast was responsible for the line of beacons which encircled the coast, where they formed a part of the defence system. Beacons came under the control of the vice-admirals during the sixteenth century. [7] Although the Staddon beacon appears on a map of the area surveyed in 1738, it was not noted when a further survey was carried out in 1784-6. [8]

An extant lease dated 1745 shows that 11 acres which formed part of the parcel of the Beacon – a quarter part of Staddon Downe – formerly in the possession of Josiah Willing, deceased, and then in the possession of Sir William Morice, was granted to Sarah Willing, widow, for the sum of £40 for 99 years and a quarterly rent of £1.6s.8d. She was also required to attend all the courts of Sir William Morice when they were held within the manor of Staddiscombe, along with other tenants of the manor. [9]

A further lease dated 1789, from Humphrey Morice, granted to William Pearse of Plymouth Dock:

All that field or close commonly called Withyhedge, quarter part of Staddon Downe, lately in the possession of William Finch or his undertenants.

A lease of the same land dated 1808 to Asinath Vine and Sarah Parsons, widows, shows that the owners of Staddon were now Pollexfen Bastard and Edmund Bastard of Kitley, Yealmpton. A lease of the Barton of Staddon, dated 1832, to Richard Popplestone, confirms this farm as being in the manor of Staddiscombe, the total acreage then being 232 acres. [10]

Staddon Fort, one of Lord Palmerston's fortifications built during the nineteenth century, was strategically placed to command a wide view of the Channel and the entrance to the Sound, and, together with the 80 feet high Staddon Wall, built in 1883 for gunnery practice, dominates the landscape at Staddon Heights. [11] From Staddon Down the land drops steeply to Staddon Point, where there is a small harbour and jetty. Close by is the Fort Bovisand Underwater Centre, which is based in the converted nineteenth century fort.

A Plan for the Defence of Plymouth prepared by Sir Richard Grenville, 1586-1588, illustrates a new bulwark on Staddon Point, which has three guns and shows the direction and range of their fire. Three hundred soldiers were needed to defend the landing at *Bove sande*. [12]

A little to the north of the harbour at Staddon Point are two cliff-side quarries; the Plymouth Quarry and the Devonport Quarry. There are two extant leases for a stone quarry at Staddon Point to the 'Commissioners for paving, watching and lighting the Town of Plymouth'; the first, dated September 1786, was granted by Sir William Morice, and the second, dated May 1833, by Edmund R.P. Bastard of Kitley. A similar lease was granted to the Town of Devonport. [13]

Just within the old Plymstock parish boundary at Bovisand is a reservoir for 12 000 gallons of water. This was used solely for the supply of ships, the water being conveyed in iron pipes by gravity to the harbour at Staddon Point. Tank vessels were stationed there for the purpose of carrying water to ships entering the Sound. Designed by John Rennie, who also designed the breakwater, it was constructed by Joseph Whidbey Esq. The whole project, including a spacious wharf and pier with a jetty, being completed in 1824, at a cost of £39 774. [14]

Staddon fulfilled another valuable service when, during the First World War, a part of the brake surrounding the coast was cultivated, probably for the first and only time, for growing corn and potatoes. Afterwards the land was allowed to return to its original uncultivated state. This was a popular place for picnicking and for picking blackberries. Although the brake formed a part of Staddon Farm people were always free to wander over it. [15]

The *South Devon Museum*, published in 1834–5, recounts a walk along the footpath from Mount Batten around Staddon Heights and an exploration of the bracken-covered slopes with their unusual plant life and butterflies. This footpath is now part of the long-distance South West Way. [16]

Staddon came into the ownership of the Ministry of Defence during the early part of the present century, Staddon Barton Farm being leased to the Westlake family.

The value of Staddon Heights and Jennycliffe for public recreation was recognised by the Plympton St Mary Rural District Council and by the Plymstock Parish Council, both of these bodies making representations to the War Department regarding public access to these areas. [17]

An official guide book, published by the Plympton St Mary Rural District Council in 1961 states that; 'Staddon Heights is now preserved to the public for all time'. Also providing an additional safeguard, the National Parks Commission (now the Countryside Commission) made a South Devon Area of Outstanding Natural Beauty (DESIGNATION) Order, dated 10 September 1959, which included Staddon Heights and the coastal land around Staddon Point and Jennycliffe. [18]

NOTES AND REFERENCES
STADDISCOMBE

1.   *Devonshire Domesday*, I, 652.
2.   John Prince, *Worthies of Devon*, I, 135.
3.   Sir William Pole, *The Description of Devonshire*, 325.
3a. *Dict. of Nat. Biog.*
4.   *Inq. Post Mort.*, I, Hen. VII, No. 78, 1485. *Misc. Inq. Post Mort.*, pt 14, No. 38, 1626.

5. Clarendon, *Rebellion and Civil Wars in England*, V. II, 442–4.
6. Cal. of the Comm. for *Compounding Delinquents' Estates*, 1643-1660, pt IV, 2595.
7. Rev. R. Lane, *The Brixton Book*, 120, MS, Plymouth Central Library, Local Studies Dept.
8. *The Kitley Records*, W.D.R.O.

NOTES AND REFERENCES
STADDON

1. *Devonshire Domesday*, I, 654.
2. *Dev. Domesday*, I, 349.
3. Sir William Pole, decd. 1625, *The Description of Devonshire*, printed 1791, 517.
4. *Feudal Aids, Devon*, 1284-6, 335.
5. Pole, *Devonshire*, 325.
6. *Dict. of Nat. Biog.*, Sir William Morice (1602-1676).
7. M.M. Oppenheim, *The Maritime History of Devon*, 6-7, 105.
8. *Plan of the Environs of Plymouth, 1735*, W.D.R.O. *The South Part of an Accurate Survey and Measurement of Plymouth and Dock Towns and the Adjacent Country*, 1784-6, British Museum, W.O.78/385.
9. *Kitley Estate Papers*, Lease No. 16, W.D.R.O.
10. *Kitley Estate Papers*, 74/358/8, W.D.R.O.
11. C.W. Bracken, file of news cuttings.
12. Defence Map, *Sir Richard Grenvyle's for fortifying Plymouth 1586-8*, P.R.O., MPF6, S.P. 46/36/4. Eliz. I.
13. *Kitley Estate Papers*, C/part Lease, 74/548/9. W.D.R.O.
14. J. & M. Lysons, *Devonshire*, 1822.
15. Mrs James Finnigan (formerly Miss Westlake of Staddon Farm).
16. *South Devon Museum*, Vols 3–5.
17. Minutes of the *Plymstock Parish Council*, July & Sept. 1930, W.D.R.O.
18. National Parks Authority /87.

Chapter Twenty

ELBURTON, SHERFORD AND COMBE PRIOR

The only archaeological evidence of early human presence at Elburton is a find of three Neolithic flint arrowheads and two scrapers.[n.1] A Roman coin found at Higher Sherford may have some link with the Roman trading post at Mount Batten.[1] Field names such as Great White Barrow and Lower White Barrow suggest an ancient burial site, possibly of Bronze Age date. White Barrow Stroll formerly linked Sherford Road with these sites. Closes of land named Firestones also indicate early occupation. [2]

The agricultural settlement at Elburton came into being on land belonging to the royal manor of Plympton, which was owned by successive Saxon kings until the Norman conquest, when it passed to William I. In the Domesday Book of 1086 Plympton was entered as *terra regis*. Then, in 1100, when Henry I, youngest son of the Conqueror, succeeded his brother William Rufus he gave the lordship of Plympton to Richard de Redvers, eldest son of Baldwin, sheriff of Devon, and created him the first Earl of Devon. [3]

Early settlement was determined by the nature of the soil and the availability of water. Elburton, with fertile soil and numerous springs and streams was ideal. The adoption of field names such as Springpits, Springfield, Wellhay and Flood indicate a plentiful supply of water. Before piped water was brought to the village in the early part of the twentieth century a public well, known as 'Gunnys', was situated at the bottom of cottage gardens to the south of the village, a path between the gardens giving access to the villagers.

Exactly when Elburton was first settled cannot now be established with certainty, although the *ton* suffix suggests it took place during the Saxon period. It was usual for groups of peasants, including freed serfs known as *kotsetlan* (cottagers), to be settled on the outlying areas of large manors, with sufficient timber from the lord's wood to build themselves a cottage and a small plot to cultivate for their own needs.[4] The eleventh century *kotsetla* had a small share in the village arable, which comprised a few acres in the open field which he could cultivate for his own profit and in co-operation with his neighbours. He paid no rent, but was expected to work on the lord's demesne farm for one day a week throughout the year and more at harvest. He was then free to cultivate his own plot and seek casual employment among his better off neighbours. Although the *kotsetla* had achieved a measure of independence he was still bound to the manor and could not move outside without permission. [4a]

The *kotsetlan* were followed by a class of men called *geburas*. These were tenant farmers with land they could cultivate for their own profit and for which they paid rent. The *gebur* was still expected to work on the lord's demesne for two days on every week of the year and for three days a week at harvest and between Candlemas and Easter. During this time he took his turn as watchman at his lord's fold. In return, the lord usually helped him to start life on his own account by supplying stock. It is expressly stated that he ought to have received two oxen, six sheep and a cow, together with seven acres already sown upon his yardland. [5] The *bur* element in Elburton's name could be taken to mean a township settled by *geburas*. The *gebur* held his house and land by copyhold tenure on the lives of two or three of his relatives. On the dropping of a life by death he was required to pay a heriot, sometimes the best beast or a specified sum of money. He held his land at the will of the lord for a term of years, and if he himself died the lord might grant the tenement to his next of kin.

As with most attempts to discover the early history of particular areas for which few documents are available, it is only possible to build up a picture in the light of those national events which may have affected their development. This principle could be applied to the mid twelfth century when, following the death of Henry I there were two contenders for the throne; Matilda, daughter of Henry, and Stephen, grandson of the Conqueror. When Stephen was crowned king the country was plunged into civil war.

Baldwin de Redvers, second Earl of Devon, rebelled against Stephen, sheltering in his castle at Exeter when Stephen, with the main body of his army, entered the city. With a strong garrison he held the castle against the royal forces. During the progress of this siege Baldwin's castle at Plympton surrendered to Stephen, the king sending 200 horsemen, with a large body of archers, who unexpectedly appeared under the walls of the castle about daybreak, the fortress being almost entirely destroyed. The Plympton manor lands, which extended far and wide around the castle, and said to be abundantly well-stocked and cultivated, were harried by the king's troops who drove off to Exeter many sheep and oxen. [6] It is unlikely the Elburton *geburas* escaped their attention, probably with disastrous loss of stock, which could have reduced them to poverty.

At the conclusion of the civil war in November 1153 a charter of Stephen, described the Treaty of Winchester, by which Stephen agreed that Henry, son of Matilda, should succeed him. Baldwin's name appears as Earl of Devon in the impressive list of witnesses to this charter, so it would seem that he had regained his former status and possessions.

These early settlements were islands of cultivation in a sea of forest, heath and waste. Under the rigorous Forest Laws instituted by the Normans, who hunted the red deer in these areas, any newtake from the waste was punishable as trespass on the king's demesne. These laws inhibited the cultivation of new land until, in 1204, the men of Devon subscribed 5000 marks to purchase from King John a Charter of Disafforestation, which covered the whole county with the exception of Dartmoor and Exmoor. It may have been at this time that more land was brought under cultivation at Elburton.

After the death in 1246 of Baldwin, eighth Earl of Devon, the manor of Plympton descended to his sister, Isabella de Fortibus, Countess of Albemarle; née de Redvers. She became known as the Countess of Devon. Isabella confirmed the charter of her father Baldwin, who, in 1242, granted a borough to the townsmen of Plympton, and in a further charter of 1262 she conferred additional privileges to the tenants of the manor, one being the right to take wood for fuel from Lee Wood in the parish of Shaugh. These rights extended to the tenants of the manor at Elburton. Both charters were confirmed by Edward I in June 1285, and by successive sovereigns up to and probably beyond the reign of Mary, 1553–1558. Another long-standing right of the Elburton tenants was that of pasturing their cattle on Shaugh Moor. [8]

When Isabella died in 1293 an Inquisition found that Hugh de Courtenay, the great-grandson of Mary, youngest daughter of William de Redvers, the sixth earl, was Isabella's heir. The Courtenays continued in succession [n.2] until their active support for the Lancastrian cause during the Wars of the Roses brought about their downfall. Thomas Courtenay, the sixth earl, was beheaded at York on 3 April 1461, his honours and estates being forfeited to the Crown. [9]

During this troubled period two incidents of local interest were recorded:

(1) In the year 1478–9 *John Hawston of Elberton was attached to answer to the Lord for yearly driving the Forest of the Prince and the cattle there agisted* (placed there to remain and feed for a period) *from Yealm Head through all the land of Stealdon and thence to a place called Quyckbeame, and thence to Redlake Head, and then to Fishlake, and from Fishlake to Hurtlake, and thence to Erme Head, and impounding them at Torrycomb in the pinfold there, to the damage of the prince yearly 40s.* The land within these bounds were in part Commons of Devon, in part Forest. [10]

(2) On 26 April 1480 a grant for life was made to the king's servant, Robert Belle, one of the grooms of the king's chamber, *of all the holdings which William Gyfte and Amice his wife, severally held in Aylberton within the manor of Plympton and which had come into the king's hands for want of lawful heirs of their bodies.* [11]

Although in 1470 the honours and estates of the earldom of Devon were restored by Henry VI to John Courtenay, brother of Thomas, the sixth earl, he died at Tewkesbury in 1471, fighting for the Lancastrian cause. After his death without issue the ancient earldom of Devon fell into abeyance, its possessions again reverting to the Crown.

Following the Lancastrian victory at the battle of Bosworth in 1485 Edward Courtenay, son of Sir Hugh Courtenay of Boconnoc (in Cornwall), was created eighth Earl of Devon by Henry VII, and an Act of Parliament restored to him the previous honours and estates of the Earls of Devon. Edward Courtenay's son, William, was married in 1495 to the Princess Catherine, sixth daughter of Edward IV. Knighted in 1487, Sir William Courtenay was actively employed in the king's service until, in 1502, he was imprisoned in the Tower on suspicion of being implicated in a conspiracy against the king. He was released in 1509 by Henry VIII and in 1511 the earldom of Devon, which had reverted to the Crown when his father died in 1509, was restored to him. He died the same year, leaving as his heir his only surviving son, Henry, who was 13 years of age.

Once again the manor of Plympton, with its outlands at Elburton, had a lady of the manor, for William's widow, the Princess Catherine Countess of Devon, was granted by her nephew, Henry VIII, all the estates of the earldom of Devon for her lifetime. By Act of Parliament in 1512 her son, Henry, took the title of Earl of Devon, and in June 1525 he became Marquis of Exeter. [11a]

Following Henry VIII's break with Rome, Henry Courtenay was regarded with suspicion by the king's minister, Thomas Cromwell, his avowed enemy. He was tried on a charge of treason, convicted in 1538, and beheaded on Tower Hill. His wife and son were kept in prison until, in July 1539, she was pardoned and released, her son being held, until in 1553 he was released by Queen Mary. Although his title and estates were restored to him, he died in 1556 at Padua in Italy. With his death the long association between the Courtenays and their manor of Plympton came to an end.

For a time the manor was again held by the Crown, being eventually divided among the descendants of the four sisters of Sir Edward Courtenay of Boconnoc who had succeeded to the earldom in 1485. As a result, the manor was divided among four owners, some of these fourth parts being again divided by sale into eighth parts.[12]

Following the division of the Plympton manor among several owners a confused situation developed. Some surveys of the manor were taken, the earliest being in 1638 following the death of Sir James Bagg who, in 1625, had acquired the barton of Saltram and the fourth part of the manor of Plympton. Bagg was heavily in debt and in 1638, not long before his death, he mortgaged his property for £10,000. After his death, his son George successfully petitioned King Charles to give him his father's mansion called Saltram, with lands adjoining, and one quarter part of the manor of Plymholme (Plympton). He later conveyed, for a valuable consideration, all his property and lands to Sir George Carteret who, by his will, devised his estate to his wife Elizabeth and then to his rightful heirs.[13]

It seems that out of the four original mortgagees of this property in 1638 only one, Sir John Jacob, survived and by his will made his son, John Jacob, executor. When Sir John Jacob died an Inquisition was taken in January 1673, whereupon the sheriff of Devon took possession of all the aforementioned lands and delivered them to John Jacob to hold until the £10,000 mortgage, with costs, was paid. John Jacob died in 1676, whereupon Sir Thomas Wolstenholme, as the surviving administrator of Sir John Jacob, was entitled to the sole benefit of this estate.

A legal wrangle developed between Lord Carteret, great-grandson of Sir George Carteret, the original purchaser, and Sir Thomas Wolstenholme, the holder of the mortgage. Negotiations dragged on until 1704, when what was termed 'a friendly accommodation' was made whereby all lands lying in Plympton St Maurice, Plymstock, Elburton and Brixton should be enjoyed by Thomas Wolstenholme, his heirs etc., on condition they confirmed all leases granted by Lord Carteret. Although Lord Carteret remained the legal owner he was compelled to grant a lease to Thomas Wolstenholme for 99 years of the barton of Saltram and the fourth part of the manor of Plympton at £5 per annum. As can be seen, the effect of Sir James Bagg's profligate ways was felt long after his death.[14]

An abstract of Sir Richard Vyvyan's (of Trelowarren in Cornwall) title, dated 1753, of one eighth part of the manor of Plympton names the Elburton tenements, their acreage, the tenants' names, the lives on which they were held and the rent.[15] It is interesting to note that some of these tenements included a half-farthing of land. This was an eighth of an acre and it is tempting to consider that these may have been the plots granted to the very first settlers at Elburton. Collectively these half-farthings are still known as 'the Commons'.[15a]

The rules of good husbandry were incorporated in the leases of Elburton tenants; one such lease in December 1807 required that after land was broken up for tillage, 16 hogsheads of good well-burnt lime to an acre should be mixed with earth and spread over the land. The lessee was not to take more than two crops of corn or other grain or anything else except turnips in each seven years of the term of the lease. The lease also required that clover seed and good grass seed should be sown and dung spread before the term expired, or an equivalent in ashes be applied according to good husbandry.

The lessees were not permitted to cut down any kind of trees or saplings nor top, pole or pare any growing trees but only such as have been usually polled and then but once in each seven years. Notice had to be given before hedges were cut in order that saplings and growing timber trees could be marked. The orchard had to be cared for and not used for pasture. The corn must be thrashed out on the premises and the reed combed and cleansed, and the straw, dung, compost and soil, used on the premises 'for the better manuring and improving thereof'.[16]

Previous to the introduction of lime as a manure the method of improving coarse and sterile ground was by the ancient system of beat-burning, whereby the turf was dug up with mattocks, no deeper than the matted roots of the grass and weeds extended, then left to dry until the herbage was sufficiently withered. This was then piled up in little heaps called beat-burrows, with a handful of straw in the centre which was set alight and kept burning. When burnt out a coarse, gritty kind of ash remained which, on a calm day, was spread over the ground. This was hard work for the husbandman, so later the spade was used in paring off rather than digging up the turf with the mattock. He also had to use the hand rake and be careful not to burn the earth. [17]

Beat-burning was superseded by lime-burning, which was introduced during the sixteenth century. An old record tells of lime quarries being worked at West Sherford previous to the reign of Henry VIII,

which continued to the year 1827, when they were removed to about a furlong northward. A group of disused limekilns can still be seen alongside the highway leading from Elburton to Plympton St Maurice. [18] Between Elburton and Billacombe there was, until the 1960s, a small quarry with its own kiln. The path along which the donkeys carted the burnt lime from the kiln to the old road could still be seen until widening of the main A379 road led to demolition of the kiln. Housing development nearby also led to the quarry being filled in. The story is told that cock-fighting, a forbidden sport, took place there and that look-outs were posted at strategic points to sound a warning if anyone approached.

Catts Hill, along which the burnt lime was carted, was the only way from Brixton via Elburton to the Cattewater until, in 1823, Lord Morley of Saltram received Royal Assent:

to make another line of road from Kitley Hill in the parish of Yealmpton, by the villages of Brixton and Elburton and from thence to within four hundred yards of the Bridge over an estuary of the sea called the Lary.

The Bridge would have been the Flying Bridge Ferry, as the Iron Bridge was not completed until 1827. A short distance to the south of Catts Hill on a high ridge lies Dunstone Wood, given to the parish in 1935 to commemorate the Silver Jubilee of King George V. [19]

Elburton once had its own archery butts, now an open space and children's play area. An Act passed in 1541 provided that these were to be put up and maintained in every parish, so that shooting at them might be practised on holy days and other times.

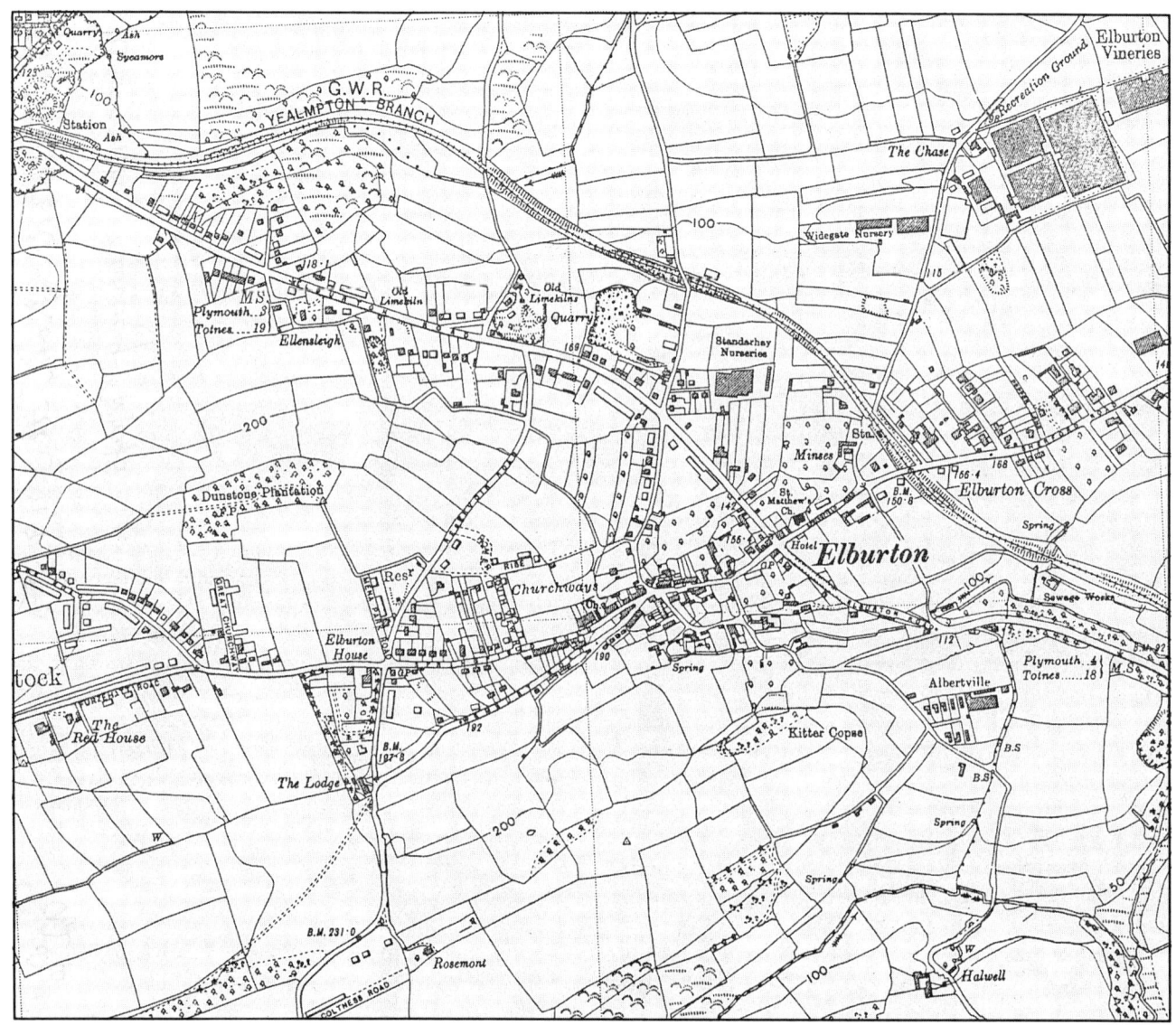

Elburton – taken from the 1915 Ordnance Survey map.

Elburton village, about 1900.

Sherford

At the time of the Domesday Survey in 1086 the manor of Sherford in the vicinity of Elburton, but lying within the boundary of the parish of Brixton, was in the possession of Judhel of Totnes:

Formerly it was held by Aluric the Saxon, but was then held by William. There were four villeins, six bordars, and two serfs, and it was worth by the year twenty shillings.

After William de Warelwast, bishop of Exeter, dissolved the old Plympton monastery and founded the priory of Plympton, West Sherford came into the possession of the priory, by charter of Roger de Nonant, baron of Totnes. The manor house of West Sherford, built by the priory, was used by the prior and canons as a grange-country house with farm buildings attached. East Sherford was given to the priory by gift of Fulco.

John Howe, the last prior of Plympton, in consideration of £40, paid by Thomas Maynard the elder, leased on 24 September 1538, to Anne, wife of the said Thomas Maynard:

the reversion of the Dominical place and Barton lands called West Sherford, in which the said Thomas then dwelt as tenant, excepting the lime-kiln and the house adjoining the culver-house there.

The Maynards held the farm of West Sherford as early as the seventh year of the reign of Henry VIII, and were then appointed bailiffs of the manor of East Sherford. [20]

On 12 January 1582, as a further token of her favour, Queen Elizabeth granted to Sir Francis Drake, for his services, the manor of Sherford in the parish of Brixton in the county of Devon, formerly the lands of the dissolved monastery of Plympton. [21] The heirs of Sir Francis Drake continued in possession of Sherford until the present century, and both farms are still in agricultural use.

Combe Prior

The earliest known documentary evidence of land at Elburton is a grant by Hugo Peverell of two furlongs of *terre de cumba* to the Church of the Apostles Peter and Paul of Plympton. Although the document is not dated it appears to be early thirteenth century. This land was situated in a valley a short distance to the south-west of the village of Elburton, and just within the boundary of the parish of Plymstock. Also, in 1264, Walter de Cumba, lord of the manor of Spriddlestone, granted to this church:

that they might take water from Cullewelle Lake and through his land of Spridelstone to their land of Combe. [22]

When the monks built their house and cultivated the land it became known as the farm of Combe Prior. There was a link between this farm and the village of Elburton by a well-defined path skirting the Commons to emerge into two lanes, one leading to the old road to Brixton and the other north to the village. Only a short length of the latter remains, but a track once led downhill to the road at Springpits and thence to the crossroads where a granite cross was mounted on an outcrop of rock. It is probable that in medieval times monks from Combe Prior travelled along this way to preach the gospel and celebrate Mass at this cross. Until the head and part of the shaft were broken off either at the Reformation or during the Puritan Revolution, this would have been a tall, slender cross with the arms either straight or tapering slightly. The massive socket-stone with what remains of the shaft has been re-sited on a triangular green a short distance west of its original position.

The priory ceased to cultivate the farm and in 1511 the then prior, John David, granted copyhold tenure to John Blake, his wife and son, of the manor of Combe Prior. [23] In 1536 John Howe, the last prior, granted a lease for 96 years determinable on lives to

Elburton Cross, resited at Fernhill Garden.

John Blake, Elizabeth his wife, and John and Christopher their sons of:

> *All that fair place at Combe Prior in the parish of Plymstock: always excepting the Prior's mansion place called Lower Combe, with the apull gardyn and a little arbor to the same mansion adjunct and a dove-house to the same mansion place belonging and all the woods, groves and quarries there with free liberty for the priors, their servants, workmen and labourers to goe and to come, to and fro all the said premises before excepting with all manner of carryages for their business necessary and profitable at their will and pleasure.*

The payment of a fine of £20 was made by the Blakes and the annual rent was £6. [24]

In 1539 Plympton Priory was dissolved and all its possessions confiscated by the Crown. A Court of Augmentations which was set up to deal with monastic property received a request from George Keynsham, Gentleman, to purchase the farm called Combe Prior with the mansion called Lower Combe. In November the same year the King, by his Letters Patent, granted 'Old Combe Prior together with Lower Combe to George Keynsham and his heirs'. [25]

One wonders whether George Keynsham realised the long-term effect of the lease held by the Blakes and their heirs, for although he now held Combe for £13 yearly in substitution for knight service, he could not legally take possession of the lands. This may be the reason why he decided in 1546 to convey the mansion and the freehold of the farm for £146.13s.4d. to John Blake and his heirs. [26] In 1555 John Blake drew up a deed setting out the ownership of Combe to himself for life, then to John, his eldest son, and then to his rightful heirs. This was not the end of the matter, for he and his son John suffered several attempts at a common recovery by various gentlemen, one being in 1581 by Thomas Barkley, who later occupied the well-known Downhorn at Plymstock.

Despite these difficulties the Blake family remained at Combe for many years, this farm heading the list of properties for the Eastern Division in the Plymstock Rate Book. Then, in 1663, Ferdinand Blake, Gentleman, and Ruth his wife, in consideration of a competent sum of money conveyed Combe Farm to Edmund Pollexfen of Kitley in the parish of Yealmpton. [27] Although the property changed hands the Blakes remained there for a time as tenants, and a John Blake was churchwarden at Plymstock Church in 1703 and 1704.

When the Hearth Tax returns for 1674 were made, the Blake family refused to subscribe. Because of this three parish constables, Thomas Cole, William Candish and Daniel Candish entered Mr George Blake's house and found he had six hearths. Mrs Joan Blake also refused and was found to have five hearths. [28]

The roof structure of an ancient barn at Coombe Farm.

Coombe Farm, Elburton.

By 12 February 1724 the Blakes ceased to be tenants of Combe, for on that date a *messuage*, barn, gardens etc. in Combe, alias Combe Prior, were leased to John Finch, yeoman, and six fields belonging to the barton of Combe were leased to Silas Bickford, yeoman. John Finch's lease was renewed in 1754, but by 1767 the capital *messuage* of Combe was leased to Alexander Edwards, and by 1800 John Harvey was the lessee. [29] Nothing more is known of the Blake family.

Carved beams at Coombe Farm, Elburton.

Combe Farm is one of the few remaining farms in the former parish of Plymstock. The old mansion house has an Elizabethan wing and another farmhouse nearby is of two periods, Georgian and Victorian. Both are still in occupation. The magnificent barn, which not so long ago still had its original high–pitched open timber roof, resembling the roof of an old church, is still in use. The dove–house vanished long ago and the old way to the village is no longer used.

When services at the Elburton village cross ceased the villagers would have used the church paths in order to attend Sunday services at the Plymstock Parish Church.

The first building for religious worship at Elburton was built at Springfield Road in 1869 as a Bible Christian Chapel. This is now the Elburton Methodist Church.

Following the end of the First World War Elburton decided to build its own church, and the Church of St Matthew was completed in 1922. Fifty years later, in 1972, Elburton was created a parish in its own right.

NOTES AND REFERENCES
ELBURTON, SHERFORD AND COMBE PRIOR

1.   C. Gaskell Brown, *Plymstock, an Archaeological Survey and Policy.*
2.   D.R.O., *Plymstock Tithe Map, 1842.*
3.   James Hine, FRIBA, *Plympton in the Olden Time*, T.P.I., Vols II & III, 1865-6, 83-5.
4.   H.P.R. Finberg, *Tavistock Abbey*, 37-8.
4a.   Finberg, *Tavistock Abbey*, 37-8
5.   F.M. Stenton, *Anglo-Saxon England*, 3rd edn, 374.
6.   *Dict. Nat. Biog.*, Baldwin de Redvers.
7.   *English Historical Documents*, V. II, 1042-89, 436-439, No. 22.
8.   J. Brooking Rowe, *The History of Plympton.*
9.   *Dict. Nat. Biog.*
10.   T.D.A., V. LXXXVI, 199.
11.   *Cal. Patent Rolls*, April 26 1480.
11a.   *Dict. Nat. Biog.*
12.   J. Brooking Rowe, *Plympton Erle*, 24.
13.   John Stevens, *Plympton in the 17th century*, Plymouth Local Studies, P7.
14.   W.D.R.O., 24-4-20, 24-4-5, 26-4-1.
15.   D.R.O., *Brooking Rowe Bequests.*
15a.   D.R.O., *Plymstock Tithe Apportionment.*
16.   W.D.R.O., *Lease, Sterts and Candishes Tenements.*
17.   William Chapple, Review of Risdon's *Survey of Devon.*
18.   Rev. R. Lane, *The Brixton Book, MS*, 154, Plymouth Local Studies.
19.   W.D.R.O., *Plymstock Parish Council Minute Book*, October 1935.
20.   Rev. R. Lane, *The Brixton Book*, 155. Rev. O. Reichel, *The Hundred of Plympton in Early Times.*
21.   W.D.R.O., *Original Conveyance.*
22.   W.D.R.O., *Grant.*
23.   W.D.R.O., *Lease*, 1511, Copyhold Tenure.
24.   W.D.R.O., *Lease*, 1536, 96 years.
25.   P.R.O., E318, No. 657. *Cal. Patent Rolls*, November 1544.
26.   W.D.R.O., *Conveyance*, 1546.

27.   W.D.R.O., *Conveyance*, 1663.
28.   *Devon Hearth Tax*, 1674, Ed. and published by T.L. Stoate, 1982.
29.   W.D.R.O., *Leases*, 74/447/12; 74/447/13; 74/447/5; 74/449/7; 74/144/27.

n.1.   The earliest dateable evidence of settlement in this area takes the form of a group of worked flints discovered in a garden in Sherford Road just west of the present City boundary. This find, made in 1965, consisted of three leaf-shaped arrowheads, five scrapers and two waste flakes. The assemblage is characteristic of the early Neolithic period (4000–3000 BC), and may represent deposits from a temporary encampment. A scatter of worked flints, including cores and scrapers, has been recorded from Hazeldene and Hazel Grove areas (west of Vinery Lane) as a result of recent archaeological survey, and indicates something of the popularity of the area with early farmers.

Small-scale excavations in 1994 and early in 1995 in an area due for housing development north of Hazel grove uncovered evidence for metal working and finds of pottery of late Bronze Age or early Iron Age date (1000-8000 BC). These traces were buried under deep soil eroded from surrounding slopes and serve to remind us of the existence of types of site not often recorded from surface survey.

Romano-British settlement is attested from at least four locations in or near Elburton, concentrated in the area south of Elburton Vineries and north of Sherford Road. The discovery of bones, and a small iron blade in association with a late Roman coin in one of these locations suggests the possibility of a cemetery locally. A multiple-ditched sub-rectangular enclosure has been plotted from aerial photographs at a location to the east of Haye farm, and north of Haye Road Nurseries. This is likely to be a defended farmstead of the late Iron Age or Romano-British period.

Although it is known that a medieval hamlet existed in Elburton itself, there has been no suspicion of further isolated settlements existing then. However, field survey by Plymouth City Museum staff in 1992 recorded concentrations of medieval pot sherds at Hazeldene east of Haye Road. These may be associated with earthwork platforms surviving nearby and might represent the last vestiges of a hitherto unrecorded medieval hamlet. The area concerned is due to be destroyed by an extension to Moorcroft Quarry across Haye Road. However, excavations are planned in advance of this quarrying, and more should be learned about the possible settlement here then. *Note contributed by Dr. Keith Ray, City Archaeological Officer, Plymouth City Council.*

n.2.   When Baldwin de Redvers, the eighth earl, died the earldom lapsed, being re-created when Hugh de Courtenay became the first earl of Devon.

INDEX

159